PRAISE FOR *THE DIGITAL M*

This book is an essential tool for anyone running digital marketing campaigns. Full of great tips and practical guides, it should be on the desk of every marketer.

Ashley Friedlein, Founder, Econsultancy and Guild

Simon Kingsnorth, once again, debunks the myth that digital marketing requires years of experience. He brings a level of simplicity and practicality that makes the trade accessible to all, which has to be a good thing.

Glen Conybeare, Global President, Reprise Commerce

The Digital Marketing Handbook is essential for every office and classroom environment given our economic reliance on the interplay of digital marketing across industries. Simon Kingsnorth captures digital and traditional elements our teaching agency actively references.

Devon S Perry, CEO, Segel Associates

The Digital Marketing Handbook

Deliver powerful digital campaigns

Simon Kingsnorth

Publisher's note

Every possible effort has been made to ensure that the information contained in this book is accurate at the time of going to press, and the publishers and authors cannot accept responsibility for any errors or omissions, however caused. No responsibility for loss or damage occasioned to any person acting, or refraining from action, as a result of the material in this publication can be accepted by the editor, the publisher or the author.

First published in Great Britain and the United States in 2022 by Kogan Page Limited

2nd Floor, 45 Gee Street
London
EC1V 3RS
United Kingdom
www.koganpage.com

8 W 38th St, Suite 902
New York, NY 10018
USA

4737/23 Ansari Road
Daryaganj
New Delhi 110002
India

Kogan Page books are printed on paper from sustainable forests.

ISBNs

Hardback 978 1 3986 0341 7
Paperback 978 1 3986 0339 4
Ebook 978 1 3986 0340 0

British Library Cataloguing-in-Publication Data

A CIP record for this book is available from the British Library.

Library of Congress Cataloging-in-Publication Data

Names: Kingsnorth, Simon, author.
Title: The digital marketing handbook: deliver powerful digital campaigns / Simon Kingsnorth.
Description: London; New York, NY: Kogan Page, 2022. | Includes bibliographical references and index.
Identifiers: LCCN 2021051521 (print) | LCCN 2021051522 (ebook) | ISBN 9781398603394 (paperback) | ISBN 9781398603417 (hardback) | ISBN 9781398603400 (ebook)
Subjects: LCSH: Internet marketing. | Industrial marketing. | Electronic commerce–Management.
Classification: LCC HF5415.1265.K564 2022 (print) | LCC HF5415.1265 (ebook) | DDC 658.8/72–dc23/eng/20211019
LC record available at https://lccn.loc.gov/2021051521
LC ebook record available at https://lccn.loc.gov/2021051522

Typeset by Integra Software Services, Pondicherry
Print production managed by Jellyfish
Printed and bound by CPI Group (UK) Ltd, Croydon CR0 4YY

For Oz and Dexter

CONTENTS

ABOUT THE AUTHOR

Simon Kingsnorth is a marketing expert with over 20 years' experience building and delivering effective marketing strategies for companies around the world. He is also the author of the international bestseller *Digital Marketing Strategy*, which is used by universities and institutes across the world.

He is the CEO of Simon Kingsnorth Ltd, a UK-based marketing agency which delivers marketing strategy, content, social media, SEO, advertising and design solutions for start-ups, SMEs and global corporations.

simonkingsnorth.com

01

How this book works

I'm going to take a guess that you bought this book to help you with your digital marketing. It's a stretch I know, but I'm fairly confident on this one. I haven't researched it, I haven't analysed it, I haven't planned for it, but I can be pretty sure. Why? Because the title of this book is pretty simple and straightforward. If you can run your digital marketing in the same way, you can be just as sure of success, and that is exactly what this handbook is designed to help you do.

So why do you need this book? Surely you can just search the internet for the answers?

Well, to some degree, yes you can. However, a little knowledge is a dangerous thing. If you don't know what you are looking for, how do you find it? If you don't know the person that wrote the blog, how do you know whether to trust them?

The *Digital Marketing Handbook* is a practical guide aimed at helping you to deliver the best possible results every time. I have worked hard to ensure you hold in your hands everything you need to know to deliver the best outcomes from your activity.

We will look at how to build beautiful websites that convert, how to create and manage high performance paid campaigns across multiple channels, how to produce engaging written and visual content and how to produce communications that deliver satisfaction and retention.

All of this will be supported by real tools and examples to help you. I have included practical tips throughout the book. Not just high-level principles, but what you actually need to do to deliver the best results for the least effort; also what to watch out for and the common pitfalls to avoid along the way. I've also included step-by-step guides for each key task so you can skip the learning phase and get it right first time.

There are also case studies of great work done by your peers in the industry for you to emulate, and some to serve as a warning of what can go wrong. Alongside these are recommendations on platforms to use. There are thousands of platforms available to digital marketers today and so these shortlists will hopefully enable you to cut through the noise and get straight to the tools that will help you.

We will also look at analysis: what to read into your data, how to set it up and what vanity metrics to ignore. There are a lot of opinions out there about marketing – from career marketeers to entrepreneurs, everyone has a view. This book ignores the opinions and gets straight to the facts to ensure you can focus on the ideas and the strategy and let this book walk you through the implementation.

My first book, *Digital Marketing Strategy*, was written to explain how to build a digital strategy and to ensure we all, as marketeers, understand the marketing, strategic and technology elements of building a successful strategy. I never expected it to go on to be an international bestseller and to be printed in so many languages and used by so many universities around the world. If you are clear on your strategy, this Handbook will help you implement it. If you are looking for more support on how to develop your strategy before you start to deliver it, you may want to pick up a copy of *Digital Marketing Strategy* to support you further.

To accompany this Handbook I have also produced a series of guides on each channel. These guides are designed to take you through everything from planning and set-up to testing and analysis. Each will give you clear instructions and what to do to maximize your results. These will be referenced throughout the book and can also be found at simonkingsnorth.com.

Finally, if you are in need of further help with your marketing, please don't hesitate to reach out to me through my website. I have worked with companies big and small, all over the world, in many industries and I continue to consult to many clients today.

Here is a quick summary of the features to look out for throughout this book:

Top tips

> TOP TIP
>
> You will find boxes throughout the book that are aimed at giving you one quick tip at optimizing the area being discussed. These are designed to help you get straight to the nitty-gritty and be able to find them again easily for future reference.

Case studies

CASE STUDY

Throughout the book you will find many case studies that show the good and the bad on a given subject. I strongly recommend familiarizing yourself with them, as we can all learn from others' successes and failures.

Platform recommendations

PLATFORM RECOMMENDATIONS

Where we get into technology and data you will find these boxes that recommend a list of some of the best platforms out there. These are useful to refer to when building your marketing technology stack and in any future tender processes.

What to watch

WHAT TO WATCH

These scary-looking boxes are designed to be exactly that! They highlight mistakes that are easily made, and indeed many of us have made, and which I want you to be able to sidestep.

Step by step

STEP BY STEP

Finally, where there are tasks to follow, you will find these short guides to help you take one step at a time to success. Think of them like a recipe – a recipe for success.

02

Building a high-converting, beautiful website

A website is the foundation of your digital marketing. It has never been easier to create one of course. There are many platforms available to put together a website in minutes. Simply choose a domain and a template and add some stock photos and you have a website. What you don't have however is a great website.

So, what makes a great website? Well, ultimately this comes down to whether the website achieves your goals or not. There are websites that are visually appealing, and it's tempting to say they are great websites, but some of the best converting websites are frankly unpleasant to look at. In fact, if you go back to the early Amazon website it was never beautiful, but it was very good at converting and cross-selling. Not that this is something to aspire to. There is no excuse today not to seriously consider design within your website. Why? Because you want your site to look good? Well yes, but more importantly because beautiful websites are more likely to deliver better brand value, content engagement and higher conversion.

In this chapter we will look at the key steps to take to put together a website that wows, engages and converts. We'll start with the planning phase.

Step one: Before you begin

Consider your goals

As we've already said, you need to know what your goal is before you plan out the website.

1. **Brand led:** Are you an established global brand who needs your digital presence to promote your online messaging in support of your broader marketing strategy?
   - For example: McDonalds, Nike.
2. **Volume led:** Are you a high-volume, consumer start-up who needs to generate millions of free sign-ups or downloads of your app or service?
   - For example: early-stage Spotify or Facebook.
3. **Sales led:** Are you an e-Commerce site that needs to sell as many products as you can in your country?
   - For example: Etsy, Amazon.
4. **Enquiry led:** Are you a niche B2B business who needs a portfolio supported by case studies, testimonials and pricing details to drive leads from prospective clients?
   - For example: a manufacturer or professional services organization.

Whatever your business model, you need to consider which of these key goals apply to you:

1. Build the brand.
2. Deliver campaigns to a large audience.
3. Provide highly engaging content.
4. Gather leads, registrations, downloads.
5. Sell products.

Based on these goals, you will need to build your site accordingly. Let's play this out with the four examples and five key goals above to see what you should be considering at this early stage to ensure you build the right site:

BRAND LED

1. Your brand is already built, so this is not a focus, but ensuring that the brand remains strong throughout is key. You should encourage and reward brand loyalty.
2. Ensure your messaging is integrated with your social media and offline campaigns to pull everything together and to be the core destination.
3. Build great content. It will be expected and demanded.

4 You should try to encourage registrations to get to know your audience and deliver deeper experiences to them.

5 Selling isn't the focus, but if you can sell more through soft-selling techniques and competitions, then this is a useful addition.

VOLUME LED

1 Brand building is essential. Keep the logo, colour and design clear and consistent. Get the language and the feel right now, as this is a critical phase for you. This should be your number-one priority.

2 This is also critical for you. Those campaigns need to go far and wide and ultimately pull people back to your website.

3 Your content may not be as essential, but it will help to convert undecided consumers and researchers and drive SEO traffic.

4 This is your number-two priority. Reasons to sign up and ease of doing this with clear signposting is key.

5 Stay away from this. You are playing a volume game. Any feeling of selling will throttle your growth.

SALES LED

1 Depending on your sector, this may not be as important. Branding is never something that should be poor, but, if you are in an industry that is very much rational in its decision making, simple clarity and accuracy can be enough.

2 Your conversion tracking and clear paths from campaigns to conversions are essential. You also need campaigns for the products and categories you are selling, so this structure is essential to get right.

3 Content will support your sales, so this is important. It will also drive new customers through SEO and social media.

4 You may want to take enquiries from undecided buyers, but generally you do not want to focus here. Push them to buy while they're in the market.

5 Number-one focus. Get those call-to-action prominent, clear and everywhere. Test the colours, language and everything you can to optimize the funnel.

ENQUIRY LED

1. As above, this may not be essential depending on your industry.
2. Your campaigns should focus on lead generation here. Build and deliver focused and highly targeted campaigns.
3. Content is queen here. Deliver lots of great content to help the decision-making process. Written content, images, video and audio plus interactive content across multiple channels are essential. This should be the bedrock of your site.
4. The number-one focus. Give reasons to believe and convert those believers into leads. Keep the forms very short and the signposting clear.
5. You're not trying to sell. You are trying to convince. Sales messaging in your content is important, but don't push too hard or you will lose the enquiry.

These five key goals give you the chance to consider the priorities in the design and structure of your website before you begin. No matter what your business, you should be able to get an early direction using this simple planning model.

Know where you stand

It is possible that you are building your website from scratch. This can be a blessing, as you have no legacy issues to deal with. It is of course just as likely that you are considering a rebuild of an existing site. In this situation, all the principles of this chapter apply, but you also have the advantage of existing data.

First you should interrogate your analytics to understand any pain points in the key customer journeys. Look for conversion dropouts and high bounce rates on key pages. Understand where call-to-action are being used versus ignored and where technical issues such as page speed or mobile optimization are causing you to lose visitors.

Alongside these quantitative measures, you also need to understand how users are responding to your design. This is where usability work is critical.

- **Heatmaps:** Consider using heatmap software on your website. This can give a clear picture as to where the mouse is hovering. This will be indicative of where users are drawn: buttons, imagery, offers. All can encourage users to move their mouse to that area without clicking. Heatmapping can give an otherwise invisible insight to your decision making on design elements that drive the right behaviours.

- **Eyeball tracking:** Not something that can be done wholesale across your website but rather with a select group of willing participants as a usability research study. This enables you to track the eye movement on users who are interacting with your site and layer this data over the pages they are interacting with. This gives more accuracy than heatmaps as a user may not move their mouse cursor to the place they are looking and there is no mouse on mobile devices. It can't be done at scale however.
- **Usability research:** Usability research is the gathering of willing participants to review your site. This can be highly valuable. You should ensure a wide demographic of individuals that matches your desired audience. The standard process is then to allow the individual to browse your site freely and see what they do. Note down any issues, behaviours and common journeys taken. Following this, individuals are given specific tasks, and you note how easy it is for them to fulfil these, along with any interesting trends. Finally, you chat with participants about their thoughts on the experience, design and any other specific questions you need to ask.

This qualitative input, when combined with eyeball tracking, can provide invaluable insights that analytics simply cannot.

Know your audience

Keeping these principles in mind, the next task is to ensure you know your website. A common mistake many new entrepreneurs and even experienced business professionals make is to believe that because you visit a lot of websites you know what makes a good website.

Well, you probably also drive a car, but do you know how to build one? Chances are you use a computer and a mobile phone, so, do you know how to build them?

The fact is we know what we like but we don't know what everyone else will like. We have to acknowledge that the only way we can be certain of delivering the best possible website is through following best practice, as proven by marketers for decades now, and to understand our audience. It only matters what works for them, not for you and I.

To understand this, we need to look at four important factors: behavioural, demographic, geographic and psychographic segmentation.

BEHAVIOURAL SEGMENTATION

Simply put, this is analysis of the actions that individuals have taken on your properties and the grouping of similar action sets into segments. This could be people's behaviour during shopping, browsing content, using social media, times of day or devices used. By understanding whether an audience member is browsing on mobile versus desktop and buying on desktop versus mobile you can optimize your design accordingly.

DEMOGRAPHIC SEGMENTATION

Possibly the most famous segmentation type, demographics deal with the signals that make up who we are, such as age, marital status, ethnicity, gender: the key signals of us as people. While they can certainly tell stories and enable some predictions, they can also be misleading. Married people may be more likely to have children, but many married people will not, and many unmarried people will. Older people may be less likely to be surfers, but some will be. There are outliers here that need to be considered carefully so as not to offend or make poor assumptions.

GEOGRAPHIC SEGMENTATION

'Geographic' is simple enough. Or is it? The obvious question is where is the individual located. However, they may be located in one territory but purchasing something in another. They could be importing goods, or booking an overseas holiday. Their language may be local to either location. Their cultural origin may not be the same as their current geographic location, for example if they have emigrated to another country. Consider the bigger picture in your geographic segmentation.

PSYCHOGRAPHIC SEGMENTATION

This is perhaps the most complex but, as with most things in life that are harder, the most insightful. Psychographic segmentation means understanding an individual's perceptions, interests and what drives them. What values would make them shop with your brand? What imagery is likely to resonate with them? What promotions may incentivize them to buy? You would expect these answers to be very different for a banker who would focus on money and a nurse who would focus on health, but that is too simple. The banker may even be more focused on children's health due to having a child with medical problems, while the nurse might be fed up with the health industry and just be working to get paid. Psychology is a vital area for any marketer to understand, even if just to a basic degree.

Following this, you should develop a further point to ensure you are able to think like your consumer and ensure your designs will be fully optimized.

PERSONAS

Combine the above segmentation outputs to create between 6 and 12 personas. This is where you create a picture of an individual with common qualities. This could be a young person who is unmarried and lives alone. They do not have a car and work in a junior job. They buy things for necessity or fun, not luxury. They are very mobile focused; very sociable. They live in a rented flat in a town centre. Alternatively, it could be a senior business person living in a luxurious country house, with another home in the city. They drive multiple cars and are married with children. They buy for necessity, fun, lifestyle and luxury. They are an online user but also spend a lot of time with offline media. They are quite sociable.

These two simple examples demonstrate how you could expect both personas to shop with you but to behave very differently, and so you need to ensure your experience is built with both in mind. Fast, mobile and cheap for Persona 1 versus easy, trustworthy and premium for Persona 2. Both can actually be achieved despite seemingly being opposites.

STEP BY STEP

Understand your audience

1. Look at behaviours from your own data.
2. Review the demographics of your customers vs other consumers.
3. Understand the geographical landscape of your customers.
4. Use psychographic segmentation to understand their motivations.
5. Develop the above in to 5 to 10 personas.

Customer journey maps

We will look at design thinking and specific technical considerations around navigation below, but before we do, it is helpful to do a whiteboard exercise to map out the journeys you are aiming to create based on the above thinking.

From your marketing channels, who will land where on your website and where do you want them to go next? It is not enough for you to organize the site into areas that you find logical. People do not jump from a logical area to a logical area. Users will follow paths that feel natural: paths of least resistance and that naturally flow from the last stage, no matter what that was. They will not all enter your site on the home page nor will their journeys always be linear.

You must be clear therefore before you build as to what these journeys are. Coming into your site via social media may land you on a content page. What is this type of user looking for and how can you give them that while driving the behaviours you want? They may be looking for more recipes or fashion ideas. You may want them to buy your cake ingredients or dresses. In this scenario, you mustn't hard sell or you will see an immediate bounce from many users. Instead, offering a range of similar products for the user to review while promoting similar items, perhaps with discounts, will likely increase sales and start to develop a relationship and some brand loyalty from that user.

Map out as many customer journeys as you can and try to simplify and merge them where possible to avoid future complexity.

Personalization

Once you have a clear view of your goals, your audience and your customer journeys you should consider personalization. This has been a key trend in marketing for many years and remains so. There is now an expectation that you only deliver relevant experiences to individuals. There is however also an increasing challenge around this due to data protection regulation which, while essential for individual privacy, makes identifying individuals harder and forces digital marketers to be more creative and scientific in their use of data.

True personalization is about ensuring the individual gets what matters to them at every stage of the journey. This includes the right advertising, the best offers and the right conversion messaging. This would later be followed by the most focused ongoing communications, but we'll come back to that in Chapter 10.

To get personalization right, you need to understand psychographic segmentation as we discussed above. What makes this person tick? Combine this with behavioural segmentation to understand how they have been behaving and you can start to recommend content that is of interest to them, provide offers that match their buying habits, change imagery to the type that makes them feel comfortable, and much more.

With this done we have completed step one. We have enough knowledge now to understand what we should be doing so let's move to the design phase.

Step two: Design

The first thing to consider from a design perspective is of course your visual identity. You should have a set of brand guidelines that detail how to deliver your visual brand across multiple channels. This should inform colours, logos and layouts. If this already exists for the web, now is a time to review it based on the design principles below. If not, this is essential work to undertake now.

While this book is not intended to go into deep detail on branding, it is important to follow core principles around brand design, from international and cultural considerations to colour co-ordination, values and tone of voice. Ensuring that your brand guidelines deliver the essence of your brand's personality is vital to ensuring consistency and authenticity. This work is not just to look slick, cool or professional but also solves many debates further down the road and affects both conversion and loyalty.

Design thinking

Design thinking is a term you may have heard of. It is an established method of working from initial concept through to delivery. It can feel chaotic and messy, but many of the best creative processes in the world are. Few artists' workshops are spotlessly clean.

The process follows four key stages and it's important that you follow each if you are to deliver the best website you can.

The four stages are: Discover, Define, Develop, Deliver.

Without knowing it, you have already achieved stage one. This is where we try to understand our audience and therefore what our challenges are.

Stage two, Define, is an expansion of the customer journey map above. What are the problems to be solved? How do we deliver what the audience wants while ensuring our goals are met?

The third stage, Develop, is where things can get messy. Here we begin the ideation. This is no longer purely based on data. This is where walls get covered in sticky notes and people start writing on any surface they can find; where there are no bad ideas and sessions can be long and tiring but fun and fascinating. How do we answer those challenges? What do we do to create design principles that solve the problems and create amazing experience for our users?

Finally, Deliver is where we put everything together and we'll look at that in step three below.

So, as we have moved into stages two and three of the Design Thinking model, now is the time to bring the teams together: designers, data analysts, conversion experts, brand owners, campaign managers, Product owners and all others with a stake in this. This is not a process you can do with one or two members of the team. Everyone who has a stake should be included and this extends to external agencies you may be working with. It is vital that all the data, expertise and opinions are in one room for heated debate and creative ideas. You also need a good moderator. Someone must take the responsibility to keep everyone on track, stop any criticism of ideas, defuse any tension and ensure actionable outputs are derived from the sessions.

The Design Thinking stage may go on for several weeks or months. You may have time pressures, but try not to rush this too much. Creativity rarely thrives when rushed. You are complete once you have solved all the problems and developed solutions to deliver the best outcomes for your users and your business.

Understanding design

Design is often thought of as subjective. Many people will tell you what good design is and is not. Most often this is an opinion and not scientific. What you, your chief marketing officer or even your CEO regard as good design is, while of course being something to consider, not the most important factor in determining good design. If all three of you agree something is beautiful but 95 per cent of your audience disagree, then, unfortunately, your opinions were wrong. So, how do you ensure such a subjective discussion results in the right outcome?

Well, the answer is quite simple. Art is a science.

Those may be the most controversial four words I have written in all my publications through the years, but bear with me.

We are surrounded by AI and robotic advancements at the moment. One robot that has stolen the news is Ai-Da which is able to create pieces of art by scanning and then sketching them. It is labelled 'The world's first ultra-realistic robot artist'. Is it truly creating something or merely copying? Is the robot really doing it or is it the code written by the humans that does it? Do any of us truly create or is it the signals given to us by others that create the art we produce? A fascinating project by the mentalist and illusionist Derren Brown demonstrated how he could use subliminal messaging to influence advertisers into creating a concept that matched one he had already produced. So, are humans just as scientific in their creativity as robots? It's a fascinating discussion, but perhaps too far from the practical for this book.

In fact, there are many rules that, when followed, create pleasing design. Truly inspirational design does need a creative eye, but if the rules are followed, any design can be professional, beautiful and effective.

Visual hierarchy

First, it is important to work out the visual hierarchy of your design. This will differ on different sections of your website but the core principle remains. If you have ever visited a website and not been sure where to click, what to read or how to get to the information you want, the chances are that it is due to a poor visual hierarchy.

The importance of the key elements of your page can be shown very clearly to your visitors through some simple mechanics. These include:

- **Colour:** Brighter colours will gain more attention than pastel or pale tones.
- **Contrast:** Strong contrasts such as black and white or contrasting colours are effective.
- **White space:** Minimalism can give the design elements much more focus.
- **Size:** Larger items will attract eyes more than smaller ones.
- **Alignment:** The brain wants tidiness, so unaligned items attract attention.
- **Repetition:** This creates patterns and therefore association of elements.

- **Proximity:** Simply by being close to something there is an association.
- **Reading:** Users read left to right in English for example.

Keeping these principles in mind, consider:

- Clear headers. They should be larger and/or bolder than the surrounding text. Align your elements for tidiness, but break this alignment occasionally where you want focal points.
- Don't use too many bright colours and stick to your brand palette where possible, but do look for focal points to break this rule and grab attention.
- Ensure your call-to-actions are bright and not lost in a crowd of other elements.
- Group your key content types together to encourage more engagement in your site.
- As a rule, sending users along a path left to right on an English language website makes sense. Also breaking this pattern occasionally can create a clear focal point. This direction should, of course, change for languages that read to the left or down for example.

Golden ratio

The golden ratio is an excellent design principle to understand. The ratio is 1.618, known as Phi in Greek (not to be confused with the mathematical constant Pi). This design rule is used widely from art to architecture. It is a common part of our everyday lives and yet most of us are completely unaware of it. The rule states that two quantities are in the golden ratio if they relate to each other according to a specific formula, as shown in Figure 2.1.

So, for example, a rectangle with a long side of 12 cm would need a short side of 7.42 cm to be in the golden ratio ($12 \div 1.618 = 7.42$).

The rectangle in Figure 2.2 with the ratio of 1.618 (A) is the most pleasing to the eye.

Rule of thirds

The rule of thirds will be familiar to any photographers reading this. Simply put, if you place a grid over an image and split it into three equal vertical sections and three equal horizontal sections you will have an image with nine distinct sections. By then positioning focal points on the corners of the

FIGURE 2.1 The golden ratio

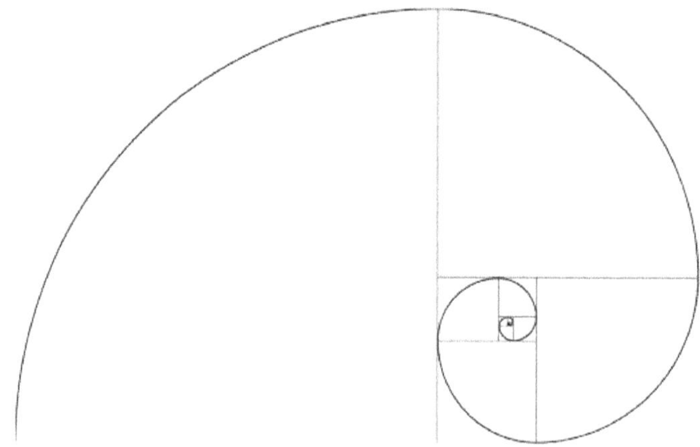

FIGURE 2.2 A golden ratio rectangle

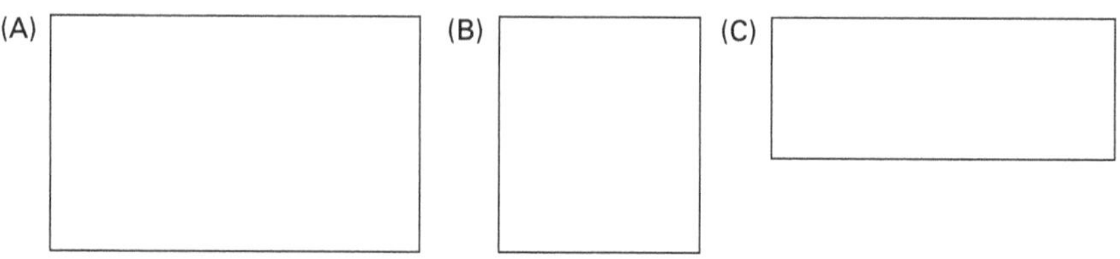

central section you naturally create a pleasant composition. Consider the two images in Figure 2.3.

The composition of the first image just feels more pleasant than the second, which seems a little messy. This is the human brain looking for the rule of thirds.

While this is easy to apply to photography, it can be harder to apply to a flexible website that works across multiple screen sizes and devices. If we stick to the principle on more design-led screens, however, we can play this out in any viewport. Consider, for example, a product page and where you might place a call-to-action, a product image and the copy and it is clear how the rule of thirds can quickly become a helpful design grid.

Hick's law

Something that every marketer should understand is Hick's law. This doesn't just apply to design but to everything you live and breathe in marketing. In simple terms it means keep it in simple terms. The law states that the more decisions a person has to make, the longer it will take them to reach a decision.

FIGURE 2.3 The rule of thirds

This is critical to remember when designing forms and navigation. You can in fact extend the law further to say that not only will people take longer to make a decision but, in today's world where patience is thin, they may never reach that decision and opt to drop out instead.

Therefore, keeping forms short and only gathering the necessary information is key. Keeping navigation simple is essential. Keeping your messaging clear and immediately understandable is vital to moving your user to the next stage of the journey.

This of course also applies to your advertising, content and much more, but it is critical for effective web design.

Fitt's law

This is an important law to understand in UX design. The law pre-dates modern UX and websites but has been used as a cornerstone of design in the modern UX world.

Fitt's law states that the time it takes a person to move a pointer to a target is a function of the distance to the target divided by the size of the target. The core understanding to take away here is that a small object further from the pointer (for example the mouse cursor) will be harder for someone to interact with.

So, it is critical that any groups of actions are located together. Login text boxes and submit buttons, for example, should be as close as possible and large enough so as not to cause irritation when trying to click or tap on them.

From this law comes the concept of the 'prime pixel' – the pixel that the next action should be closest to as that is where our user's cursor is. In reality we can't fix that pixel in one place when designing a website as a user will move their mouse around, hence why we should keep related items close together. We can, however, consider the 'magic pixels'. These are the four corners of the screen: furthest from the centre and the least effective place to put anything of importance (Figure 2.4).

Gestalt design laws

The Gestalt principles are fascinating laws of human perception that show how we group things together that have no real relation but that help our brains to process what's around us. As a child you may have seen faces in the shadows of your bedroom and even today you may see animals in the clouds. These strange occurrences are your brain trying to assign patterns to the things your eyes see in order to process things effectively, often for survival reasons.

FIGURE 2.4 Magic pixels

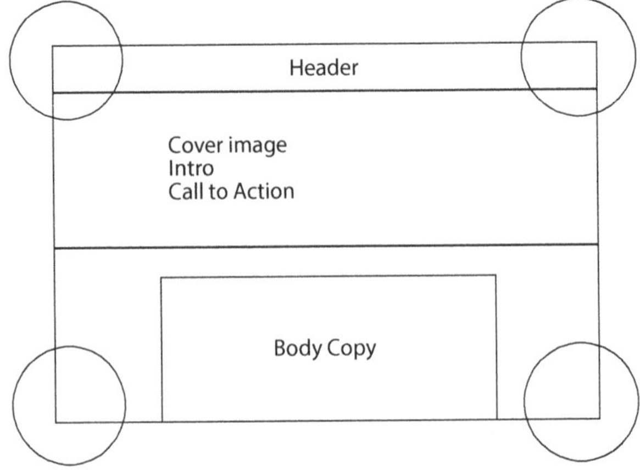

These same laws can be used to make websites more pleasing to the eye.

LAW OF CLOSURE

We humans don't like unfinished work. If you show me the World Wide Fund for Nature (WWF) logo, I see a panda. This is not a complete drawing but I can see where the lines are to make a panda so my brain constructs a panda rather than just seeing the individual shapes for what they are. This rule can be applied cleverly to websites to create images that complete themselves.

LAW OF COMMON REGION

We associate items that are included in the same region. This is very common in the websites you use every day. From posts on social media to Google's search results pages. Once you group items together with boxes, shading or spacing it becomes much clearer to the user how the items are related.

LAW OF FIGURE/GROUND

This design rule is most famously known through the faces/vase drawing. If shown on a black background, the vase stands out as a white shape. If the background is white, the faces stand out as black figures. By using colour and contrast in this way you can control which elements come through prominently as figures and which disappear as background.

LAW OF PROXIMITY

Quite simply, items that are grouped closely together are associated together. Having large spacing between distinct menus and content items but keeping those items in close proximity within the group gives a clear signal to the brain.

LAW OF SIMILARITY

Also a relatively simple Gestalt law. If items look the same, we group them the same. This applies to a great deal of things in life, but with websites it is important to ensure you don't have competing groupings. Try to create distinct styles for the different key elements of your site.

Colour

An understanding of colour is of course important. And don't be mistaken in thinking this, or any of these other design principles, should just be left for your designer to worry about. Being able to assess whether a colour scheme truly works should be the role of every marketer, from those with a technical focus to the end decision maker.

The colour wheel is the place to start. By looking at this we can establish which colours are complementary by looking at those opposite each other on the wheel, such as blue and orange, or purple and yellow. The colours of your brand will of course play a part, but for accenting, highlighting or image selection these combinations can really draw the eye.

Monochromatic colours are also a great way of staying on brand while giving a soft distinction between elements. Analogous colours do the same but with more distinct variance.

Split complementary, triadic and tetradic colours are a great way of building a palette to be used throughout your website. This can inform your section design, navigation and call-to-actions with ease. I recommend further research of these colour relationships.

As well as the colour wheel itself, it is important to appreciate the science of colour. This refers to both psychological and physical science. You may have noticed, for example, that blue is a very common colour. I'm sure you could name 10 brands with a prominent blue without even trying, for example Facebook, Twitter, LinkedIn, Ford, Ikea, Samsung, BMW, Philips, PayPal and KPMG. This is no coincidence. In fact, according to Canva, blue is by far the most popular colour for Fortune 500 companies. The colour blue gives a sense of calm and trust. It's safe. It's also a colour that can be seen by people who have colour blindness, which is apparently why Mark Zuckerberg chose it for Facebook.

Red on the other hand indicates passion, love, energy, excitement but sometimes anger and 'stop'. Green often promotes nature, health and freshness, whereas black gives a feeling of quality, sophistication, formality but also drama and darkness.

There is a too much detail to delve into in colour science here, but appreciating the subliminal meaning of colours and their relationships is important to delivering great design.

Imagery

From video to static photos to infographics, imagery can make or break a design. So, what makes good imagery?

First, quality is key. Poor-quality images, no matter how beautiful the composition, will destroy trust and in turn harm every performance metric on your website. In the age of Ultra HD, a poor-quality image will not be tolerated by a large percentage of your audience.

Second, images must have a purpose. Putting an image in simply to break up the text looks like exactly that. It is a waste of space and another element a user has to navigate past. Every image should be part of the story. It must have a reason to be there. You should ask yourself: how does the image add to the narrative? This is not to say that images should not be used to break up long text, rather that they should but only if they can play a role in the story being told on that blog or service page.

People in photos make a big difference. Humans are social animals. If we weren't, we would have become extinct millennia ago. We love to see other people.

CASE STUDY: GOOGLE

I will retell a case study that Google told me many years ago.

A company wanted to achieve conversion on its website so it tested imagery on its home page. First, it added a human interacting with the product as the main image rather than just the product. This increased clicks on the conversion button. Then the company made the human smile. The clicks increased again. Then it changed the adult human to a baby, and more clicks. Finally, it made the smiling baby look at the button, and even more clicks.

This use of science to test and learn how images play a part in improving your website is critical to success. By no means are images simply there to add some colour.

Finally, you may have brand guidelines that dictate the use of photography only or illustration only. These sorts of prescriptive rules are unhelpful. If you have guidelines like this that restrict creativity and testing, you should challenge them. Sometimes consistency can add tidiness to a website. However sometimes mixing photos and illustrations is exactly the sort of break that attracts the eye and makes something stand out.

Think of the film *Who Framed Roger Rabbit*. Not only was it groundbreaking from a cinematic perspective, it was also beautiful to watch because of the opportunities presented to the creative team by having this freedom.

Signposting

Along with ensuring to keep your navigation simple, as we mentioned above, you should also ensure there is clear signposting throughout your website.

Consider where you want people to go next and use the design rules above to accomplish this. Consider the Google baby example, the Gestalt laws and your goals. How can you use these to give clear signs to the user about what to do next in order to read more, sign up, buy now?

Mobile first

This almost goes without saying today, but do not design purely for desktop. Every site should be designed for mobile first. It may be the case that more than 50 per cent of your users or even 90 per cent of your users prefer their desktop, but if you don't optimize mobile you will not only lose the other 10 per cent, but Google will punish you in the search results and then you lose the 90 per cent too.

Responsive design is essential so ensure that all your design work is considered across multiple devices and standard resolutions. We'll discuss future-proofing and the technical considerations around this below, but you must ensure this is considered from day one and not an afterthought.

Design trends

Finally, it is worth keeping an eye on design trends. This is generally one for the design team, but, again, it helps to have an understanding of it.

> TOP TIP
>
> Set aside some time every month to look at the website designs that are winning awards and gaining industry interest. Follow and subscribe to industry publications on- and offline to keep a finger on the pulse. Ask your agency to update you on trends. These trends can shift quite fast and, while you don't want to be redesigning your website every six months, you may see elements that you want to test and bring into your design as part of the gradual evolution of your site.

One of the trends to watch out for, for example, is how users set up their devices. Many currently choose dark mode. This can simply be due to personal preference, the light conditions they work in or their personal sensitivity to light, or many other reasons. It has also become quite popular on some app designs as it saves device battery. This mode could change the feel of your site so is worth noting.

Step three: Information architecture

Information architecture is an essential step to go through pre-build. This is where you organize the content of your website to ensure there is a logical hierarchy that works for user journeys and the needs of the visitor.

There are several different models of information architecture, which we will take a quick look at now.

Single page

This is one simple, often long, page with everything you need. Very few websites are able to use this structure as it offers little scope for easy navigation to products, services and other key information and journeys. It also has little SEO value due to the minimal content it can hold.

Flat structure

This structure allows for multiple pages, all of which sit at the same priority level. A home page would be equal priority to any other page on the site. This can work for small sites such as simple brochure-ware websites where journeys are very limited. It will not work for most sites however due to the lack of clear structure for a user.

Index

This is a common structure where you have one home page and all other pages sit a level below that. Again, this is for relatively simple sites but adds a little more structure to the content.

Hierarchy

Finally, there is the hierarchy, which is common among most larger sites and has multiple levels of structure below the home page with content organized into categories and grouped accordingly. You may choose to keep these categories entirely separate to focus the user journeys or allow them to interact for deeper engagement in your site.

When planning your architecture model and set-up, you must go back to step one and consider your findings and decisions around customer journey mapping and design thinking. It is essential that you consider the user needs and the journeys you need those users to take as you build your hierarchy.

A single focus is always sensible when driving a goal. Try not to have distractions within your journeys that could allow users to drop out. Messages about other products that can't be bought as part of this journey, adverts for other companies or links to other areas of the site can all cause drop-off. Keep your journeys focused, minimalist and simple.

Having said this, cross-selling is important. In fact, any cross-promotion, not just of products but also of related content, is useful. It can help to inform users and support them in decision making. It can create more loyalty and deeper engagement across your site. It can also create an increase in referrals. Therefore, while keeping your conversion journeys simple is critical, broadening your cross-selling on products and content areas of the site is important.

CASE STUDY: AMAZON

Amazon have long been giving us all a masterclass in cross-selling. Using their core app and website as an example we can see many simple but effective uses of the method, from 'People like you bought this' to 'People who bought this, also bought this.' There are also recommendations based on your wish lists and recent browsing habits. Some of this is shown while browsing and some post purchase. Some is shown on your home page and some on the specific product pages. Each item shown is incredibly easy to add into your basket, and thus the overall income from each shopper increases.

Methods of developing information architecture

There are several methods you can use to help you find the right architecture for your content.

TOP DOWN AND BOTTOM UP

This approach is relatively simple and encourages you to look at the content from two different angles.

- First, the top-down approach starts with your goals and the purpose of your website, from which you build the content accordingly. This is a very logical approach and you will have this understanding already from step one.

- Second, the bottom-up approach starts with your content and looks at the relationship between the various topics and how they should therefore relate together.

By putting these two outputs together you can establish the best overall journeys and logical structures for your content.

CARD SORTING

As with design thinking above, this involves writing down all of your content and working out how it would all fit together. Differently from the method above however, the best route here is to allow users, visitors, customers and colleagues not involved in the project to go through this. How would they arrange the cards? What journeys make sense to them? Let them lay down each card in a way that makes logical sense to them, then look for trends and learnings that you can apply to your architecture.

WIREFRAME

Finally, building a wireframe of your site and going through user testing will show clear issues and popular journeys before you go into the full build phase. This can save many months of reworking and is strongly advised to be a part of your website build process. This would come after you have made many of the decisions from the previous activities and should be focused on ironing out any last issues that remain before final build and launch.

Content considerations

For design reasons, it is worth keeping your text minimal. Too much copy will cause frustration. Consumers have never before been so impatient and unwilling to work hard at buying from you. Why would they when they can buy from someone else quickly and easily? When considering your copy length, keep in mind that you must find a copywriter who can deliver complex messages in a simple and easily understandable way. You also need to consider however that copy that is too short will harm your SEO success. Focus on the right length to remove the risk of thin content as defined by Google and other search engines but not so much as to be frustrating for the user.

Step four: Build

You should now know your customer, the journeys they take, your goals, how to set up your information and what design you feel comfortable with.

Finally we get to build this all into a reality. But beware, this is where a lot can go wrong. The best designs from the best designers can transform into disastrous websites if the build phase isn't properly implemented. We will now consider all the key points to focus on during this build phase.

WHAT TO WATCH

When starting work on the design phase, ensure you consider how the project will move to the build phase.

If your agency is designing your website, and your internal technology team or another agency are building, you must get them together at the start of the process. If a technology team does not have a design eye and no help from the design agency, then a unicorn can quickly turn into a Shetland pony. (No offence intended to Shetland ponies!). Link the design and build phases together from day one or the whole project can end up with compromises and failures despite the greatest designs and hardest work from you and your teams.

The foundations

Your domain name will be for the long term. You may already have this established, but if you are just founding your business, you should consider the future of your business and not rush into a domain that will need altering later. A *.com* domain will give more status and international performance than a local one. However, local domains will be more relevant in each region (more on this below). Try to avoid long or complex domains with hyphens – these can perform poorly on search engines, be confusing for users to type in and also give a poor professional impression of your business.

Ensuring your website is registered with Google Search Console and Bing Webmaster Tools is vital for keeping track of the search engine's view of your site. This will ensure your pages are in the search engine results and will report on any issues that you can then resolve quickly.

In order to do this, you will need a sitemap, so preparing an XML version of your sitemap is essential. This should include every page on your site, including the importance and frequency of updates of each page. This will help the search engines to focus on the right areas. We'll touch more on that in the next chapter.

Hosting

When considering your hosting options, you should start by considering your business goals. If you are likely to be producing a large website with many images, videos or products, such as a new website or ecommerce site, you will need plenty of scope for scalability. If you have high levels of traffic or intend to scale quickly, bandwidth is important. Finally, look at the additional features on offer, such as backups and security options. These can be invaluable when something goes wrong.

Compatibility

We have mentioned responsive design already. This remains critical to success. Some websites are now getting 100 per cent of their traffic on mobile. Most social media sites have well over 90 per cent mobile usage and this is only growing. Mobile first is essential to user experience and SEO, as we'll discuss in the next chapter.

Browsers are also ever changing. Chrome is now a major player when not so long ago it didn't exist. Such is the power of Google. Microsoft's browsers continue to be well established and evolving. Firefox also remains a major player and there are many more. Ensure you test on multiple browsers – do not assume they will all interpret your build the same way.

Ensure too that you understand the browsers, resolutions, screens and devices that are commonly used now and likely trends coming soon so that you have a site that looks beautiful and functions well for every user.

Integration

Analytics is one area you must include in your site from day one. Without a functioning analytics platform you will not be able to make any decisions around future optimization of your performance. There are many platforms available, from free to expensive, and even the free platforms offer considerable benefits. We'll look at setting your analytics up and more on data and testing platforms in Chapter 9.

Integration with social media is another key area today. Sharing is an essential part of any online platform and your website is no exception. You should be encouraging your visitors to share products, blogs, videos, static pages; anything that could be of interest to their friends, family or colleagues. Whether it's newsworthy content to Twitter, recipes to Pinterest or business tips to LinkedIn, you should be looking for social sharing at as many touchpoints as possible.

Review services are another essential area. With the power of the consumer at an all-time high, it is essential to be able to display review scores both on your website and off it, such as in search engine results. Claiming ownership of your business on review sites, encouraging reviews, managing those reviews closely and integrating them with your website can deliver a level of trust that greatly increases conversion.

Finally, consider any other tools you work with that could benefit from integration on your your website. A good place to start would be your marketing automation suite or email platform. Gaining sign-ups for email communications is great, but also tracking users' journeys through your website and other properties is essential for every marketer today to be able to fully optimize spending and results.

Localization

International considerations for global businesses can be very complex. Below we take a look at the key considerations.

- **Translation:** Consider how you will handle translation. This may include internal resources, but there are also many reliable translation services, including some built into content management systems (CMS). One other consideration here is to try to avoid text within images. You don't want to translate that image 20 times when you could just translate the text once.
- **Responsive design:** We have already mentioned this of course. In the context of localization, sites can come in many different languages, and responsive design quickly enables your templates to work with different lengths of content and even directions of characters.
- **TLDs (Top Level Domains):** We will cover this in more detail in the next chapter, but for localization it can be enormously beneficial for SEO to use ccTLDs for your different country content. For example *.uk*, *.it*. Using one standard *.com* domain simply tells search engines that your site is neutral. In an age where localization is key, local domains can play a big part in the success of your international strategy.

- **Consistent language:** Try to create content that is consistently in the same language. Even if you encourage user-generated content, try to ensure it is written in the same language as the page. This can help search engines to understand the true targeting of the page.
- **Cultural considerations:** You should also consider cultural differences. The same phrases and words may not make sense in another language or may even be offensive. Currencies may be different and even user behaviours. Your visitors may prefer different search engines, social media channels and devices. This is especially true when we look across continents.

Security

Security is an ongoing concern and I'm sure everyone reading this book will be able to remember at least one company that has had a digital data security leak in recent years. As these attacks are becoming more sophisticated, you must consider the security of your online channels. Any e-commerce site, organization that processes payments or data, or any company with significant brand awareness must focus on this as a priority.

Ensure you have an SSL certificate, review the security features of your hosting service and ensure your developers have delivered the right security framework. This is something you must not leave to chance, so understanding security and engaging with an expert here is highly recommended.

Single sign-on is another route to consider as part of security. Facebook, Google and many others offer this option and you may consider developing one for your own properties if you have multiple platforms. This is convenient for users, however, anything that is simple for users is simple for hackers. Single sign-on is also potentially a single point of failure. There is enormous value in this for gated content or platform logins and it has become very common, but be careful if considering it for your own system.

Images

Ensure your images are optimized for speed and quality. File formats are complex and you should ensure you understand them. There are also new formats being introduced on a semi-regular basis, so staying up to speed is again important. When choosing an image format, consider lossless versus lossy compression, vector versus raster quality, and browser support, as not all browsers support the same image types. WebP is a major trend to follow: this is a Google format that is still finding its feet but is likely to become mainstream.

Summary

If you consider all of the above and follows steps one to four, you can be confident in creating a high-performance, beautiful website that hits your goals. But never stop there. You should always be testing, learning, optimizing and testing some more. A project to create the best website for your business always has a start date but never has an end date.

PLATFORM RECOMMENDATIONS

- CMS;
- Wordpress;
- Wix;
- SquareSpace;
- Gator;
- Zyro;
- Weebly;
- Zoho;
- BiCommerce;
- Your Domain Host.

03

Optimizing your website to deliver top SEO results

Search engine optimization is one of the broadest and most complex areas of marketing. It can be enormously frustrating and enormously rewarding. Much like social media, the goals can often be muddied and the techniques for delivering against those goals a little mysterious.

To excel in this field, you need to have a scientific understanding of code and technology, a creative understanding of content, a good PR head to generate meaningful links and an all-round skillset in project management. That's a tough ask for any single person and so building a team or working with consultants or an agency is often the right solution. However, you cannot lead that agency unless you at least have a grounding in the core areas.

In this chapter we will look at the main areas you need to understand and should be considering with your SEO strategy to optimize your performance.

What you need to know

The are many considerations in SEO. You are surrounded by a lot of jargon and a lot of acronyms. This is simply because there are so many levers to pull from coding changes to content frequency. Before we get into the tactical implementation, we are going to look at the foundations. These are the things you must understand and act upon at the very start.

The SERPs

The SERPs are the search engine results pages. In other words, the pages on Google, for example, where you see the list of results after you search for something. This is the battleground. This is where every SEO expert is trying to get their site to its best prominence.

That is a very carefully selected set of words. It took me a few minutes and a few rewrites to finish that last paragraph. Why?

Well, it is not simply, 'Get to position 1.' What does that actually mean? Position 1 on what keyword? For whom? In what territory? Also, what about those definition boxes we see? Video listings? Local business listings? Quotes? Recipes? Where SEO used to be simply about chasing that top position, there are now many ways to maximize traffic to your site. It is still the case that 90 per cent of traffic goes to sites that are listed on page 1. The position 1 slot on any keyword is 10 times more likely to receive a click than the site in position 10. In fact, position 1 tends to get significantly higher click-through than position 2. From positions 2 to 10 there is a gradual decline, and then a huge drop off to page 2 and beyond. This data is regularly backed up by research such as that by Backlinko (https://backlinko.com/google-ctr-stats).

Competing on those number-one positions for the keywords that drive volume therefore remains important, but using the real estate of the SERPs to jump above your competitors through those rich content boxes we mentioned above is a great way to win.

You also need to understand that the volume term isn't the only one that is important. If you sell car insurance, perhaps the term 'cheap car insurance' is the one that drives the most volume? That may well be highly competitive and, while you should certainly drive to optimize around it, you should also look to optimize for the huge range of other keywords that your competitors may be missing. 'Car insurance Birmingham', 'Ford car insurance', 'car insurance for over 50s', 'car insurance discounts'. The list is practically endless and through building a broad strategy you can gain significant volume of niche customers, land them on a page dedicated to their specific need and increase your conversion significantly. We'll consider more around this as we work through this chapter.

The knowledge graph

We have mentioned these rich-data boxes a few times now. This is where the knowledge graph comes in. This is the knowledge base that Google maintains through connecting together distinct facts from sources across the internet.

These pieces of data are then used to fill specific boxes with key information related to searches. Not only would this work for a search like 'Sauron', but it can also make assumptions based on your intent and deliver likely outcomes. For example, if we search for 'the bad guy with the ring', Google provides us with Sauron as the answer.

Now this isn't just for well-known demons. Your company can get involved in the knowledge graph too. We'll look at this below.

It's also important to understand the downsides of the knowledge graph. According to several pieces of research, the knowledge graph can actually decrease clicks. This is simply because it answers the question, therefore making it unnecessary to click on a site. So, understanding where the knowledge graph may impact your keyword targeting is important. If you target a keyword with low CTR (click-through rate) due to the knowledge graph answering the query, you stand a good chance of being unsuccessful.

Algorithms

A word that was largely unknown to the public 20 years ago is one that is now on everyone's lips. Algorithms affect so much of day-to-day life now across search engines, social media and the devices we interact with day in and day out.

Search engines have always been notoriously secretive about their algorithms. It is impossible to get the exact rules around how Google works from anyone and these rules change regularly, often with very little or no notice. So how do you keep up?

Well, there are many clear ranking factors for SEO, which we will look at below. You should be monitoring these and working on improving them at all times. Beyond those however there are two key principles to making those algorithms love you.

BEHAVE YOURSELF

A phrase you will hear crop up in SEO is 'black hat'. This refers to search engine optimization techniques that are designed to deliver the best search ranking by manipulating the system: effectively by cheating.

Black hat techniques from the last 20-plus years of SEO include writing keywords over and over again in white text on a white background; stuffing the same keyword into your content over and over again so it reads badly but optimizes the page; putting competitor brands into your meta keywords tags to be ranked on their brand searches or buying hundreds of links from cheap little websites to improve your link volumes. None of these old techniques work any more, but they are an obvious way of illustrating the point; clearly demonstrating no interest in the right outcome for the user, just in manipulating the algorithms for your own gain.

Anything like this that is trying to trick the search engine should be avoided. First, because it is our duty to try to deliver the best results for consumers. If you'd like to be more selfish about it, however, then, second, because you have a high chance of being kicked off the search engines. This can kill businesses. I have seen companies go out of business from this exact outcome. It can be extremely difficult to get listed again and, even if you do, you will likely have to build your SEO up from the bottom again.

BE HUMAN

Don't optimize for Google, Bing or any other search engine. Optimize for the human. It's important to understand the ranking factors of course and appreciate how the search engines work. If you are focused on those rules alone, however, you will always be a step behind them. Instead, if you focus on the best possible user outcome, you will be aligned with the search engines and can stay a step ahead of them. This means that when a large and surprise algorithm changes, you won't need to react because you'll already have it covered.

This means ensuring your site has valuable, fresh content on a range of relevant topics. Doing things that generate good PR across reputable sites that are ideally also willing to link to you. Ensure too that your site loads quickly and is clean and easy to navigate.

Focus on principles like this and you have your best chance of success.

Ranking factors

As we mentioned above, there are many ranking factors to consider. In *Digital Marketing Strategy* I developed a very simple model called the SEO triangle (Figure 3.1).

This simply shows us that the core ranking factors can be split into three groups – Technical, Content and Links. This adds some structure to how we consider tackling the ranking factors and how we assign value and effort to each area.

If we look at some of the core ranking factors in Figure 3.2, we can see how this works.

These change and so it's important to check in on them every 12 months as a minimum. Fundamental shifts are unlikely in a short period of time, but can certainly happen over a longer period.

FIGURE 3.1 The SEO triangle

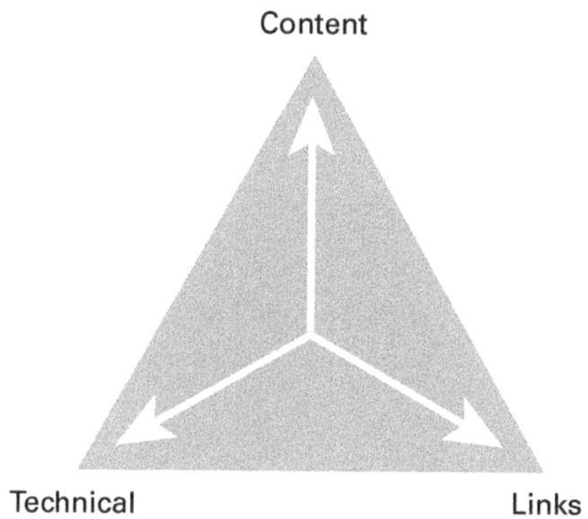

FIGURE 3.2 The ranking factors

Technical	Mobile friendliness
	Structured data
	Page speed
	Internal links
	URL relevance
	Site security
Content	Relevance of page content
	Meta tags
	Consistent, regular content
	User engagement
	Local content
	Social signals
	Relevant keywords within site
Links	Quality of linking sites
	Domain authority and trust

As we look at Technical, Content and Link strategies below, we'll dig into how we problem-solve for each of these factors.

Foundational tools

The final parts of the foundations are the key tools you need to work with. We'll discuss the full tech suite for SEO later, but at this stage, we just need to look at the core platforms.

First, you should register your site with the appropriate search engines. To do this, you will need to create or use an appropriate account to log into tools such as Google's Search Console and Bing's Webmaster Tools. This is where you register your site and monitor core data.

Using these tools, you will be able to see how many pages your site has indexed; mobile usability; searches on which your site is returned in the SERPs alongside clicks on those keywords; any errors in your site; site speed and many other key factors for your SEO monitoring. You will also be able to see any penalties you are given by Google. If you are avoiding black hat techniques then you should also avoid penalties.

Through these tools you can submit a sitemap to show the search engine the pages of your site and their priority. You can also ensure your robots.txt file is accepted and you can start to analyse early results.

Your sitemap should be created in xml format and include every page on your website. The following information is important:

- the url of each page: <loc>http://www.mywebsite.com/mypage</loc>
- the last time the page was changed: <lastmod>2021-03-06</lastmod>
- how frequently the page is changed: <changefreq>monthly</changefreq>
- the relative priority of the page on your site: <priority>1</priority>

This is then read by the search engines and they should go on to check every page. They will take this data as an indication of how regularly to check. It will not fully dictate to a search engine how to rank pages (the search engine will decide that for itself) but it will give an initial boost for a new site and enable the search engine to have a sense check at all times.

You may create this yourself or your CMS may do it for you. You should make sure you understand which set-up you have. You can also use the excellent tool Screaming Frog to create the sitemap for you or through plugins like the WordPress SEO Yoast.

Robots.txt files, on the other hand, are designed simply to tell search engine crawlers what to crawl and what to ignore. They include simple 'allow' and 'disallow' commands to specific folders of your website to ensure only the right areas are crawled. This helps to avoid any unnecessary indexing of irrelevant content. This same file can also tell search crawlers where your sitemap is located.

An example of a robots.text file may be:

```
# Group 1
User-agent: Googlebot
Disallow: /directory1/
```

```
# Group 2
User-agent: *
Allow: /

Sitemap: http://www.mywebsite.com/sitemap.xml
```

The above example prevents the user agent known as Googlebot from accessing anything in directory1 or any of its subdirectories. All other user agents can access everything. It then shows the location of the sitemap. While the two groups and their formatting are essential in a robots file, the sitemap location is optional but recommended.

Alongside these core areas you should also register with a local search such as Google My Business. This will ensure you are contributing to the knowledge graph. Ensure you complete this accurately and follow the guidelines or you will struggle to get it approved. Also, if there is already knowledge graph data on your company, products, brand, senior staff or any other directly relevant factor, you should claim this knowledge graph. Once that is done, you can suggest edits to maximize your SERP real estate and click volumes.

Once you have completed these core foundations you can start the research and planning phase.

SEO research and planning

It's vital at this stage to be clear on your goals and it's important to understand that 'Get to position 1' is not your goal.

Your goal may be sales (such as an e-commerce site), leads (a service company) or simply traffic (a content portal). This should be what you use as your measure of success. This doesn't mean you should lose sight of your ranking, your website performance, your content engagement or any other signal of SEO success, but you must stay true to your real business goals.

This means that having the number-one position on a number of keywords that drive lots of traffic to your website is great, but if your goal is leads and that traffic doesn't generate leads, then you have failed. And vice versa: if you achieve a great number of leads without ranking number one for any keyword, you are doing a great job.

So, how do we ensure we meet our SEO goals? We need to understand where to focus. We should be looking to include the right keywords in our URLs, page headings, content, alt tags and anywhere relevant (without repeating them too often). We'll touch on all of those later in the chapter, but, in the meantime, how do we find out what those keywords should be?

This is where keyword research comes in. Keyword research is going to give us the direction we need to start optimizing our site. It can tell us what people are actually searching for, how many people are searching for it and who are they. It can tell us how they want that information presented to them and what they value most. There are a number of methods and we'll look at those below, but first it's important to appreciate intent. This applies to a great number of areas of marketing and is especially important in search (organic or paid).

If I search for 'cats', what is my intent? It could be I want to buy a cat. Or I want to learn about cats. Perhaps I want to watch funny cat videos. Maybe I want to watch the musical *Cats*. Maybe I have a friend called Catherine, or Cat for short, and I want to know how many people are called Cat. Ok, that last one is a stretch, but the point is that you don't know the intent of such a broad and generic search term. If people were to search for 'best cat food' or 'buy cats near me', suddenly we know a great deal more. The first search is likely to be a cat owner, pet sitter or at least knows someone who is a cat owner. The second is someone who probably wants to buy a cat for themselves (as cats are rarely bought as presents outside the immediate family). Google describes these intents as:

- 'know' (find information);
- 'do' (accomplish a goal);
- 'website' (find a specific website);
- 'visit-in-person' (visit a local business).

So, keeping all of this in mind, let's build it out to look at an example of a pet-food store. What questions do we need to ask ourselves as we begin to consider the right keywords to target?

What types of pet food are people searching for?
For dogs, cats, gerbils? Flavours? Dry or wet?

Why?
Because they want healthier food for their pet? Because of news about an issue with a product?

When are people searching for pet food?
Time of day? Day of the week? Month of the year?

Who is searching for it?

Women or men? Adults or children? The wealthy or less well off?

Where are they?

Local? National? Regional? International?

How are they searching?

Typed or voice? Desktop or mobile? What words and phrases?

These questions help you to truly understand your audience and their intent. From here you can start to create keyword assumptions that relate directly to the needs of your consumers.

That is not going to get you to a full and complete list of course. You don't know what you don't know. In order to expand on the results of this initial phase you must use some tools. There are a few tools available online that can take keywords and give you related keywords with predicted volumes. I've listed some of the main ones to consider below.

Google Keyword Planner

It seems strange to look in an ad platform for organic insights, but within Google Ads is a Keyword Planner which is the go-to starting point for keyword research. It isn't perfect, but it can be a great way of gathering a large keyword set quite quickly. If you have Google Ads running, you can also use your historic performance to inform your SEO of course.

Google Trends

An excellent tool for monitoring changes in specific terms. As the world changes, consumer behaviours change. You will see gradual and sometimes immediate shifts in performance of keywords and you will also see clear seasonal trends for many terms. A key part of the keyword research arsenal.

Moz Keyword Explorer

Moz has long been an important tool in SEO. Their Keyword Explorer tool provides monthly search volume and SERP features (like the boxes mentioned above).

Semrush

Semrush is an excellent tool for many areas of digital marketing and it will feature in numerous places in this book. The platform has a dedicated SEO dashboard that can inform your strategy from keywords to links and technical issues.

Soovle

This tool looks across multiple sources such as Google, YouTube, Bing, Yahoo, Amazon and others to provide a much wider range of results than many other tools can offer. Keeping the context in mind for the channels is important.

Jaaxy

Another tool that provides a very wide range of keywords alongside competition. It also provides an indication of how many websites are trying to compete on a given keyword.

There are many more of course but these tools will give you a good starting point.

After using these tools, your initial keyword list is likely to expand. For example, you may now also have:

- Healthy cat food;
- Food for old dogs;
- Pet food shops in Philadelphia;
- Food for indoor cats.

This gives you the chance to shape great content around these terms and start to edge ahead of your competition on highly relevant keywords. Terms such as 'food for indoor cats' may also be significantly less competitive. Competing on a wide range of less competitive, more niche terms may deliver your goals much more easily than trying to push up one more place on the primary volume keyword.

The difficulty of ranking on a specific keyword is called, perhaps unsurprisingly, 'keyword difficulty'. The primary keyword in an industry or for a product is likely to have a very high keyword difficulty. Large brands with a great deal of PR and large websites are difficult to topple from the top for these terms. Keyword difficulty can also be increased if the SERPs are crowded with the rich boxes we have already mentioned.

Working in a challenging scenario such as this can mean a need to focus on these niche or long-tail keywords. A long-tail keyword is one that is highly targeted and often involves a specific phrase rather than one or two direct words. An example would be 'Where can I buy a blue coat in Rome' rather than 'coats'. If you sell beautiful blue coats in Rome, the first search will not only give you fantastic click-through rate and conversion but it will also be less competitive and easier to rank for. It's a win-win.

In actual fact, high-volume terms such as the 'coats' example may even be so generic as to be worthless. Just because I search for coats doesn't mean I want to buy one as we've already discussed regarding intent above. The long-tail approach is therefore a strong way of winning for any business but especially one that is out-spent by, and less well known than, the big brands.

Finally, we need to take a look at our keywords through a few different lenses to kick out variations of the terms we have discovered during our research.

- **Trending:** Is this keyword a long-term focus or a current trend? If trending, then you may need to prioritize quickly but not build your long-term strategy around it. Are there any other keywords that have associated trends you could ride on the back of?
- **Immediacy:** Could using the terms 'now', 'today' or 'in January' change the intent or meaning of a keyword and expand your list?
- **Needs-based:** Think about the needs of the searcher. Are they trying to solve a problem? Are there other ways to solve that problem that you can also create keywords around?
- **Product type:** Quite simply what variations do you have? Large and small. Blue and green. New and old models. Cheap and premium. Wool and leather. Consider every variation and separate out the keywords.
- **Locality:** Never has local search been more important. 'Near me', 'in my town', 'in Shanghai' – consider every likely variation that's relevant.
- **Action:** What is the specific action someone is looking to take? To find out information? To buy or enquire? To visit a shop or other location?

Technical SEO

Technical SEO has always existed as one corner of the SEO triangle. It is an area that marketers are often least comfortable with as it leans much more towards technology professionals rather than marketing professionals. Indeed, many SEO practitioners will be technically minded and trained but with a good marketing and commercial brain rather than marketers who trained to become programmers.

The reason is that technical SEO can be very complex in places and, while the principles remain the same – deliver a fast, clean, clear and easily indexed site – the complexity in getting there can be significant.

Google has always sought to bring the best websites to the top of its rankings, but how do you define best? The only constant in SEO is that this definition keeps changing. The infamous algorithm changes from Google are ultimately about redefining this to ensure that a Googler will get to their desired outcome as quickly as possible.

Also, the user experience of your website has never been more important. Google is very focused on page experience as a measure of success and current and future optimizations are likely to focus on this. This doesn't mean content- or link-based SEO is any less important, but it does mean you cannot compromise on the quality of your website UX any more.

Part of that means sites that have the right content, which we'll look at later. Part of it means sites that other websites see as valuable and therefore link to. We'll look at that later too. The third part is whether they are technically good websites. If I click that link, will it load in a reasonable amount of time? Will I be able to easily navigate that page? Will I know what I'm looking at or will things be misleading or shift position just before I click on them?

Some of the more important technical considerations have been transformed into what is now known as 'core web vitals': the key signals that a website is operating within Google's guidelines. We'll start therefore by taking a look at these.

Common causes of CLS issues:

- Images;
- Ads;
- iFrames;
- Embeds.

How to fix: Set dimensions and reserve space for anything that will load.

Core web vitals

The core web vitals can be found within the Experience section of Google's Search Console. The platform will quickly show any URLs that Google considers of poor quality and those that need improvement. From here you can dig into exactly what the issue is and then take that insight to review your code and eliminate the problem.

Another way to find out this information is to run a Lighthouse test through Google Chrome.

> USING LIGHTHOUSE
>
> In the browser, select Options > More Tools > Developer Tools.
>
> At the top of the right-hand bar, you can find Lighthouse.

Generating a report on mobile or desktop here will give you an in-depth list of how your site is seen from a technical perspective by Google. You will receive screenshots of every stage of loading and a report into every code issue and how much load time it is causing, alongside any other concerns in the technical build of the site. Each will be rated with a traffic-light system to show serious issues, concerns and items that pass the test.

Let's look at the three metrics that make up the core web vitals, as shown in Figure 3.3.

LARGEST CONTENTFUL PAINT (LCP)

LCP measures how long it takes for the largest piece of content to appear on the screen. This could be a section of text on the page or an image. So, this is not looking at the full load of the page but rather the largest and therefore potentially most important element.

This can be relatively simple to optimize against. If for example you have a large image or video and a relatively small amount of copy, you could just reduce the file size or improve the format to make it load faster. Of course, it's not always this simple, but with some investigation and by using the tools mentioned above you can find, isolate and improve the issue. The

FIGURE 3.3 Core web vitals

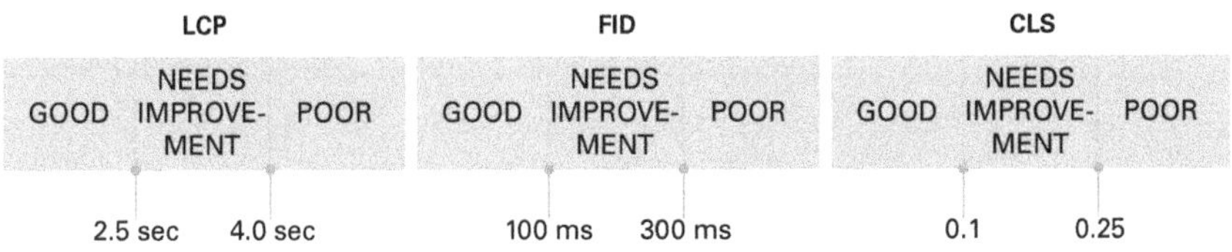

loading screenshots as seen in the Lighthouse report are a great way of identifying the largest piece of content as is Google's PageSpeed Insights.

You should aim for the LCP to be within the first 2.5 seconds as you can see in Figure 3.3. If it is taking up to 4 seconds, you should be looking to make improvements, and beyond that you have a serious issue that you should solve as quickly as possible.

There are many causes of poor LCP, which can include slow server response times, render-blocking JavaScript and CSS, slow-loading resources and issues on client-side rendering. Tackling these will involve minifying CSS, deferring non-critical CSS, optimizing images, compressing files, using server-side rendering and minimizing JS.

Ultimately, you should ensure you do not load more than you have to (for example WordPress plug-ins, CRM code), keep the code minimal and tidy, and optimize any files for size.

FIRST INPUT DELAY (FID)

FID, rather than focusing on load time, focuses on interaction time. It is a measure of how long it takes the site to react to the first interaction taken by a user. An interaction is a broad term but means a firm action such as a button click rather than a more passive action such as a scroll or pinch.

We have all experienced the website that looks fully loaded but you just can't click on anything. Why not? Because it is still loading something in the background. This causes enormous frustration and immediate bounces from many users.

As you can see in Figure 3.3, the times here are very tight. This FID score should be under 100 milliseconds. 100–300 ms needs improvement, and slower is a serious issue. This means that you again need to minimize the work being done on the load of your site to ensure it becomes interactive very quickly. JavaScript can be a common cause here, so take a look at what is being loaded and if it can be improved or removed.

Now one important thing to note is that not every page is about interaction. Content-focused sites such as blogs may not be trying to push you into a call-to-action. They may be entirely about reading the content. Certainly, many pages on most sites will be focused on this engagement rather than action approach. On those pages, FID is not relevant and may actually be a distraction. It is important therefore to appreciate where to use this and not to apply it to the whole site in a blanket approach.

CUMULATIVE LAYOUT SHIFT (CLS)

CLS is a factor that has become more common in websites over recent years and I believe is one major reason Google have focused more on page experience. So, what is it?

Have you visited a website and it starts to load...? You see something interesting and go to click on it and as you do it shifts down the page and you end up clicking on something else? Or you are reading a long article and it keeps shifting down the page as things load and move the page around. This can often be caused by ads, which are there to monetize the content and therefore enable that website owner to produce the valuable content that brought you there, but it's incredibly irritating and can render this great content so annoying that you leave the site.

Besides ads, you should be conscious of any other large elements that you place on your page that may shift other items around. Images, call-to-actions and promotional boxes can all be guilty of causing CLS issues. It's essential therefore to optimize your images and specify the attributes of them so as to be clear to the browser what space they will occupy.

The measure for CLS is not in speed or interaction but in severity of movement. The more the page shifts around, the higher the score. Google considers anything below 0.1 to be fine, while 0.1 to 0.25 needs improvement, and over 0.25 is a serious concern.

Google have openly said that all three scores need to be in the green range for a rankings boost. That doesn't necessarily mean this should be your core focus. You should always be focusing on the best user experience and perhaps that won't always line up with the core web vitals on every page of every website. However, it is definitely worth taking a serious look at these numbers and assessing if you can improve them, as it is likely to become only more important over time.

CASE STUDY: A FASHION COMPANY

The challenge

A fashion company was struggling to get traffic to its website. The website itself was well designed and the conversion rate was strong. However, traffic just wasn't arriving from organic sources. By conducting an SEO audit, they found that their technical SEO standards were good, but the content could be improved and the volume and quality of incoming links was low. They needed to address this.

The solution

The company decided to embrace link baiting. They were aware that buying links or in any way trying to inorganically create links is not what search engines like to see. They therefore created a piece of content that was designed to entice other sites to link to them. This link baiting involved a tool where users could design their look. Using a 3D model, users could choose specific outfit options and colours to preview their fashion choices. Many of these were linked to the company's products. This was a tool that anyone could use, would attract the right audience type and enabled a direct increase in sales.

The results

Over the next six months, this became the second most visited page on the site and contributed 21 per cent of the company's sales. It also played a major role in improving the company's SEO performance as they moved from page 3 to page 1 on their primary target keyword.

Structure and hierarchy

As we've already discussed, Google is assessing the technical signals from your site to determine its experience for users. One area that is sometimes overlooked as a key signal generator is the site structure.

If a site is logical and clear, users will very quickly be able to understand where to go and what to click on to find their way around. If it follows a clear pattern and uses best practice, your experience signals will be good: strong click-throughs, good engagement, more pages per visit. However, if your site is confusing, long dwell times and high bounce rates are likely signs of frustration. With a poor structure, Google will see these signals and the SEO results will be negative.

As you know, the more appealing your site to users, the more appealing it is to search engines. Google's algorithm uses information from searchers to rank your site. If your site has poor CTRs and low dwell time, it will not perform well in the SERPs. By contrast, when a user finds a site that they like – a site with great structure – they don't bounce and they stay longer. An accurate site structure can reduce bounce rate and improve dwell time, both of which will lead to improved rankings.

Two of the most important benefits of a great site structure, beyond simple user experience, are:

- **Better crawling:** If your site has logical paths and good internal linking, search robots can quickly establish the full site structure, meaning no missed pages or confusion about which pages are the correct ones to rank on a specific subject.
- **Enhancements such as site links:** Google will decide if your site is worthy of site links. A poor structure means Google cannot be confident enough in your site to give an accurate view to searchers. Site links give you extra real estate on the SERPs and that can be invaluable.

Website hierarchy is something you should plan out alongside your information architecture, which we'll discuss later in this chapter. You should consider who is coming to your website and why, including who you want to come to your website and why. This determines the outcomes you need to provide for those visitors and therefore the clear paths you need them to take. You can then take your work on keyword research and apply that to creating content that attracts those individuals to your site.

By putting the outcomes together with the content plans you can create a simple skeleton of the structure that takes users from content they are interested in to outcomes they are looking for.

Try not to over complicate this. As with anything in marketing, the simpler the better. It should not go deeper than it needs to. In fact, you should aim to keep the most important content at the top of the structure. For example:

MyWebsite.com/Important-Content

Rather than:

MyWebsite.com/Catalogue/Products/1/Important-Content

NAVIGATION

Within any conversation around structure, we must mention navigation. The structure itself is great for the robots, but the user also needs to move around it logically. As a result, a clear menu that can be easily found and navigated is critical.

Mega menus, hamburger menus, minimalist menus: you will find different routes employed by different websites here. So, which is right for you?

Mega menus: For sites that showcase very large and complex businesses or product catalogues, a mega menu can play an important role. If a user may want to get to a very wide range of products, businesses or topics quickly and it is very difficult to determine that from the user data, then this is a good option.

However, if you can keep your menu smaller and simpler, you should. Avoid mega menus if they do not add real one-click value to the user. The desire to showcase all your pages and products can be tempting, but do not force options onto users for your benefit – only for theirs.

Hamburger menus: This is a common method that works very well on mobile devices and has become very common. This three-lined icon that hides the menu and expands upon click is great for small spaces. It can also be employed on desktop to great effect. However, if you are looking to push your users to a specific page, you should surface it and this approach doesn't allow that.

Minimalist menus: This is an increasingly common approach that is the opposite of the mega menu. Many sites now are showing only two to three links at the top. This ensures the user focuses only on the ones you want them to. It can be extremely effective at controlling the journeys your users take and therefore driving leads and engagement but be careful not to trim too much and leave your users confused about how to get to key content.

TOP TIP

Reviews

The power of the consumer today is enormous. According to Inc.com, 84 per cent of people trust online reviews as much as they trust their friends, and 91 per cent of people read reviews. This plays a much bigger part than SEO of course, but getting reviews across multiple channels enables you to get a review score extension added to your search results. Google will decide to do this when it feels there are enough reviews.

If you're confident in the quality of your products and services, then this should play a key role in your SEO plans.

Structured data

We will not go into deep technical details about structured data in this book. I would recommend you look at Google's developer tools and help pages to understand this in more detail. What we will discuss is the importance and benefit of this approach.

Google always looks to provide data in a structured way. In fact, 'to organize the world's information' is their mission. Therefore, helping them to do this is only going to benefit you.

Structured data enables you to tag your website in a way that helps Google to understand specific features that exist within your content. This could be for books, products, articles, events, job postings, restaurants, local business listings and much more. Because each element of the item is tagged, Google is able to return results about the item by its unique elements. For example, a product can be tagged with:

- product name;
- product image;
- product description;
- brand name;
- brand logo;
- aggregate rating;
- price;
- other fields.

This makes the product page no longer just a listing on your website but a fully quantified addition to the Google database, enabling each element of the product to be searched for uniquely.

This approach can also apply to FAQs and much more, enabling results to be returned in the SERPs even where your organic listings are not particularly strong.

The power here is quite clear, but you must follow Google's guidelines. You can use their Structured Data Markup Helper Tool to help with the tagging code and the Rich Results tool within Search Console to see what tagging is working or having issues on your site.

Tagging

Heading tags are an important consideration when building your site. Each page should have an H1 tag and this represents what the page is about. While there have been reports that Google does not care how many H1 tags you use, it clearly creates a stronger hierarchy and is therefore sensible to take this approach.

The title of your page is generally an H1 tag. The subheadings of your content and sections of your page should then be H2, H3 and H4 tags. Each can be given its own style via your style sheet and you should consider an H2 to be of secondary importance, H3 of tertiary importance and so on. This greatly helps with readability, navigation and SEO.

You should also make sure every image has an alt tag. This is not only to help SEO but also for accessibility reasons. Accessibility itself is important to ensure everyone can read your website. There are many criteria to meet around the use of colours, sizes of font and tags, and this is one. From an SEO perspective you will also be rated poorly if your images are not tagged, so ensure you complete this simple piece of work when uploading images to your site.

Meta tags are not as important as they once were, but they still have their place. Gone are the days when you could stuff any keywords you want into the meta keywords tag and rank for them. However, the meta description tag remains important. Is this because you can cram it with keywords? No. Having your keywords in there is certainly a good thing, but this is less about directly improving your search rankings and more about improving your click-through rate.

A good description should be highly relevant to the page, include the correct keywords in a natural way and have a call to action. All within the 160-character limit.

There is no actual technical limit here, but beyond 160 characters your description will be truncated and will therefore lose some of its value. Screaming Frog is one of many tools that will easily help you stay on top of your meta descriptions.

CANONICAL TAGS

These were introduced in 2009 and are important for everyone working in SEO to understand.

Duplicate content is not something Google likes. You should avoid creating multiple versions of the same page, either on your site or across multiple sites. You should also of course avoid duplicating anyone else's content.

However, there are times when duplicate content can play a role. For example, a brand that wants to publish a story to all of its subsidiary sites. Also, from a technical perspective, the http and https versions of a site or the www and non-www versions.

Google reads all of these as duplicate pages and so we need to tell Google which to consider as the original page – the one that should rank for this content. Google will actually determine this by itself, but sometimes – believe it or not – Google can get it wrong. It can't actually say for certain where the original content is or why it should be that page. Assumptions can be made, but they may be incorrect.

As a result, you can add a canonical tag to your page. This tag can confirm to Google that the page is the correct version or it can tell Google that another page is the correct version.

You may need to implement this using the actual canonical tag itself, which you can find with a quick Google. Alternatively, you can implement it through many popular content management systems via their SEO plugins. For example, the Yoast plugin on WordPress.

Http status codes

One of the less glamorous areas of SEO is status codes. They do however remain important for any SEO practitioner to understand. Before we move on to content SEO, we will take a quick look at four of the key codes to understand.

301

By returning a 301 code on a page on your website you are telling the search engines that the page has permanently moved to a new url. This is helpful when sunsetting an old page or redesigning a website. This ensures that the SEO value of the old page and any external links pointing to it are transferred to the new location.

302

This is a temporary move of a page. This tells the search engine that the page is somewhere else for now. Perhaps because some work is being done on it. The page will be back. No SEO value is transferred and if this stays in this status for too long, Google will change the code into a 301.

404

The infamous status that the page cannot be found. You should ensure you have a designed 404 page that clearly instructs users where to go if they come across this.

503
Your site is likely to be down. This may be due to huge volumes (such as release of tickets for a popular concert) or a server issue. The site will be back up. Again, you should look at designing a specific page here to inform the user.

Content SEO

The second corner of the SEO triangle is content. It has never been more important or more broadly defined than it is now. Everything from video and audio to PR and infographics is covered within content. It is then distributed via websites, social media, printed publications and many more channels besides. We'll get into content strategy more specifically in Chapter 7, as here we focus purely on the role content plays within SEO. In this section we will look at some of the core approaches to creating content that search engines love.

Research

First, we need to decide what we're going to write about. This will be part of our Content Calendar approach (see Chapter 7) and must include content that we know our audience want to read/watch/engage with. We have already discussed keyword research and this again plays a major part in this starting point.

Alongside that, you can also review user-generated content sites online. Reddit is a great place for SEO content research. What are people talking about, asking about, debating? Whatever your product and industry, chances are there is something here that is being discussed. This may not show up clearly in your keyword research but it's clearly a hot topic among some of your audience.

Another tool to consider here is one that has grown significantly in recent years. AnswerThePublic.com gives a view as to what questions people are specifically asking. It splits them into the what, how, why and other key formats before directing you to the results for each. This can inspire Q&A-format content that you may have missed.

Once you've completed this SEO-focused keyword research you need to write content that focuses on that keyword. That's not to say that you should write a lengthy article with that keyword in as often as possible. In fact, keyword frequency is a delicate balance. A few mentions on a page will help give a clear signal to the search engines about the topic of the page, but too many mentions looks like you are trying to over optimize your page, which will give negative signals. Try to be natural in your language. Do try, however, to get your keywords mentioned early in your content. This makes it very clear what you are talking about.

What's cool about this technique that is you get to see keywords that people are searching for right now. Which means these terms aren't super-competitive (yet).

Produce

Now comes the hard part. Producing your content. For written content, you will find that length plays a major factor.

Anything below 300 to 400 words would be considered thin content. This is to say that Google will generally consider it of no value. The more content you have like this on your website, the more likely that Google will consider you to be offering little value to users.

Longer content is therefore much more valuable, but it does take more effort to put together. Where a short-form piece may be 400 words, a long-form content article is more likely to be 1500 to 2000 words. A blend of both is therefore a good balance, but you must have a piece of long-form content on the key topics or you will fail to compete.

Within this content you should make the structure very clear. For example, you should create subtitles to break up the piece. These should use H tags as discussed above. Important points should be in bold and call-to-actions should be very clear.

Somewhat surprisingly, you should also link out to other relevant sites where you can. It may seem counter-intuitive to send your visitors to another website, but this is a clear signal that your site is playing a role on the internet of helping people to find the information they use. Remember Google's mission statement and it will make sense.

You also need to consider how easy your piece is to read. Not everyone reading it will use the same native language as you. Not all will have the same education or regional dialects. Keeping sentences and paragraphs short, avoiding jargon and writing in a neutral dialect will help your page be more readable. Try to ensure sentences are not repetitive and they lead onto the next sentence naturally.

One technique used by many successful content writers is to start with extra-short sentences. Ask a question and answer it very quickly. Your article can get into more detail and explain the why, but you have quickly solved the problem for the user – great.

When designing content pages, you should take the approach that newspaper editors learned many decades ago. Keeping your copy in blocks that are not too wide makes it much more readable. Wider blocks mean much more chance of the reader losing their place. This is why newspapers are much easier to read than books.

Within this format you should also include other content types. We have mentioned video and audio above and will go into YouTube and podcasts later in the book. Featuring video guides, interviews and quick tips that break up your content also really engages users. You can explain something in 10 seconds in video that may take a couple of minutes reading in the written form. This helps your user, and ultimately your SEO, a great deal.

Beyond this, other forms of content that help users solve issues can be enormously helpful.

We will discuss link baiting below, but one of the ways of attracting users to your content is by directly solving a complex issue for them. This can be done in the form of a simple tool. Content such as tax calculators and mortgage calculators have been hugely popular for many years. They solve a complex issue quickly and therefore users will want to visit you, and other websites will want to link to you.

Also consider what you can write that applies to a niche audience. Locality is important. A huge percentage of us are looking for local services online, and satisfying that through great content is an excellent way of helping a niche audience and therefore delivering great search value to many internet users.

Finally, consider your cornerstone pages. These are the critical pages on your site; the ones that make up the focal points of your structure. Each one of these should be the best it can possibly be. SEO content is by no means just about blogs. Your core pages should have the same treatment as the more frequent content, so ensure you apply all of this to every product, service and corporate page necessary to deliver your brand strength.

Keep it alive

Once you have your content you need to keep it alive, which you can do through a few methods.

First, you should promote it. I don't mean pay to advertise it but share it on your networks. Social media is an obvious place to begin and this will give you a kick=start and a location where it can grow in popularity quite quickly.

> TOP TIP
>
> *Never stop*
>
> You should refresh your content regularly.
>
> Once a piece is written, you should not consider it finished. It's worth revisiting content on a regular basis. This is of course greatly dependent on the resources available to you, but if you can rewrite your content annually to update stats and changes to the industry or product, then you will keep it highly relevant and timely.
>
> Google is always looking for fresh content.

Link strategy

Links are the final corner of the SEO triangle. The logic goes that, if your site is being linked to by a lot of other respected sites, it is probably doing something valuable. This makes sense.

Volume of links is therefore certainly a factor, but so is quality of links. Simply getting thousands of links from poor-quality or brand-new websites will not help you here. That is definitely the easiest way to gain links, but it is of no value and, in fact, can attribute negative value.

We have mentioned black hat techniques a few times in this chapter. They crop up again here as there have been, and remain, many ways to try and manipulate Google into ranking your website via link building. I would strongly recommend against this. In fact, I have myself been involved in several projects for clients who have had to spend a lot of money and time trying to remove the remnants of a previous black hat link-building strategy, often resulting in their removal from Google altogether.

You should avoid link exchanges. You should never pay for links for SEO purposes. Any paid link should have a 'nofollow' tag associated with it to tell Google that it has no SEO value. You should not list yourself on as many directories as possible and you should never create your own sites just to link to other sites that you own. The way to drive links to your site is through natural means.

But that sounds very slow. Well, natural doesn't have to mean passive. There are many techniques you can use to drive links to your site, from the right sites and well within Google's guidelines for link building. Building these links organically, steadily and relevantly can pay huge dividends. In fact, if you look at the best performing sites in any area of search, you will see a huge correlation between links and ranking.

Before we get into the techniques, we should touch on domain authority. DA is a measure of how relevant a website is for its given industry. It was developed by Moz, but other similar measurements exist in tools such as AHRefs and SEMRush. These authority scores usually relate entirely, or to a great deal, to the inbound links that the site has. This includes the volume of links and the authority of the sites linking. If a website therefore has many links from sites with 50-plus (out of 100) DA it will be passed a great deal of 'link juice', which will in turn score it highly. If it has few links, its score will be low. If it is linked to from a great deal of sites with a DA of 10, it will start to look like a very poor website. This is an essential factor to understand when deciding which sites to target for link building.

So here we will look at some of the right and wrong strategies to use for link building.

Buying links

This is a case of finding sites that look successful and paying them to link to your site. Many will reject the offer but some will take the money. As mentioned above, if you don't add a 'nofollow' tag then you're breaching Google's guidelines and may be penalized. You should avoid this approach.

Foundational organic links

Here you add links to the obvious, easy places. Forums, blog comments, business directories. These are very low value simply because they are so easy to do. In fact, doing too much of this could result in a Google penalty. Do this to a limited extent and ensure it doesn't make up a high percentage of your inbound links.

Broken link building

This involves finding a broken link, recreating the content on your site (and ideally improving on it) and then telling everyone linking to it to link to you instead. You can use Archive.org (a great resource for many reasons) to find what used to be at a broken link. You can then ask the owner of the broken link you found to point to you instead. Your success rate will be limited and it can be quite a lot of work, but this has some limited value here.

Simply asking

The most obvious route, but if you are aware of high-value sites that you want to link to you and you feel you have content that is truly compelling for their audience, why not ask. You do of course need to give them something. Not money, but something of benefit to them. You could link back to them. You could mention their brand in a positive way. You could write a case study about them. There are many options. This is ultimately a sales exercise.

Digital PR

Write compelling content and distribute it to journalists and publications either directly or through aggregated services. This may result in some pick-up and hopefully links. If you get pick-up, be sure to check for links and ask for them if they are missing. Many online publications have great domain authority and so a compelling story can work wonders.

Link baiting

We mentioned this above. If you create content that people really want, you will naturally gain links. Calculators are a great place to begin but with any other tools that solve problems, or long-form content that goes above and beyond your competitors, you will see links developing naturally over time.

Resource link building

Finding resource-focused pages and getting them to link to you is another great technique. These pages exist purely to link their users to great external resources on a given subject. You can find resource pages on a specific subject by using search modifiers. For example, if you were searching for resource pages on marketing you would type: marketing intitle:resources inurl:resources.html.

You can then reach out to these resource pages with the high-quality and relevant content that you have to benefit their users.

Link penalties

As mentioned above, if you receive a lot of poor-quality links, you are likely to suffer rather than reap any benefits. If this continues for some time or gets materially worse or you are found to be link buying, you have a good chance of receiving a Google penalty. This can involve a serious decline in your search rankings and perhaps removal from the search engine altogether. If this happens, it can be months or even years until you return and you may never return to your previous success. These penalties have put many companies out of business and radically affected the success of others. This is one of many reasons why black hat techniques should be avoided.

Disavowing

Links are however not entirely under your control. So, what if poor sites start linking to you? This will bring down your link profile and could harm your SEO.

Thankfully there is a solution. Google has a Disavow tool. Quite simply, you can identify poor-quality links through any SEO tool that you use, save these into a document and upload them to this tool. This means that rather than having to try to remove all of these links, you are simply telling Google that you do not want them to count towards your SEO profile and they will be ignored, ensuring no negative impact from them.

If this is aggressively happening at scale you should try to find why and where and stop it. This can be difficult, but it can save a lot of work and worry further down the line.

Reporting

We have talked repeatedly about how all of the techniques from this chapter can improve your search engine rankings so clearly that is the number-one metric to focus on.

SEO reporting is an area that needs careful thought, and you need to ensure that your boss understands what you are reporting on but more importantly, why you are reporting on it. I have seen many frustrated SEO professionals over the last 20-plus years who are delivering phenomenal results but are being criticized and pushed in the wrong direction by their manager. Why? It's simply a question of training and communication.

So, what does a good SEO dashboard look like?

To begin with we must take a step back and remember what we're trying to achieve. Visits? Leads? Sales? Whatever our ultimate goal is, it should feature within our KPIs. If SEO isn't delivering against our goal, then why are we doing it? There are exceptions to this. Perhaps you are a celebrity who is trying to retain a strong public profile. Your website isn't trying to get you movie deals but to ensure you maintain your celebrity status. However, for the vast majority of websites your core business goals should be the number-one concern for your SEO dashboard.

Ultimately, even if you don't rank on many keywords, don't have a great volume of high-quality back links and don't get a lot of traffic but all of your traffic converts into sales and that is growing 100 per cent month on month, then your strategy is working.

Key performance indicators (KPIs)

- **Goals/leads/sales:** As said above, this is likely to be your number-one focus. Every other metric is a means to an end. If they all contribute to this outcome for your business then, while you can improve them, they are doing their job.
- **Visibility:** This is the percentage of traffic your site is getting as a proportion of all the traffic available for a given search term or group of terms. For example, if you rank second on a keyword you will get around 25 per cent of the traffic and so your site visibility for this keyword is 25 per cent. Across all of your keywords you can quickly understand your overall visibility.
- **Keywords ranking in top 3, 10, 20, 100:** Tools like Semrush will tell you how many of your keywords are in the top 3, top 10, top 20 and top 100 results. This is beneficial to understand whether you are ranking for the right terms and how this is changing over time.
- **Site health – core web vitals:** We have of course mentioned these already. Every SEO report should track these and react quickly to any changes.
- **Traffic:** Depending on your strategy, this may be more or less relevant. Huge volumes of the wrong people are not helpful here. As page experience becomes more important, bringing the wrong people to your site will mean low engagement and therefore a poor SEO signal to Google.

- **Links:** You should maintain a view on the quantity and quality of domains and pages linking to your site. Are these within the targets mentioned above or do you have an increasing number of poor links within your profile? Of the poor links you have, what percentage are disavowed?
- **Indexed pages:** Are all of your pages indexed? Are there any indexed that shouldn't be? Is your canonical set-up correct?
- **Top-ranking pages:** Which pages on your site are performing best from an SEO perspective? Which are driving the most traffic?

PLATFORM RECOMMENDATIONS

Finally, there are many great SEO tools and we have mentioned many of them in this chapter. They are:

- AHRefs – great for link SEO;
- Screaming Frog – great for site audits;
- SEMRush – a wide range of tools around links, content and technical SEO;
- Search consoles – Google and Bing offer tools to monitor performance and react;
- Moz – wide ranging SEO toolkit with everything you need;
- Google Analytics – overview of organic performance on your site;
- Google My Business – essential for local SEO;
- Structured Data Markup Helper – a great tool to help with structured data.

04

Managing paid search for cost-effective results

Paid search is a channel that goes by many names. It's sometimes known as PPC (pay per click), but this applies to a method of payment for many channels so is not entirely accurate. It's sometimes called SEM (search engine marketing), but this could also include SEO, so again it's misleading. Paid search is really the term of preference here.

Whatever you call it, it has long been established as an important channel for many businesses and one which can deliver huge success if understood and managed correctly. It is however a complex area and so understanding how to optimize it effectively is critical for success. While you can toy with social media as you work out your strategy without any cost impact (although potentially some brand impact), anything you do on paid search without full optimization is wasting money.

This chapter first looks at ensuring you have a solid grip on the channel, how it works and why it works that way. Then we'll look at some specific techniques that will ensure that your paid search campaigns reach their full potential.

There are a lot of metrics to consider within paid search and it is vital that you do consider them. This channel is hugely measurable and you should be analysing every metric and pulling every lever to maximize your return on investment. The jargon and measurements can be quite extensive, so I'm not going to go into basic definitions such as clicks and impressions – I will assume you have this baseline of knowledge. Instead, we will address them as we go through the chapter. But let's start with a look at one of the more mysterious metrics that we need to understand before we begin, as it affects our entire strategy.

Quality score

Ultimately, when a user searches for a keyword that you are bidding on, there are two ways that a search engine decides on where to place your ad. The first is the bid, and we will look more at bid strategies later in the chapter. The second is quality score. What is quality score and how do you optimize for it?

Well, first let's understand just how important this is. Quality score is not just a nice metric to tell you that your ad is doing well. It actually serves as an adjustment to your bids, enabling your ads to outperform lower-quality ones and drive much better performance for your budget. In fact, if your ads achieve a quality score of 10 (out of 10) this can mean that your ads cost half as much as they would at the Google benchmark score of 5, as Google will favour your ads due to relevance to the user. If, however, your quality score is 1, it could mean bids are adjusted to 400 per cent of their planned bid, as Google doesn't want to show them as they seem irrelevant to the user. Disaster. So, with that in mind, let's take a look at what quality score is in more detail.

Quality score is ultimately a metric of relevance. Are your keyword, ad and landing page – the full user journey – relevant to the person searching? If so, great – you'll get a top quality score. If not, you need to make changes to benefit from this.

This is the most important lesson you will learn on paid search:

> To ensure you get the best quality score possible, you need to ensure you have your user journeys optimized.

So how do you do that? Well, you need to create specific keyword sets, ads and landing pages. It's a lot of work, especially when Google offers the option to dynamically create the ads for you. The trick with paid search, however, is to put the hours in. By creating tightly grouped keywords in ad groups, writing ads specifically targeted to those keywords and landing the user on a page about that specific subject you will deliver excellent quality scores not to mention fantastic click-through rates and conversion rates, ultimately leading to the best possible ROI.

We'll dig into more detail on this as we work through the chapter, but in a nutshell that is the approach to paid search. Be specific and put the effort in and you reap the rewards.

It's worth noting that within your Google Ads account you may not find quality scores. Google does not always show them by default. Therefore, you may need to go into your keywords report, click the Columns button above the keywords, find it there and add it to your report.

Account structure

Now that we understand this mysterious metric, let's get into the structure of a good paid search account.

Let me add that I am focusing on Google here. Why? Simply because Google has the vast majority of the market share for search in most territories. First, because if your approach works on Google it is likely to work elsewhere, for example Bing. And second, because Bing has a tool that enables you to import your Google structure, so this way round makes the most sense.

Ad accounts are broken down into Accounts, Campaigns and Ad groups. You are likely to have only one account for your company, but you may have many accounts if, like me, you run an agency or if you have multiple businesses that you run within your company structure.

Campaigns are where we get into the detail of what we're selling. At this level we are focusing on the logical top level of our product structure. Perhaps we are a clothing store and we have campaigns for dresses, trousers, shirts and blouses, sweaters, shoes, skirts, hats and so on. This gives us a very quick snapshot of our product portfolio and how it is performing.

However, when someone searches for a dress, are they just typing 'dress' and looking at everything that shows up? Very unlikely as the choice would be overwhelming. They probably have something in mind. A summer dress, an evening dress, a white dress, a dress with stripes, a long dress, a warm dress. The options are significant. Think back to the quality score relevance. If someone searches for a white dress and we show them an ad for a black dress, will they click? No. So, we need to take a step below campaign level.

This is where Ad groups come in. Now we can really start to separate out these different options we looked at above. We create an ad group for white dresses. Within this we have a range of keywords associated with this search, and we'll look at those in the keywords section below. We'll then write an ad specifically about white dresses and point them to our white dresses landing page to ensure it's as fully relevant as it can be.

There we go. That is a great experience for the user, will result in top quality scores, great conversion and the best performance we can deliver. All we have to do is repeat that approach for the other terms. There may be a lot, but you can start small and build up from there. Don't take the easy route – it leads to a place you don't want to be.

Keywords

Now we have the core of our account set up, we can begin to populate the keywords. Before we do this, we must conduct our keyword research. We already covered this in Chapter 3 so be sure to read back and understand the approach.

Once we have built a good set of keywords, we then need to consider other options. Google will automatically show your ad for similar terms that you may not think of, but you mustn't rely on that. You should consider options around the edge of the keyword set you develop. Let's explore this now using our white dress example.

- Our starter keyword – White dress.
- Shopping intention – White dress shop, buy white dress.
- Budget focused – Cheap white dress, expensive white dress.
- Ego focused – Fancy white dress, premium white dress, luxury white dress.
- Branded – <Your brand> white dress.
- Product variants – White skirt, ivory dress, white silk dress.
- Occasion – White summer dress, white dinner dress, white wedding dress.
- Local – White dress shop near me.
- Mis-spelling – whyte dress, white dres.
- Negative – White dress table, Marilyn Monroe white dress.

You can see how the term 'white dress' can expand significantly into a wide variety of keywords. This list is by no means exhaustive. You can expand a term into at least a hundred variations quite quickly. You then need to consider whether one ad can realistically cover all of these terms.

If someone searches for white summer dress and white wedding dress, should they see the same ad? Probably not. You can instruct Google to dynamically insert the keyword that the user used into your ad to make it more relevant. That can solve the issue, but it can also create other issues. You lose control as soon as you use any dynamic functionality, so my advice is always to manage it yourself and be disciplined. In this scenario I would separate wedding dresses into an ad group of their own. They would be likely to have a separate landing page anyway, so it seems like an obvious choice.

Generic, brand and competitor keywords

These product-related ads are what we would call generic search terms. The other types of search term are brand and competitor. Brand keywords are, unsurprisingly, bidding specifically on your brand name. This may seem odd as surely your brand name comes top of the organic search listings anyway. Therefore, if someone clicks on the ad rather than the organic listing, you're simply paying for traffic that would have come to your site anyway but for free.

This is certainly one possible scenario. Brand bidding is not always worthwhile, but there are scenarios where it can be. Perhaps you are having an SEO issue and your site is not being returned where it should. If you're not to be found when someone searches for your brand, there is a strong chance that a user will click on one of your competitors instead. Perhaps your competitors are bidding on your brand name. You may be losing customers to them. You will have more success bidding on your own brand so you need to protect yourself. Or perhaps your brand name is very close to something else – an animal, political movement, vegetable for example. Maybe it's difficult cutting through the noise.

Competitor bidding is also rather obvious and we've already mentioned it above. Bidding on your competitor terms can be a great way to acquire customers who are searching for someone else. They may be brand neutral and just happened to remember your competitor first. It's a sensible strategy; however, you must be careful not to start a bidding war. Depending on the depth of your competitors' pockets, you may find yourself trying to outbid them on your brand terms or driving bids up on generic terms. Is the amount of traffic you steal from their brand searches worth the impact on your overall account? It can be difficult to weigh this up without testing, but it is rarely a good idea to be too aggressive. If you start to actively steal your competitors' customers or mention them in your ads, you run the risk of getting into a paid search war, and nobody wins in a war.

Coming back to generic keywords, you may find that the keywords you want to bid on are expensive. Perhaps it's impossible to make them profitable for your business model. That can be a real challenge when those terms are clearly driving more traffic than the cheaper ones. One way to tackle this is to look at long-tail keywords.

Long-tail keywords

Long-tail keywords are the terms that are generally longer phrases or sentences. They are often unique and there are very few of them every month. If there are very few searches for them, then why would you target them? Because there are millions of them. In fact AHRefs (https://ahrefs.com/blog/long-tail-keywords) analysed the 1.9 *billion* keywords in their US

FIGURE 4.1 Google's autocomplete suggestions for 'white dress in'

database and found that 92.42 per cent of them get ten searches per month or fewer. It's also not necessarily true that long-tail keywords have lower search volumes. It's very often the case, but not always.

So, it is strongly recommended to include a wide range of long-tail keywords in your ad groups. By having hundreds or thousands of these you will be able to deliver the same volume but at a much lower spend than simply bidding on the big volume terms.

So, what is a long-tail keyword? Well, considering our white dress search again, we would be looking for longer searches including white dresses. A great way to find these is to look at Google's autocomplete, such as in Figure 4.1.

From here, we could expand this to:

- white dress near London;
- white dress with white shoes;
- white dress with low back;
- what's the best white dress.

And so on. AHRefs and other search tools are also great for suggesting keywords and of course you can use Google's keyword planner itself.

We mentioned negative keywords briefly above. It is important sometimes to include negative keywords as they are often associated with your brand or product but have no relevance to you.

If, for example, you didn't sell wedding dresses then actually adding 'wedding' as a negative keyword would make a lot of sense for your white dress ad group as we can say with some certainty that people search for white wedding dresses to a certain degree every month. If you're not sure, you could again use Google's keyword planner to get an estimate of monthly search volume, just to check.

Match types

Now that we have a keyword set that is extensive, includes long and short tail, perhaps includes brand and competitor terms and is broken down into targeted ad groups, we need to understand match types.

At the time of writing, there are three match types on Google. The reason I make this point is because until very recently there were four. Broad match modifier has been incorporated into Phrase match. For those of you that had been using BMM, you should look at the impact of this on your campaigns immediately.

The three core match types are: exact match, phrase match and broad match.

Exact match

Exact match is the tightest way of controlling your keywords. This technique is a great way to ensure you are not returning your ads on search terms that may not be related to your business. On the flip side however, it also restricts your visibility as you won't show on similar terms that you may not have thought of. Again, let's use our white dress example. Using 'white dress' as an exact match would return your ad on search terms such as 'white dress' and 'white dresses'

> TOP TIP
>
> *Focus your journey*
>
> Be as tight as you can. A search for red socks should show me an ad for red socks and land me on a page about red socks. Not white socks. Not red shirts. And certainly not a full clothing catalogue. Paid search managers that get this right will deliver significantly better returns than the others.

Phrase match

Phrase match gives a level of precision while allowing similar searches to play a part. The phrase of your keyword should appear, or at least one that has the same meaning. So, a phase match for 'white dress' would return your ad on searches such as 'white dress near me', 'white dress for clubbing' and 'company selling white dresses'.

Broad match

Broad match will return your ad on anything related to any of your keywords. This enables your ads to show a lot but also means the relevance of your ads is likely to be very low a lot of the time. 'White dress' here could return on 'white skirts', 'dresses for women' or even 'dresses for sale in UK'.

Google may also take into account the user's search history, other keywords in your ad group and even the content of your landing page to try to ensure better relevance.

At this point you should have a keyword set in the hundreds if not thousands. These should be separated into campaigns and ad groups with some thought about what landing pages they are going to point to.

Bidding strategy

Let's now take a look at the bidding strategy. In order to effectively deliver your ads against the keywords you have selected, you will need to understand how to budget and bid effectively.

Budgeting is quite simple. You can set a daily budget in Google and you will not spend beyond that. You may spend less depending on your bid strategy. Google will then charge you periodically, depending on your account and billing set-up.

There are numerous bid strategies available, and use of them should be based around your goals. Depending on whether you are trying to gain content engagement, brand uplift or sales, you will want to be using the right strategy.

You can choose to manage the bidding yourself or to use Google's machine learning based automation. Let's look at the options available to you.

Manual bidding

Where it all begins. Manual bidding is the simplest strategy to understand and it simply means manually setting bids for your keywords. This gives you a great level of control, but does rely on time spent on analysis and research to best understand the playing field and whether you are delivering the optimal result. Also, you may not have access to all the data that Google has, so you may struggle to optimize as well as the automated routes but, if you can develop a strategy that works, you can beat the AI.

Enhanced CPC

When selecting manual bidding you can tick the box to enable enhanced CPC. With this option you are adding a degree of automation to your manual strategy. Google will adjust keyword bids where it sees an opportunity to deliver better click-throughs and conversions from a keyword. This should result in better results but also increased spend. If enabled, you will want to watch closely for any concerning trends. If manual bidding is your preference, then it is worthwhile starting without enhanced CPC and adding it later to understand the impact.

Maximize conversions

Here we take our first step into full automation. If you are comfortable that you have a budget and you simply want to spend that amount and get the most conversions from it, then this is a great option. You will need to ensure you have your desired conversions set up and we'll touch on that below. If your conversions are leads, sales or even specific non-commercial actions on your website, this option is a sensible one to choose. However, it may not be the best route for profitability, as it will simply spend all of your budget to try to get conversions. Maximizing conversion value may be better for those with more focus on that.

Maximize conversion value

This bid strategy takes the same approach as above but focuses on the value rather than the quantity of conversions. Again, you need to ensure you have the right set-up in place. Your conversions need to have accurate values assigned to them. Is a specific conversion (sale or lead) worth $10 or $100?

Google will optimize towards the better return, so this setup is critical. The return on ad spend (ROAS) from this strategy can be excellent if implemented well.

Target CPA and target ROAS

These strategies have been in place for a long time. In 2021 Google decided to reorganize the automated bid strategies into the two maximize options above. Within those, target CPA and ROAS metrics can be set. For those with existing campaigns, they will automatically be moved across when the migration occurs. A target CPA ensures you have a level of control over what you are willing to pay for a conversion, whereas a target ROAS aims to maximize conversion value.

Maximize clicks

This strategy quite simply does what it says. The aim is to spend your budget to maximize the number of clicks on your ads. If conversions are not relevant for you and you just want as many people as possible visiting your website, this can be a good fit. It may result in you overspending on some clicks to get your budget spent, but it is a great low-maintenance alternative to manual bidding.

Target impression share

This is a relatively new option and an interesting strategy. You can choose to target the advertising slots at the top of the page to ensure maximum exposure of your ads. The danger here of course is a bidding war. It can be extremely expensive to compete on these top terms, so profitability may quickly become a problem. This is therefore best used when your goals are around awareness rather than efficiency. You will want to set a maximum CPC here to avoid nasty surprises.

Cost per view

Finally, if you run video ads, you can use CPV bidding. This is of course used for bidding on video ads on YouTube. With this bidding strategy you pay for video views and other video interactions including clicks on any call-to-actions, cards and companion banners. You'll pay after 30 seconds of viewing, or view completion if shorter than 30 seconds.

Audiences

Audiences are a great way of focusing your ads on the right people. Your ads won't just randomly show: they'll show to the right people at the right time. Not only that, but you can understand how those audiences react to your ads, and exclude audiences that don't fit.

Before you start this process, you should try to understand your audience. You may have already gone through this exercise when conducting brand research or customer surveys. If you haven't, or are unsure how to progress with it, I would recommend picking up a copy of my book *Digital Marketing Strategy*, which will take you through everything you need to build your full strategy from start to finish. You don't need a full understanding, as you can test and learn here, but you need a baseline starting point.

When selecting audiences, you can choose for them to be used for targeting (incorporated into your campaign to focus your adverts) or observation (simply to monitor and be able to react to if you feel a need without affecting your campaign). From here you can then choose audience types that fit your advertising strategy. The audience types available are:

- **Affinity:** These individuals show an interest, passion or behaviour around a specific topic. It may be a hobby or professional interest but they have a relationship with it. They could be technology lovers or fashionistas.
- **In-market:** These users have been exhibiting behaviours related to shopping for a specific type of product or service. They could be in the market for what you offer right now.
- **Detailed demographics:** You can monitor the age groups, income levels and gender of groups of individuals and adjust bids where you see opportunities and trends developing.
- **Remarketing:** People that have interacted with your website can be remarketed to. This option is available through the Audience Manager in the top menu and can be used to remarket across all of Google's platforms.
- **Customer match:** Again via Audience Manager, you can upload lists of your customers into Google. You must ensure you follow data protection laws here and you will also encounter increasing issues with privacy, especially with recent changes to iOS. Once this is working however it can be a powerful way of targeting individuals that know you well with highly tailored messages.

- **Similar audiences:** Also via Audience Manager, you can target users similar to those in your campaign or similar to those visiting your website. These lookalike audiences have the potential to be the people you may otherwise struggle to identify.

CASE STUDY: AD GROUPS

The challenge

A company had been running paid search for a little over a year with a small local agency. They received traffic to their website, but did not track leads or sales directly from the activity. They had never challenged the agency or reviewed performance. Upon appointing a new agency, a review was done and it became clear that the campaign was not optimized to deliver the best results.

The solution

The new agency reviewed the full set-up and discovered that the previous agency had been using dynamic ads. This option ensures that your ads can be highly relevant to the audience by automating the ad copy, targeting and landing page. However, no other ads were set up and, at this stage in the company's marketing journey, their website was very small. As a result, the dynamic ads had very little content to pull from and very few landing-page options.

The new agency set up ad groups that focused on each of the company's products and target segments. They built ads that were tailored to each of these and built landing pages specific to each ad group. The dynamic ads were left to run, but the new ad groups made up 90 per cent of the spend.

The results

As a result, click-through rates increased from 1.9 per cent to 13.2 per cent. In the meantime, the agency developed a new website for the company that was far larger and more tailored so that the dynamic ads could work harder.

Exclusions

Finally, you can exclude audiences. Perhaps your white dress is only suitable for adults and so you want to exclude anyone who is in-market for children's clothing. Thinking like this can further improve the effectiveness of your advertising.

Now we have a solid keyword set, a clear budget and a bid strategy. Before we come to building the ads, let's ensure our landing pages are fully optimized.

Landing pages

We have already looked at what makes a great website in Chapter 2, so we just apply that here and we're done, right? Wrong. Unfortunately, we're going to break some of our own rules here. It may seem like we are contradicting ourselves, but actually we're not. What we're doing is focusing the user's attention and experience on what matters most to us and should, if we've got this right, also matter most to them.

When we are trying to guide a user through a journey to a specific goal, such as a lead form, sale or engagement, we need to be single minded. By being focused on that one goal we can ensure that the individual is not distracted, does not get lost and ultimately gets to the destination they are looking for. Whatever their intent was from our initial planning – we are going to focus on that.

To do that we will keep the good principles of clear signposting, a fast website, clean design and much more from Chapter 2. However, we will also remove items that you would normally find on a standard web page.

Our landing pages should not be accessible from the rest of the site as they offer no value beyond what can already be found in your core content. They should not be findable by search engines as they are duplicating content that we have written about in much more detail elsewhere. They should, on the flip side of the coin, also not be pointing anywhere else.

We want this user to stay in this journey, so, creating landing pages that pull back the navigation, strip back the mentions of distracting blog posts and remove all unrelated services are the ones that will deliver results. If this user sees an interesting article while trying to buy your product, they may click and follow a chain of thought, never to return.

We therefore remove menus, hide blogs, strip back content and focus on the action we want them to take. Let's get this user to convert first and then we can get them to engage in our content, buy more from us and develop a real relationship with us.

Your landing page should be simple. Strong call-to-actions. It must directly relate to the keyword and ad they have clicked on. Here, following our example, should be a selection of white dresses. No black dresses.

No white scarves. Or, if your advert is pushing a specific white dress, we should only be seeing that one dress. It should be incredibly simple to buy, book or enquire here. And the benefits must be clear.

Consider some marketing psychology techniques here, such as:

- limited stock;
- offer only valid for three hours;
- 'Your friends bought this';
- 'As seen on TV';
- review scores.

All of these techniques can add a little extra to your conversion.

Also, I refer you back to the case study about the baby in Chapter 2. This example is one you can employ here. Don't feel you need to find a smiling baby, but the principle is clear. Keep your call-to-action clearly signposted and positive. Make your buttons green and, if in doubt, test and test again. Never stop testing your landing page. This should be continuous. You can use tools such as Unbounce and Instapage for this.

Now that we have a clear, stripped down, well signposted and conversion-focused landing page, we can finally look at the ads themselves.

Ads

Writing ads for paid search is an art form. But as, arguably with many art forms, there is a science to it. Here we will focus on the best way to get your ads to perform as well as they possibly can.

As we're at the final stage, we have already talked about quality score and therefore tying keywords to ads to landing pages. And as we now understand the elements either side of the ad, all we have to do is add the filling to the sandwich.

For copy we therefore have to ensure we include the keywords that we are targeting and that the landing page discussed. These should already be the same. Thankfully, Google gives us a lot of help here. The ad-creation tool will show you the relevant keywords and tick them off when you include them within the ad. Also, as you build the ad, Google will give you a real-time score, from poor through average and good to excellent. If you don't reach 'good' with your editing, you need to keep going until you do or you are not likely to perform particularly well.

When building your ad, you can select the URL that the ad will point to but also a custom URL that is just for display purposes. This is the URL that the user sees in your ad but has nothing to do with the destination. For example, we could be landing our visitors on the url:

https://myfashiowebsite.com/products/10110/31-64-ghp/dress-types/long/white

But we can set our display url as:

https://myfashiowebsite.com/whitedresses

A great signal for a user to click through.

We should then add multiple headlines that Google can rotate and optimize against. They should include keywords from our ad group and be highly relevant. At this stage we also need to consider our typing style for the first time. There are three things you should keep in mind here:

1 Keep it very benefit led.
2 Try to include call-to-actions where possible.
3 Capitalize Every Word In Every Sentence Like This.

TOP TIP

Do not forget negative keywords. These can be enormously valuable in preventing wasted spend. Think very carefully about what you offer.

If you are a payment services provider, you may not want people searching for payment protection insurance. Perhaps 'insurance' would be a negative keyword for you.

If you are a business consultant, you might want to remove people searching for 'business consultant salary' or 'business consultant job', as they are unlikely to be looking for your services.

Add these in and you could improve your performance instantly.

That last point may seem a little odd. It reads in an unusual way and surely it can't make a difference. Well, in reality it does make a difference and it always has. Do not go over the top though. TOO MUCH OF THIS, or ToO MuCH of tHIs can result in punishment from Google as excessive capitalization is against their guidelines.

Try to write around 10 to 15 headlines and then move on to your descriptions. Here you should retain the capitalization approach from above and write four compelling reasons for people to pick you over anyone else. Call-to-actions, unique selling points and reasons to believe should all feature here as they would in any effective marketing campaign.

Finally, you have the option to add tracking, and we'll discuss effective tracking in Chapter 9. From here, assuming you have reached at least 'good' on your score, you can move on to adding extensions.

Extensions

There are many options available to us with extensions. These are effectively features that power our ads to the next level. They may enable us to take up more real estate on the SERPs, add extra promotional messages to our ads or even complete the lead on Google itself.

- **Sitelink:** These extensions enable you to showcase the key pages on your site that can drive sales related to your strategy. You may wish to showcase services, products or benefits here, such as offers.
- **Callouts:** These are short messages that will be appended to the end of your ad. They can feature short selling points, such as 24/7 service, to help strengthen the ad.
- **Structure snippets:** Here you can structure specific lists of items to appear below your ad. These could include holiday destinations or lists of services.
- **Image:** Add an image to your ad to pull the eye to it. This could be a logo or product image. Visuals often catch the eye more than words. Pictures speak louder than words.
- **Dynamic image:** Another version of adding images is to enable Google to pull images from your site. This can be more powerful, but again takes a little control away from you, so you will need to review and monitor it appropriately.
- **Lead form:** This is a short form (which can be pre-populated by Google) to capture the lead without it touching your site. If your website is not optimized, this can be a great option, but it also lessens the user's chance to learn more and reduces upsell potential.
- **Location:** Highly relevant for many businesses, adding the location of your shop can be very powerful in converting local customers.

Reviewing and testing

Once you complete your ad, it will need to go through a review cycle. If you make any edits to an existing ad, the same will happen. Using foul language, brand names or poor capitalization are examples of where your ad may fail or not be allowed to run at full pace. Keep an eye on your ads for this approval and try not to edit them too often.

To avoid constantly editing ads for testing, you should run multiple ads in the same ad group. Once you have some distinctly different ads that give you a chance to test offers, headlines, call-to-actions or extensions, you can rotate them.

You can choose how you do this at the campaign level or at the ad group level. The options are to rotate evenly or to let Google optimize for the best performing ads. It is usually best to let them rotate evenly to begin with so you can get a feel for what is working and what is not. Automatic optimization when there is zero data can be very misleading. Once you get a feel for clear winners you can add a new test and again rotate evenly until a winner shows.

WHAT TO WATCH

Do not go too broad in your search terms.

It's tempting to think that your ads and keywords are good, so let's go for as much traffic as we can, and only the right people will click on the ads.

The issue is that you will get the wrong people clicking for certain. And your relevance will be very low. Your click-through rate will be through the floor, and you won't have the data to understand why.

Keep your account focused and manage it closely for the best results.

If you don't have the time for this approach, you can ask Google to optimize for you. The AI is smart and will generally do a good job of choosing the best ads, but it wouldn't be wise to trust it 100 per cent yet.

RSAs and ETAs

You should also understand ad types. The method we have described above is for responsive search ads (RSAs). These enable Google to rotate many options and for you to get the best outcome. Expanded text ads (ETAs) also exist and these are effectively limited versions of the responsive ads (three headlines and two descriptions). So why would you use ETAs? Well, less is sometimes more. Responsive ads give a great range of options but not a great deal of visibility on which options have worked. ETAs give you a lot more control and a clearer understanding of what works.

RSAs are likely to return for more long-tail keywords, but will spend more to try to achieve the same result as they are not as targeted. ETAs will give you more control but less testing. Ultimately this choice is down to you, but the sensible outcome is to have a blend of both methods.

You can of course focus your ads on specific countries and at specific times of day or days of the week. This can be very relevant for your business, but is largely built on your broader strategy than any effect on paid search, which is a global 24/7 channel.

At this stage you should have a fully set-up account with keywords, ads and landing pages ready to go. But before you hit *Enable*, let's quickly touch on a bit of admin.

Linked accounts

At this stage you just need to ensure you have everything connected. Turning your ads on without the proper set-up can lose you data. Ensure you have your Google Analytics attached to your Google Ads account. You can do this through Linked Accounts in your settings.

Here you can also attach Salesforce, YouTube, Search Console, Zapier and others. This will ensure all the platforms talk to each other. Pull your goals through from analytics to serve as conversions for your campaigns, and monitor your keywords within analytics.

Once you're all connected and confident that every item is showing accurately, it's time to be brave and get that account started.

Reporting

But wait, how do we know what success looks like?

You have a number of dashboards available to you now – all filled with KPIs. This now comes down to the goals of your campaign. You should look to build a dashboard that is meaningful and enables you to react quickly to trends. The higher the budget the more important this is.

You could use Google Data Studio for this, or you can use many other great analytics tools or even something as simple as Microsoft Excel. I would warn against the latter – not because it's not a great tool – of course it is – but it wasn't built for this purpose and there are simply a wealth of advertising dashboards out there.

Here are the KPIs you should build into your dashboard, wherever you choose to build it:

- **Cost:** Spend in the period, on the ad group, on the campaign.
- **Commercial:** Conversions, conversion rate, cost per conversion, average conversion value.
- **Channel:** Impressions, clicks, click-through rate.
- **Efficiency:** Cost per sale (if sale and conversion are different for your business), return on ad spend.
- **Detail:** Top keyword by each of these KPIs.
- **Competitor:** Share of voice, top placements.

Each of these metrics should look at the figure for the period, the change versus the last period and the difference versus plan. Ideally you would look at the change since the last period and the changes since the same period last year. This enables you to see seasonal and business growth changes separately. Therefore, a 13-month rolling chart is valuable.

These metrics should also be separated into campaign and ad group level to understand where the strengths and weakness lie.

Finally, you should look at pulling out material changes since the last period. Ad groups, keywords, demographics that have shifted materially. This enables you to start thinking why.

Comparing your data with Google Trends can be powerful to tell a story of your performance versus the market

Remember that reporting is not about numbers – it's about insights. Always ask yourself 'So what?' and make sure your report answers that.

05

Running display advertising that delivers brand value

Display ads are a part of our everyday internet life. They used to be just simple banners, but over the years, they have evolved to include different media, such as images, animated images, videos and immersive experiences, across numerous placements such as pop-ups or in-stream video ads.

Display advertising is usually altered based on a user's demographics, surfing history and behaviour, and the more targeted it is, the more effective it becomes.

While display ads can be an excellent investment to grow your brand, if you don't know how to use them effectively, you're going to waste money. When you apply all the specific insider knowledge, choose your display ads and placements wisely and target the current audience, they can yield great results.

Key things to understand about display ads as we begin:

- Display ads are usually designed to entice customers to engage with them somehow, like clicking to go on a website, and perform a specific action, such as filling out a form or buying products. But they can simply be used to have your brand enter the viewer's subconscious mind and become familiar.
- Several display ads are much more complex than the static banners of old, although these exist and can still be effective. Some display ads include interactive elements to prompt viewers to engage directly with the ad, for example investing their time filling out a simple form, answering an interesting question, or even playing a mini-game, all within the ad.
- Google and Bing are the platforms used to create display ads.

This chapter will cover some of the most critical aspects of display advertising and insider tips to help you grow your brand.

Step one: Before you start

Be clear on your objectives

Before committing to a campaign, it is vital to define your objectives clearly. You must understand what you are attempting to achieve with a campaign; otherwise, all your efforts will be in vain, with no means of understanding whether or not the campaign was successful.

Customer journey

The customer journey describes the stages a customer goes through prior to, during and after becoming a customer with you. They go from the Awareness stage to Consideration to Conversion to Loyalty (see Figure 5.1).

Let's look at how display ads can be used to drive the customer along the journey. Knowing the stage of the customer journey that you're targeting is crucial in creating suitable ads and developing creativity that helps your ads fulfill their objectives.

AWARENESS

In the awareness stage, the prospect gets to know that your brand exists and what products or services you offer.

FIGURE 5.1 The customer journey

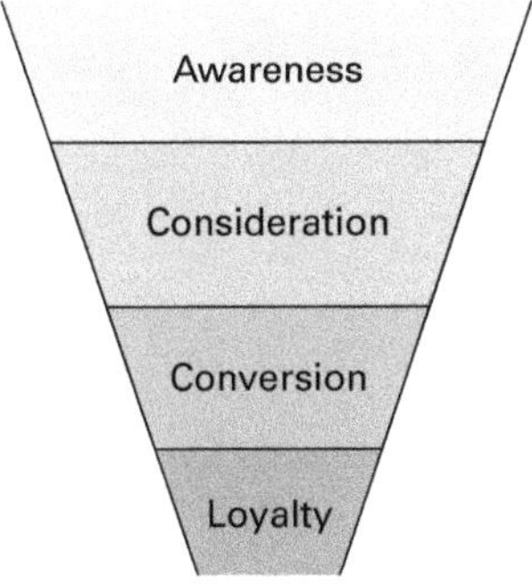

Display ads are perfect for the awareness stage because they are a form of presence, making the brand visible in the customer's daily life and activities in the same way a billboard or magazine ad might. They're not directed to people who are already looking for you. They exist to reach potential new customers wherever they are on the internet.

Display ads have a massive advantage over search ads, which is the vastly higher volume of impressions. That builds brand awareness, and if you're paying for ads on a cost-per-click basis, these impressions don't even cost you anything extra. That is your chance to introduce yourself, build the recognition effect and gain business down the line. According to the *Global Banking and Finance Review*, 71 per cent of consumers are more likely to buy a product or service from a brand name they recognize.

The key objectives to guide creativity for an awareness-stage ad are:

- Capture attention and spark curiosity.
- Have an emotional effect.
- Get across your brand name and logo.
- Show what kind of product and service you are offering.

An example of an awareness ad could be a banner letting you know that a particular show will be playing in your local theatre, including a picture, date and location (Figure 5.2).

FIGURE 5.2 Example of an awareness display ad

CONSIDERATION

During the consideration stage, the prospect compares your brand with others, evaluates it, and draws (hopefully favourable) judgements and conclusions. They're interested in your brand's promises, but now they want to check if the reality lives up to the hype. A consideration stage campaign focuses on how the brand is better than competitors, how it is unique, or why it is the best choice. Search ads commonly cover this stage because prospects may be Googling and actively seeking information, but consideration-type display ads can also be effective. Search ads have a median CTR of 1.55 per cent, over three times the median CTR of display ads, which stands at 0.44 per cent (Smart Insights, 2021), so I advise you to run both types of ads at this stage and compare results.

The key objectives to guide a consideration stage ad are:

- Build trust.
- Establish your USP and stand out from the crowd.
- Show why your brand compares favourably.
- Build authority by aligning with people or institutions that the target audience already trust or think well of.

An example of a consideration-stage ad for the theatre show could be the same as the awareness ad, but with the addition of a few five-star graphics and reviews from well-known publications, such as, 'Stunning musical extravaganza' – *The Guardian* (and Figure 5.3).

FIGURE 5.3 Example of a consideration display ad

CONVERSION

During the conversion stage, the prospect becomes a customer.

Conversion is a vital objective for display ads only when retargeting is used. A typical conversion ad with discount codes, for example, isn't going to yield a high click-through rate if it's targeted to people who don't know the brand or product exists until they see the ad – there are no last touches to build up trust and establish a relationship.

On the other hand, conversion-type ads to people who've visited your site, are subscribed, or have additional knowledge of the brand through actions you can measure are 76 per cent more effective (WordStream, 2020). They're a powerful way to recapture cart abandoners, with customers 70 per cent more likely to follow up their abandoned purchases if they've seen a display ad (Baymard Institute, 2020).

The key objectives to guide creativity for a conversion stage ad are:

- Prompt the prospect to act.
- Make it easier for them to say 'yes' – by providing a discount, for example.
- Add a sense of urgency or scarcity.
- Personalize an offer based on what they already like or buy where possible.

An example of a conversion stage theatre ad might be, 'The show's nearly in town! Limited time discount. Claim yours now!' (See also Figure 5.4.)

FIGURE 5.4 Example of a conversion display ad

LOYALTY

The final stage is loyalty. After you spared no effort in achieving the desired outcome and gained a customer, you want to keep them and maximize their LTV (lifetime value). A loyal customer will not only come back to make more purchases but also become an ambassador, likely to engage in word-of-mouth marketing on your brand's behalf.

High-quality customer service has been cited as an essential factor for staying loyal to a brand by as much as 96 per cent of customers (Microsoft, 2017).

But what about ads to generate loyalty? In the theatre example, the venue could target previous visitors with an ad promoting a special member's pass that gives them 15 per cent off all future tickets.

Know your options

After taking a look at the customer journey and deciding what stage your viewer is in and where you're looking to drive them to, you need to understand your options for achieving this. You can do a lot with display ads, for example:

- capture email addresses for a product launch;
- provide live discounts or information on new drops;
- expand over the whole screen for an immersive, more emotional experience;
- prompt people to phone you with an in-ad call button;
- install an app or take action in the app.

As you can see, the possibilities are vast regarding engaging viewers in your ad and brand. Think specifically about what you want to achieve with each advertisement in the campaign and how this campaign sits in your business regarding your more comprehensive marketing campaign and objectives.

Choose your audience

Before you design your display ads, you need to know who you're targeting; not just to choose targeting options but also to make sure the creative is also targeted at the correct groups.

TOP TIP

Rich ads

The richer your ads are, the more likely potential customers engage with them.

Advertisements that include rich media outperform simple banners by 130 per cent (Admixer, 2021). In digital advertising, rich content can consist of videos, pictures, animations or audio. All audio, interactivity and visuals serve the purpose of grabbing attention – perfect for awareness – and entice users to click – perfect for consideration and conversion.

SEGMENTS

It's likely that your product or service has a segmented market with numerous different types of consumers. Look through your existing segmented customer avatars and think about whether to target all the segments with different ad creative or a particular segment at this time.

Consider the following example. A pizza chain wants to increase its awareness and orders with a particular segment – basketball fans. It creates display ads to sit alongside basketball content in the run-up to a big game, prompting more basketball fans to become aware of the pizza chain, then runs conversion ads to these fans the day before and the day of the game in order to get more orders.

Think of new segments you can add and how your brand is relevant to them. To create more segments, you can consider crossover audiences that might be interested in your brand and products.

Creating display ads for specific groups of people can feel more personalized to a potential customer, making them more interested in your brand.

You can aim to increase awareness within a new segment. A successful display ad campaign run on YouTube by a vegan company raised their brand awareness among their target audience – millennials – by as much as 48 per cent using targeted display ads (Google Ads, 2018). That is an excellent example of reaping the benefits of display ads by knowing who your target audience is.

Analysing your segment

When thinking about your segment, consider the following:

- What are the drives, aspirations, and fears of this segment? How can I capitalize on these in ad creative?

- Going back to the pizza example, we could identify that the primary goal of this segment is to have fun on the night of the basketball game, eating food with friends and family while celebrating. That can easily be incorporated into the ad campaign.
- What do we want the target audience to do next? How can we make that happen?
- Are we covering every aspect of the customer journey? Are we giving the audience enough touchpoints to allow them to decide to become customers with us?

Plan your measurement

We've already talked about how important it is to set goals for your ad campaign. At the planning stage you should also consider the measurement you'll use to evaluate the success of your campaign. You'll be looking at specific metrics to create KPIs (key performance indicators) to measure your success.

> TOP TIP
>
> Measuring your campaign and analysing data is one of the essential steps to a successful ad campaign. If you ignore the data, you're throwing away the time, effort and money spent on a campaign.

Objectives and measurements go hand in hand.

Gathering and analysing all the relevant data from your campaign can help you create even more successful campaigns in future. Metrics that are not directly relevant to your objectives can still be used to understand the other parts of the funnel and the overall picture. This topic will be further discussed later on in this chapter.

The metrics and KPIs you choose will depend on the goals you set for your campaign. When you create your display ad, you'll be asked what your objective is. These may include, for example:

- views at the awareness stage;
- clicks or form-fills at the consideration and conversion stage;
- add-to-cart, bookings or purchases at the conversion stage.

The advertising platform will show you how well you perform in these areas using simple metrics and provide you with a whole host of other metrics to understand ad performance in more detail.

However, when it comes to raising brand awareness, the measurement becomes trickier. To know how well your awareness campaign worked, you can't rely solely on ad platform analytics. That is because people may have seen your ad and not clicked on it but subsequently followed you on social media or looked you up on Google, maybe even a couple of days later. To get a good feel for how well awareness campaigns are working, you have to look at a few different indicators. You can:

- compare social media growth during the campaign in comparison with other periods of business;
- compare website traffic with previous numbers;
- conduct 'social listening' to see where your brand is being mentioned online.

When it comes to assessing brand awareness, there is no one-size-fits-all solution, and each brand has its means of knowing where they stand and what they want to achieve with their campaigns. You can consider metrics provided by the ad display network that show direct effects of your campaign, and metrics outside it, to show effects the ad platform would not show you. (See Table 5.1.)

TABLE 5.1 Metrics inside and outside ad campaigns for each buyer stage

Performance goal	Metrics in ad campaign	Metrics outside ad campaign
Awareness	Impressions	• Site views • Social media reach
Consideration	• Clicks • Lead form fill • Lead magnet download	• Search volume for brand name keywords • Number of social media follows, comments, clicks or likes
Conversion	• Add to cart • Purchase	• In-store visits • Add to cart and purchase not driven by the ad
Loyalty	Repeat purchases	• Customer LTV • Shares of content on social media • Fewer complaints in reviews • Fewer customer service contacts

Remember that performance goals should be strategic in nature while metrics are quantifiable. 'Become more popular' isn't an actionable statement that can be easily tracked. Comparatively, a metric like 'Reach 500 views' is concrete and specific.

WHAT TO WATCH

View-through attribution is one of the most controversial topics in digital marketing.

If an ad displayed to a user isn't clicked on, but then the user later visits the site, it counts as a view-through impression. Such users are usually tracked through cookies, and businesses can know when they return to their website.

The controversy surrounding attribution lies in the time period between when the user initially saw the ad and when they decided to visit the website. Can a visit from a user who saw an ad on your website weeks ago be attributed to that ad? Or does the user have to go on your website shortly after seeing the ad for it to be considered a success?

Digital marketing experts are divided on this issue. Many attribute impressions with site visits even after weeks have passed since the user saw an ad. Others insist that the visit should take place within days or even hours after exposure to an ad.

View-through attribution analysis yields a wealth of information that can be used to make better-educated decisions about marketing strategy, channel selection and budgetary control. While it can straddle the line among organic and paid advertisements, the extra value it provides at both ends of the consumer journey far exceeds this lack of perfect clarity.

You should get to understand the benchmarks of each metric you've chosen to measure at this stage. Standards across digital marketing, your industry and your previous advertising campaigns can help you gauge how your display ads are performing. For example, a CTR of anything over 0.4–0.5 per cent is considered good for banner ads.

You should also prepare for split testing at this stage. You will want to make different iterations of your ads or targeting to test which set of ads works better. You can then push more budget into these while removing it from lower-performing ads. You should continue the optimizing process to keep improving your display ad ROI.

Step two: Create amazing ads

Creating display ads that effectively communicate your brand values and lead to more conversions is no easy feat. This section will cover some of the most essential aspects of display ads that can help you create unique advertisements that yield outstanding results for your business.

Understand the media you will need

The first step to creating a good display ad is knowing which types of media you will need. In today's world, people access the internet on phones, tablets, laptops, desktops and more, which all come with different presentations of content to fit screen sizes. The digital marketing world has adapted to this by offering various types and sizes of ads.

There are two major categories – static image ads and responsive display ads. Responsive ads guarantee that your ads will be viewed in their best shape and form based on the display size and capabilities.

Advanced format options

There are several advanced format options that Google offers. These options include asset enhancements, auto-generated videos and native formats. Understanding these options is essential to have suitable, responsive display ads.

- With the asset enhancements option, Google might change your content to drive better ad performance. Such modifications can be different, including cropping images, zooming in on focal points, dropping text to highlight other aspects of an ad, and so on.
- The auto-generated videos option lets Google create clips by combining various content that you provide, such as headlines, images, logos and descriptions. Auto-generated videos also aim at increasing the reach of your ads. If you provide video content for your responsive display ads, the auto-generation won't occur. You could test your videos against auto-generated videos to find out which perform better.
- Finally, native formats will change and adapt based on the website design they're shown on. This option integrates your ads into the website's overall feeling and can feel less 'forced' for a potential customer. This option helps your ad reaches more publishers, thus improving its performance.

Creating a list of various types and sizes of media is crucial, so you know what assets you have to create or ask your creative team to organize. Once you decide which options you will use for your campaign, you can commit to the most critical aspects of your display ads. You can find out the ad sizes required from the ad platform network of choice.

> TOP TIP
>
> Video advertising can yield excellent results for your brand. In-stream ads that appear on YouTube videos on mobile devices are 84 per cent more likely to capture viewers' attention than TV advertising (Ipsos/Google, 2017).
>
> Video ads have a 48 per cent higher conversion rate than static ads (Marketing Dive, 2020). Creating different video ad sizes can help you reach more audiences across devices and stand out – square videos can particularly grab attention. When working on a video ad, your first goal should be to immediately capture the user's attention. If the user doesn't enjoy the first three seconds, you'll have lost them.

Consider your audience-brand connection

When working on display ads, you should always have your target audience in mind. Once you determine your audience, consider their placement in the sales funnel discussed at the beginning. Knowing where your target audience fits in the funnel can help you create specific content to ensure that the audience moves forward in the funnel.

- **Awareness:** Your job here is to get it clear in your potential customers' minds that you exist, highlighting your name and logo and brand feel, and what you offer.
- **Consideration:** You can highlight some of the services you provide in your adverts to make them more memorable. Display ads might benefit from highlighting a problem and proposing a solution that your business can provide.
- **Conversion:** For retargeting the customers that left your website without making a purchase, you can focus on offering them various offers or discounts to tip them into the sale.

- **Loyalty**: With display ads, you can create a longer-term connection with your customers by showcasing your brand values that resonate with them, upsell them on more of your services, or offer discounts, insider passes or similar perks.

Create best-practice visuals

Having cohesive visuals for your brand is a must when creating display ads. In an awareness campaign, you're looking to make a visual imprint that will root in viewers' minds so that your brand seems familiar. That means keeping consistency across ads in colour and design is critical. You should create ads in the same colour scheme, style and visual feel as your landing page to take advantage of this familiarity and increase conversions.

There are some key aspects to consider when creating images, videos and text for your ads. Let's go over some of the good and bad practices.

IMAGES

Do:

- Use high-quality, crisp images.
- Use images that you have created rather than stock images where possible, though both are fine.
- Stay within your existing brand identity.
- Think of how to stand out on different websites – how will the images be eye-catching enough to warrant a click?
- Include images with people – these perform better, especially when the people are close to the camera, and if they're happy (Datasine, 2019)
- Keep the margins square and the borders translucent to allow pictures to fill the whole aspect ratio.
- Use images that create feeling and emotion where possible, as marketing campaigns containing emotional content perform twice as well as those that contain rational content (Neuromarketing, 2009).

Don't:

- use obvious stock images;
- use poor-quality images;

- overlay text (especially by over 15 per cent);
- use false buttons;
- use illegal or offensive imagery (check the guidelines of the advertising platform to ensure you remain in their rules);
- use inverted colours or excessive filters;
- use images with a mirror reflection.

VIDEOS

You have three to ten seconds to capture users' attention.

Do:

- Use an attention-grabbing opening that appeals directly to the viewer's pain points or desires.
- Vary the elements used, for example people, text, images and slides interspersed – this can increase viewer attention span because of the variety.
- Keep it short and straightforward.
- Convey the most crucial message.
- Make sure your videos work without sound.
- Consider including subtitles, but make sure these are big enough to be viewed on mobile or tablet as well as desktop.
- Consider your buyer journey stage.
- For brand awareness and consideration, LinkedIn advise positioning yourself as a thought leader, telling your brand story and sharing stories of customer success. For conversion, they suggest showing a quick demo of your product, giving a sneak peek of your webinar or previewing your event, for example.
- Ensure your video is in the proper format and is within duration compliance.
- Give a lot of attention to the script – as much as you would to copywriting.

Don't:

- start with lengthy introductions – the main content of your ad won't even get seen;
- bombard the user with too much information – this will create confusion, which can cost you clicks;
- utilize out-of-date elements.

Master copy and scripting

Several copywriting elements can be included in display ads, including the headline, sub-headline, body text and call-to-action. The general rule for display ad copy is to keep it as simple as possible. Customers are more likely to respond to visuals with a short amount of text.

Copywriting is its own discipline, and we cannot adequately cover all best practices here. However, one common method used in copywriting is the AIDA formula:

Attention: Grab the attention of readers.
Interest: Create a point of interest so they can see the ad is relevant to them.
Desire: Spark desire in the reader by mentioning or implying a benefit.
Action: Include a call-to-action.

This is a tried-and-tested formula that produces results. I would recommend you learn more about copywriting, and possibly outsource to a skilled copywriter. But prior to that, applying AIDA to your campaigns is a solid start.

Step three: Keywords and targeting

In this section, we look at how to get your ads in front of the right people.

Master your keywords

Keywords are one of the most important things to master with display ads to ensure ads end up on the right users' screens. Any internet marketing strategy should begin with keyword research. For content campaigns it's all about SEO and rankings, but here it's about ad placement. Google finds relevant websites that feature your chosen keywords, and also target your ad to audiences interested in your chosen keywords.

STEP BY STEP

Create keywords for your campaigns

1 Create separate ad groups for your products or services, so they can be targeted by differentiated keywords. For example, if you sell both tents and

hiking boots, these would need to be split into separate ad groups as they would use different keywords.

2 Select keywords that might appear on sites where your customers would be browsing.
   - Long-tail keywords are effective in particular (two to three words).
   - Choose 5 to 20 keywords.
   - If your brand is well-recognized, include branded keywords.

3 Use the Google Ads 'keywords' feature to gain more ideas.

Target your ads: your audience

We have touched upon the importance of the correct targeting of your ads several times in this chapter. There are different types of targeting that you can use to maximize your campaign results.

Ad targeting is a critical component of a successful advertising campaign. You may have created the ideal ad, but you must display it to the right people at the appropriate time to achieve your objectives. Google Advertising allows you to target your ads in a variety of ways.

Audience targeting is based on:

- demographics;
- affinity;
- audiences with similar interests;
- remarketing;
- in-market;
- custom intent.

Once you've defined your audience's interests, wants, habits and goals, you may determine who your audience will be for a particular campaign or ad group.

Audiences are groups of individuals with distinct interests, intentions and demographic information. This information is collated from a number of places and datasets, including page visit history, past searches, purchase activity, location data, and more. These can then be used by the ad platform to optimize bidding and targeting for your ad campaigns.

Audience targeting can be divided into several sub-categories: interest targeting, custom-intent targeting, demographic targeting, time-based targeting and remarketing.

INTEREST TARGETING

Interest targeting allows you to reach customers who have a proven interest in products or services that you offer.

Affinity audiences are one such example. With affinity audiences, you can target people based on a comprehensive understanding of their lives, interests, and behaviours. Affinity audiences have shown a qualified enthusiasm for a particular issue, allowing advertisers to target the individuals who matter most with their products or services.

> **HOW TO SET UP AN AFFINITY AUDIENCE**
>
> You can target your ideal niche audience simply by using URLs and interests. Finding the audiences page under an ad group of your choosing, click the 'What their preferences and patterns are' area, and you'll notice an opportunity to create a Custom Affinity Audience at the bottom.

In-market audiences allow you to reach customers who are on the lookout for the products you offer and are judged by the ad platform as being at buying stage. Their search history might be filled with products like yours, which means they're interested in buying products you offer and actively considering their options.

CUSTOM INTENT TARGETING

Custom intent targeting will aim to reach people with specific keywords that might be interested in purchasing your products. That is where you can use keywords to reach new consumers. You can also target people who have viewed specific URLs/apps/YouTube content.

When building custom intent audiences, keep the following five search parameters in mind:

1. In-market keywords.
2. Primary competitors.
3. The number of searches.
4. Keywords used by competitors.
5. Pages of competitors.

You may reach your ideal users and target audience through display and video ads with specific intent audiences. You may also divide these audiences into multiple categories based on the keywords and landing sites you want to target.

DEMOGRAPHIC TARGETING

Demographic targeting considers the personal attributes of your target audiences. Demographic targeting can be based on age, gender, location, device type, and numerous other options.

Users' demographic information is collected by search engines depending on their account preferences and behaviour. Advertisers may then utilize this data to add demographic targeting to their ads campaigns, allowing them to zero in on a very particular audience.

Demographic targeting can be used to reflect the particular segment avatar you're looking to reach – you may have gender and age on that list.

Location can be helpful if you operate a business that offers local services, such as a barbershop. In this case, you want to target people that are in the vicinity of your business. If you don't select the specific location, you will be wasting money by offering your services to people on the other side of the country.

Device type can be helpful – for example, if you're looking to drive app installs, you will not display your ads to desktop users.

STEP BY STEP

How to set up demographic targeting

Using Adwords, you can have access to the new Detailed Demographics in six simple steps.

1 Access your Google Ads account.
2 Choose a Campaign from the list on the left.
3 Choose Demographics from the left-hand menu.
4 From the top of the page, you can now pick demographic targeting groups.
5 Tick the box next to each demographic category you wish to target.
6 Enable your demographic targeting by selecting the blue Edit drop-down menu. You may also exclude demographics and change bid adjustments here.

TIME-BASED TARGETING

Time-based targeting allows you to capture the attention of certain people during a specific period. A great example of time-based targeting would be a coffee shop running its ads in the morning when people rush to the office and want to grab a coffee on their way.

> STEP BY STEP
>
> *How to set up time-based targeting*
>
> Apply time and day targeting to show your ad exclusively at particular hours and days of a week.
>
> 1. Choose whether this ad's time and day settings will be based on the user's local time or Eastern Time. The 'user's local' time refers to the time of day when the user receives your ad.
> 2. Choose the days of the week when your ad will be served by checking the boxes. Days begin at midnight and conclude at 11:59 pm.
> 3. Check the boxes next to the times of day when your ad will be served.
> 4. Save.

Time and day targeting is very effective for campaigns involving time-sensitive items, like tickets to sporting events or advertisements for a television series that airs on a specified day.

REMARKETING

Remarketing is a method of reaching out to people who have previously interacted with your website or mobile app. It enables you to carefully place your adverts in front of these audiences. At the same time, they explore Google or other search engines or partner websites, therefore increasing brand recognition or reminding those audiences to make a purchase.

Remarketing targets people who have already visited your website without purchasing or having their email otherwise captured.

STEP BY STEP

How to set up remarketing

1. To utilize remarketing on the display network, build a campaign with the campaign type 'Display Network' and the goal 'Drive action' > 'Buy on your website' selected. Continue to configure your campaign, then click Next.
2. Create an ad group after you've completed the remaining campaign elements. Click to expand the 'Audiences' section under 'People: people you want to reach' and select the remarketing lists you want your campaign to target using the 'Remarketing' audience selector.
3. You have the option of using remarketing lists you've developed. To establish your remarketing list, first add a 'first-party audience source' to the Audience manager.

Content targeting

You can also target users with content targeting. This strategy uses different variables to deliver relevant ads to the right users. This technique uses keywords of your ad, page keywords, and the page's content where your ad is displayed to match it to the right audience.

TOPICS

You can use content targeting based on topics. With this path, numerous variables are considered, such as text, structure and content of different websites that can deliver your ads to the relevant pages based on topics.

PLACEMENT

With placement targeting, you can choose specific websites that you know your customers often visit. This strategy doesn't require any keywords and can be done on a whole website or particular parts.

STEP BY STEP

How to set up placement targeting

1. Go to your Google Ads account and sign in.
2. Select 'Display campaigns' or 'Video campaigns' from the navigation menu.

3. Choose the campaign you wish to change, then an ad group inside that campaign.
4. In the page menu, select Placements.
5. Select the pencil symbol.
6. Select the appropriate targeting for your placements.
7. In the box that appears, choose a placement type.
8. Select the places you wish to target by checking the boxes next to them.
9. At the bottom of the box, you can select 'Enter multiple placements' and enter the URL for each placement. Then, click the 'Add placements' button.
10. Save.

CASE STUDY

The challenge

A fitness company had been using organic channels for many years and this had helped them reach a good level of growth. However, they needed to accelerate this growth and in 2017 they first entered into the world of paid advertising.

The solution

Their initial focus was on Google Ad campaigns in four countries and this quickly moved into remarketing ads that targeted website visitors who added their products to the cart but didn't make the purchase. They also targeted similar audiences to those that visited their website to find new potential customers.

This remarketing technique enabled them to quickly find the most likely purchasers and bring them directly to a relevant page on the site where they could complete their purchase or discover new products.

The results

The company saw over 50 per cent revenue growth year on year as well as improving brand presence and site traffic. Remarketing increased sales from Google Ads by over 100 per cent while conversion rates increased by over 10 per cent. (Google Ads, 2021)

Step four: Track, evaluate and optimize

Track your data

When running display ad campaigns, it's imperative to keep track of the progress you make. It can help you see where the gaps are and lead to a better strategy in the future.

Conversion tracking is vital if you're running a conversion-based campaign. There are different types of conversion tracking to cover specific actions taken on your website (purchases, signing up for a mailing list, and so on), phone calls made to your business, app installations, and so on.

To set up conversion tracking, you need to add the relevant tracking tag or code to your website or app code. When a customer clicks on your ad and takes the desired action, Google recognizes it and records it as conversion.

Once you get the relevant data on conversions, you should analyse it, to compare it against industry benchmarks and previous ad campaign results.

There are several additional data categories that conversions can reveal, including:

- cost per conversion – the average price per conversion;
- conversion rate and total conversion rate – how often an ad click leads to a conversion;
- total conversion value – the sum of conversion values;
- conversion value per cost – estimated return on your investment;
- conversion value per click – total conversion value divided by the number of eligible clicks;
- value per conversion – how much each of your modifications is worth;
- conversion value rules – the combined value for each conversion action.

The 'All conversions' section in Google Ads shows data for all conversion actions, including other particular conversion sources that weren't included in the 'Conversions' column.

The number of cross-device conversions across your conversion activities is reported in the 'Cross-device conversions' field. Cross-device transformations begin with clicking an advertisement on one device and finishing with a conversion on another.

Understanding the time of the conversion can be useful. All the metrics in the above list are recorded based on the click but not the time of conversion – a prospect could have clicked on an ad last week, but only converted this week. The conversion will still be recorded as happening last week.

The view-through conversions section shows you the number of customers who saw your ad, didn't interact with it, but later completed a conversion on your website. That differs from the usual conversions section, which only counts customers who have interacted with an ad and completed a conversion.

Evaluate and optimize your campaigns

Once you get a hold of the relevant data, you can analyse your campaign to see how well your ads perform. If there are any flaws in your campaign and your ads aren't showing where you want them to, you can take relevant actions to optimize your campaign.

But how do you know what your numbers mean so you can evaluate them effectively? The best thing to do to make sense of your numbers is to compare them as follows:

1. The first thing you can do is to compare ad placements with each other. Based on the data you receive, you can increase the bid for a particular placement if you believe it has the potential to perform better. Or vice versa – exclude specific placements if the conversion rate is unsatisfactory for you.
2. You can also compare split tests to support the well-performing ads to get more conversions and disable the underperforming ones. That can help you to maximize gains with your budget.
3. If you have already run similar campaigns, you can compare the results with your previous achievements to better understand where your current campaign might be lacking.
4. Comparing your results with industry benchmarks can give you a good idea of where your competitors stand with ads similar to yours. If your campaign is severely underperforming compared with others, you might reconsider some of their strategies.
5. Additionally, you can compare your targeting choices to determine which ones work best and avoid those that haven't led to desirable results. If certain topics you've chosen or specific demographics don't lead to relevant placements and, ultimately, conversions, you can exclude them going forward. You can also create split tests to optimize your ads.

Remember, the key to successful targeting is trial and error. You might discover certain links between topics that you might not have thought of before. Or the target demographic you were aiming to reach isn't that interested in your products.

You can use your findings as a blueprint for any future campaigns. Learning what works for your brand helps you optimize results going forward.

References

Admixer (2021) How to stop worrying about rich media ads and start using them, available at: https://blog.admixer.com/rich-media-ads/ (archived at https://perma.cc/G87L-8ZKB)

Baymard Institute (2020) 44 cart abandonment rate statistics, available at: https://baymard.com/lists/cart-abandonment-rate (archived at https://perma.cc/G858-7RQW)

Datasine (2019) Which images make the most successful Facebook ads?, available at: https://datasine.com/blog/which-images-make-the-most-successful-facebook-ads/ (archived at https://perma.cc/M9V9-ZF85)

Global Banking & Finance Review, 71% of consumers more likely to buy a product or service from a name they recognise, available at: https://www.globalbankingandfinance.com/71-of-consumers-more-likely-to-buy-a-product-or-service-from-a-name-they-recognise/ (archived at https://perma.cc/CSZ8-ZG77)

Google Ads (2018) How Schmidt's Naturals engages millennials on YouTube, available at: https://ads.google.com/home/success-stories/schmidts-naturals/ (archived at https://perma.cc/EBS2-SKUL)

Google Ads (2021) Learn how Google helped WIT fitness become a global brand, available at: https://ads.google.com/intl/en_uk/home/success-stories/wit-fitness/ (archived at https://perma.cc/F42F-Z3FT)

Ipsos/Google (2017) Data suggests visual attention to advertising on YouTube mobile is higher than on TV, available at: https://www.ipsos.com/en-us/news-polls/google-ipsos-advertising-attention-research (archived at https://perma.cc/64LR-UUUQ)

Marketing Dive (2020) Video ads drive a 48% higher sales rate than static ads, study says, available at: https://www.marketingdive.com/news/video-ads-drive-a-48-higher-sales-rate-than-static-ads-study-says/586025/ (archived at https://perma.cc/U2DV-WTXE)

Microsoft (2017) State of global customer service report, available at: http://info.microsoft.com/rs/157-GQE-382/images/EN-CNTNT-Report-DynService-2017-global-state-customer-service-en-au.pdf (archived at https://perma.cc/VYH4-J9T2)

Neuromarketing (2009) Emotional ads work best, available at: https://www.neurosciencemarketing.com/blog/articles/emotional-ads-work-best.htm (archived at https://perma.cc/3NX2-NT99)

Smart Insights (2021) Average CTRs display and search advertising – 2021 compilation, available at: https://www.smartinsights.com/internet-advertising/internet-advertising-analytics/display-advertising-clickthrough-rates/ (archived at https://perma.cc/F9VU-R6WX)

WordStream (2020) 7 Super-creative, crazy-effective retargeting ad ideas, available at: https://www.wordstream.com/blog/ws/2016/04/13/retargeting-ad-ideas (archived at https://perma.cc/YW37-9QNS)

Bibliography

Hubspot (2021) 2021 marketing statistics, trends and data – The ultimate list of digital marketing stats, available at: https://www.hubspot.com/marketing-statistics (archived at https://perma.cc/BPR3-64Q4)

Yotpo (2018) What makes customers brand loyal?, available at: https://www.yotpo.com/blog/customer-loyalty-survey-data/ (archived at https://perma.cc/DL66-S7RB)

06

Managing affiliates and partnerships to deliver highly targeted leads

Affiliate marketing is another creative strategy to boost the reach and impact of your business. Widely used and effective, this marketing strategy is applied by 80 per cent of businesses and generates 16 per cent of all e-commerce sales in the United States and Canada. In today's digital age, about 15 per cent of all digital media's revenue comes from affiliate marketing (BigCommerce, 2021).

Affiliate marketing is a commission-based strategy and revenue-growth model combined in one approach. In affiliate marketing, a business rewards affiliates, or official brand ambassadors, for every customer they introduce to their business. Your affiliates may be advertisers, merchants or even customers receiving discounts in exchange for their marketing efforts. By building an affiliate programme, your business can effectively grow revenue, sales and customer acquisition.

The benefits of affiliate marketing include:

- **Low marketing and ad costs:** In affiliate marketing, you will depend on your affiliates to run your ads, and come up with the marketing creative, from your provided assets. You will cut significant costs by not having to hire an advertising team or purchase advertisement space.
- **Low risk:** No more investing money in advertising campaigns without being sure of ROI. Since affiliate marketing is commission-based, you will only have to pay money when your affiliates' marketing efforts are successful, which obviously lowers risk.
- **Targeted traffic:** Your affiliates choose to go into business with you. If the affiliate takes a chance on your brand, there is a high likelihood that their

audience will also be attracted to your brand. This saves you the guesswork of finding your target audience.

- **Flexibility:** You can take it slow or jump in with your affiliate programme. Depending on the success of your starting affiliates, you can easily expand your programme while accepting little additional risk.
- **High ROI:** Affiliate marketing has one of the highest ROIs across all marketing strategies.

There are numerous types of affiliate marketing and you can use any or a combination of these approaches:

- **Content marketing programmes:** Affiliates create and share online material that promotes interest in your brand, for example Instagram influencers, YouTube content creators.
- **Coupon-site programmes:** Affiliates have their own coupon code to encourage their audience to engage with your brand.
- **Review-site programmes:** Affiliates increase your brand's visibility by reviewing it on certain sites.
- **Traditional media:** Affiliates promote your brand via traditional media, such as through televised commercials.

For the rest of this chapter, we will look at the steps for starting your own affiliate programme.

Step one: Set objectives

There are many factors to consider when starting an affiliate programme. To filter through the options available, it is important to set marketing objectives. Even though affiliate marketing is low risk and low cost, you should still determine objectives specific to your business to be able to measure success and boost ROI.

Of course, the bottom line is more sales, but you need to decide which metrics to track. You have a few options:

- sales volume – the quantity of units sold in a certain reporting period;
- sales value – the quantity of products delivered multiplied by the fixed price in a certain reporting period;

- average order value – the average amount spent every time a buyer places an order;
- size of affiliate network – the quantity of affiliates in the programme.

Be specific

After picking your metrics, you should get specific about your customers and product lines. What are your objectives here and how specific, or targeted, can you make these marketing objectives? Take a look at these prompts to guide your thinking:

1. Do you want to promote a particular product or service lines?
2. Do you want to reach new segments of your brand? How would you define these segments?
3. Do you want to strengthen sales in existing segments?
4. Do you want to create multiple campaigns and offers to address different objectives?
5. Do you want to respond to particular events in your industry or in society at large?

CASE STUDY: B2C TRAVEL START-UP

The challenge

A growing B2C travel start-up had been running effective social media and paid search advertising for a few years. This was delivering some growth, but it had started to slow in recent months. Their SEO had not been delivering results and it would take some time to fix this as they were a long way behind the competition. They needed to find a way to address these issues or continue to lose business to the competition.

The solution

A new CMO joined the business and quickly ran an audit of all the sites that ranked in the top two pages of Google for the primary keywords. Those that were not journalism or competitor sites were identified as possible affiliates, and communication channels were opened. As a result, two of the top-five ranked sites became affiliate partners of the company. In this negotiation, the company was able to gain a leading position over its competition on the ranking pages, therefore ensuring strong opportunities from SEO traffic while the company developed its own SEO strategy.

The results

As a result of building these direct affiliate relationships, the company was able to attract customers it would have otherwise lost due to poor SEO, and at a controlled cost. Affiliate marketing became the second biggest provider of leads as well as developing useful industry relationships for the company.

Step two: Select network

Once you've set your objectives, you should decide whether or not you will work with an affiliate network like Awin. Of the available options, CPA (cost per action) networks are the most popular choice. Working with an affiliate network is optional. You can always choose to run the affiliate programme independently. To help with your decision, let's set out the pros and cons of using an affiliate network.

Pros of affiliate networks

Affiliate networks eliminate a lot of the guesswork and infrastructure-building necessary for affiliate marketing. Most importantly, affiliate networks offer:

- reporting systems and tracking tech;
- affiliate management to ensure ethics and brand guidelines are being followed;
- established relationships with experienced affiliates, which increases your chance of finding super affiliates.

> TOP TIP
>
> What is a super affiliate?
>
> These affiliates will become your business's greatest marketing asset. Super affiliates generate a significant percentage of an affiliate programme's activity, sometimes accruing more results than hundreds, even thousands, of small affiliates combined. Due to their reach, super affiliates are in high demand. In order to acquire super affiliates, your business will have to sweeten the deal through favourable commissions and conversion rates (Marketing Terms, 2021).

Cons of affiliate networks

Even though these pros are attractive, you must also consider two minor cons:

- set up costs;
- override, which can be up to 30 per cent of what affiliates earn (10 per cent commission paid out to affiliates would become 10 per cent commission and 3 per cent to the affiliate network, or 20 per cent commission paid out to affiliates would become 20 per cent commission and 6 per cent to the affiliate network); this can represent sizeable amounts of money when sales figures are high (for example, $5,000,000 in sales on a 20 per cent commission deal for affiliates would mean $300,000 override for the affiliate network).

When considering these cons, you must still consider the amount of money and time that you will save by opting to use an affiliate network instead of starting from square one on your own.

Popular affiliate marketing networks

If you decide to use an affiliate network, CJ Affiliate (Commission Junction) and Awin are two popular options.

CJ AFFILIATE

The largest affiliate marketing network in existence, founded in 1998. Their website, cj.com, includes a whole page of informative case studies you can use to see if their strategies match your objectives.

AWIN

Awin has over 225,000 active affiliate partners all over the globe. Furthermore, Awin has a programme for entry-level businesses and start-ups that offers their services with no set-up costs. (See Awin, 2020.)

Step three: Determine structure and payment terms

To be able to determine your structure and payment terms, you need to run some calculations and make sure your plan is viable and sustainable over time.

Calculate a price that makes sense

Consider the following factors when calculating price (Crazy Egg, 2016).

- **Shift through your price options:** Will you charge per click, per lead, or per sale? It is important to avoid CPM (cost per impressions) as impressions do not necessarily correlate to sales. The key challenge here is to convince your affiliates that this programme will fulfil them even though you're emphasizing clicks/leads/sales over impressions, which are the easiest to achieve.
- **Conduct a competitor analysis:** By analysing your competitors, you can see what works and what doesn't without reinventing the wheel on your own. Extrapolating from your competitors can help you determine the way you manage commissions and these commercial arrangements. To kick-start your thinking, here are two prompts:
  - How much are your competitors paying their affiliates?
  - Which of your competitors' standards are suitable for your market and industry?

Finalize your calculations

Now it's time to think about the numbers and set your commission. This section provides a series of calculations you should use to guide your commission rates.

1. DEFINE CPA (COST PER ACQUISITION)

Simple version:
Marketing spend / Number of customers = Cost per customer

More accurate version:
$1000 ad spend brings 200 visitors, which is $5 per visitor

If you have a conversion rate for these visitors to turn into leads at 20 per cent, then you would have 40 leads, and your cost per lead (CPL) is $25. If 15 per cent of leads convert to paying customers, then you would have six customers, and your CPL would be $167.

This gives you a solid figure to work from in terms of paying commission per sale, per lead or per click.

2. DEFINE CRR (CUSTOMER RETENTION RATE)

The formula for CRR is:

CRR = ((E – N) / S) × 100

Where E is the amount of customers at the end of a particular time period, N is the amount of new customers gained during that same period, and S is the amount of customers at the start of that time period.

So, if you started with 500 customers at the beginning of the quarter, and had 600 customers at the end of the quarter, but 500 of those are new customers, then your CRR would be 20 per cent, which is quite low.

Conversely if you started with 500 customers at the beginning of the quarter, had 450 at the end of the quarter, 50 of those being new customers, then your CRR would be 80 per cent, which is high.

The higher the CRR, the higher commissions you can afford to pay your affiliates, because customers spend more time as customers and therefore have a higher customer lifetime value (CLV).

3. DEFINE CLV

Customer lifetime value is how much you expect to make from one customer throughout their time with you as a customer.

The calculation for CLV is:

Average sale value × Average number of repeat transactions per customer

So, if your average sale value across all your purchases is $40, and the average number of repeat transactions per customer is 6, then your CLV would be = $240.

The higher this number is, the more you can afford to pay your affiliates, because you know you're going to enjoy further revenue from that customer later down the line.

Other considerations

There are a few other questions that you can ask yourself to make your calculations even more specific/targeted:

- If the affiliate program is based on acquiring subscriptions, will you make one-off or recurring payments?
- Will you pay affiliates more for engaging with new customers instead of existing ones?

- Will you pay based on last touch, first touch attribution, and 'assists'? Or will you vary compensation for 'introducing', 'influencing' or 'closing'. This is a tricky consideration as you must balance fairness, making your affiliates feel valued, and prioritizing the affiliate marketing that most aligns with your objectives.
- Will you increase commissions based on performance, that is, auto-scaling commission?

Step four: Determine programme rules

Our next step concerns building a contract for your affiliate programme. Your affiliate programme agreement, partnership agreement, Terms of Service, Terms and Conditions or Operating Agreement will be the contract that regulates your business relationship with your affiliates. If you work with a network, it will have operating rules for your affiliates to follow within the network.

But you should still outline additional, individual programme agreements for your affiliates. This step is an important way to regulate your affiliates and protect your brand.

By setting up programme agreements, you will ensure your brand, products and services are marketed ethically and in line with brand values. These agreements protect you from affiliate fraud and discourage bad affiliate behaviour from undermining your marketing strategy. They also inform your affiliates on the best practices to achieve your business's specific objectives. All in all, these programme agreements allow you to communicate with your affiliates and hold them accountable. Without these agreements, you risk losing money and harming your brand.

> TOP TIP
>
> Brand protection is the advisable practice of protecting your most desirable assets from theft or misappropriation.
>
> To effectively protect your brand, you must identify anything and everything that makes your programme 'unique and distinct' from that of your competitors. These assets may include your content, media campaigns and your website. Another asset to keep in mind is your reputation. While intangible, your reputation is inextricably linked to your marketing, so be sure to prioritize it.

Once you've identified your assets, you must ensure every aspect of your affiliate programme is organized to protect these assets. Your assets should guide your thinking toward setting up institutionalized protocols. As the protector of your brand, you cannot compromise on what can and cannot be done by your affiliates. Luckily, you can use your programme agreements to effectively communicate your expectations to your affiliates and avoid catastrophe (Affiliate Insider, 2021).

Structure of a programme agreement

For your agreement, you can easily follow a set outline (AM Navigator, 2021) while adding aspects specific to your affiliate programme.

AFFILIATE AGREEMENT

Foreword

Your foreword should frame your entire agreement. Use this space to discuss the purpose of the agreement and to assure your affiliates that you will always assume best intentions. It is best practice to keep this section under 250 words for brevity.

Terms and definitions

Especially if you want your programme to be accessible to new affiliates, it is well-advised to provide a short list of industry terms. Like the foreword, you should keep this section brief to avoid overwhelming your affiliates.

Summary

More likely than not, the summary is the only section that your affiliates will read closely. Take advantage of their undivided attention! In about 10 sentences, explain the type of content you do not want associated with your brand, the type of affiliates you will not accept, the requirement for affiliates to comply with FTC's endorsement guidelines, behaviours and practices you disallow or penalize.

Enrolment

In this section, you should describe your acceptance process. Specifically, you should be forward about what kind of content would be inappropriate for your brand. Depending on your brand, you may have more stipulations than other companies. Here are some examples of inappropriate content you can list: explicit sexual content, violent content, Ponzi schemes, illegal content, discriminatory content, and so on.

Affiliate disclosure

To follow the FTC, you must require your affiliates to disclose their relationship to your company. In this section, make it clear that you reserve the right to terminate your partnership with affiliates if they fail to disclose.

Trademark policy

The purpose of this policy is to deter trademark violators. In your policy, be clear that affiliates can only use your trademark for expressly authorized purposes of your choosing. You should also specifically prohibit any font, colour and logo modifications. For a good example of this policy, check out Amazon's Associates Program Trademark Guidelines.

Policies on promotional methods

In this section, your goal is to discourage your affiliates from using misleading or false information to increase sales. Your policies here should cover all aspects of marketing at your affiliates' disposal. While the following list is not exhaustive, it should kick-start your thinking:

- Content: Require your affiliates to provide readers with true, accurate information without exaggerations.
- Videos: Create special rules for unboxing or how-to videos and require approval before your affiliates post online.
- Coupons and discounts: Make it clear that affiliates can only share coupons/discounts provided by the programme and prohibit any modifications to these coupons/discounts.
- Incentivized traffic: Prohibit the practice of paying online users to buy your product.
- Mobile apps: Establish a requirement to approve in-app ads to avoid forced clicks or other scams that will frustrate your customers.
- Paid search campaigns: Provide a list of keywords to bid on or avoid and an inventory of marketing materials.

Affiliate rights and obligations

You may decide to only cover obligations in this section. In summary though, you must communicate somewhere in your agreement that affiliates have the right to get paid for qualifying actions and are obligated to comply with this programme agreement.

Merchant rights and obligations

In a similar vein to the previous section, here you should list your right as the merchant to monitor affiliates, modify the programme agreement, and take measures against affiliates who do not comply. You also have an obligation to pay your affiliates for qualifying actions.

Relationship of the parties

This section is optional, but you can use it to reiterate that the affiliates are independent contractors.

Warranties and representations

Here, you must stipulate that this agreement coming into effect means that your affiliates represent your brand.

Payment policy

You should use this section to let affiliates know what methods you use to track and process payments, the value of the commissions you pay for each qualifying action, and how/when you make payments.

Terms of the affiliate programme agreement

In this section, you should describe when the agreement becomes effective and when/how the agreement can be modified or terminated.

Disclaimers

The disclaimers section should be an opportunity to explain that your company offers no implied or express representations or warranties regarding your affiliate programme.

Liability

Your agreement must clearly state that you are not liable for any damages or losses.

Indemnification

In this section, you should explicitly request your affiliates to hold your company harmless.

Confidentiality

This section is another opportunity to protect your brand. Here, you request any information exchanged with affiliates to only be used within the scope of this agreement.

Remedies

Only include this section if you want to establish consequences for when your affiliates violate this agreement.

Limited licence

You can include here a separate clause regarding your affiliates' right to use your company's trademarks.

Miscellaneous

Include this final section if you need to clarify any other points in your agreement.

Step five: Collate marketing assets

Affiliate marketing assets are marketing materials you supply to your affiliates so they can promote you. You can also allow them to create new marketing materials using your existing assets. If you allow your affiliates to make new marketing materials, it may be prudent to require them to seek your approval before publication. Whatever you decide, you should include your regulations in your affiliate programme agreement.

Typical affiliate marketing assets

- Image or HTML5 banners:
  Best specs (AffiliateWP, 2016):
  - Width × height in pixels: 300×250, 728×90, 300×600, 468×60, 160×600.
  - File size: 40 KB is recommended for a faster load time.
  - Recommended file formats: PNG (preferred), JPG, GIF.
- Text links.
- Videos.
- Social media posts.

- XML product feed.
- Widgets.
- Advanced form-based links.

Best practices for affiliate-created assets

While there is no wrong way to have affiliates create assets, there are a few best practices to consider in your planning. For one, you should devote a page of your website to brand assets to ensure that your affiliates' marketing materials are consistent. This page should include your logo, brand colours, fonts, product shots/imagery and specific copy or content for their assets.

Step six: Track, manage and optimize

So now, your affiliate programme is up and running. You may think your work is done, but the truth is that you must consistently track the work, manage and optimize your programme. While less work than managing your advertising in-house, affiliate marketing is still not a hands-off approach.

If you work with an affiliate network, the network will provide you with advanced analytics. They will handle the tracking, and they may even provide you with a resource manager. If you're not using a network, you'll need to collect your own data.

Managing and optimizing are the key goals here. As the manager of your affiliates, you can keep them engaged through various touch points, ensuring they feel fairly compensated and valued. Excellent management requires you to engage with your affiliates on a daily or weekly basis.

TOP TIP

Pay attention!

You will be tempted to let your affiliates run free, but resist the temptation to release the reins. Stay focused on your goals. Don't sit back for a month, as irreparable damage can be done by just one poor affiliate in that time. Keep a watch on it daily and always think about how you can improve your programme. Add new affiliates, remove poor ones, check your assets and so on.

As a result of being so involved, you will know first-hand if your marketing is meeting your objectives. What's more, ideas for optimization will come to mind as you track and manage your affiliate marketing efforts.

Why tracking and measuring is crucial

If you let your affiliate programme operate unchecked, you run the risk of missing out on potential opportunities and squandering your investment. For instance, without measuring the success of your affiliate marketing, you will not be able to identify your super affiliates.

> WHAT TO WATCH
>
> In order to make sure your numbers are always accurate, you must validate your sales. This protects you from scam artists and from overvaluing your assets.

What data you should track

KPIS

With so much data at your fingerprints, you may not know where to start. Here are a few KPI categories for you to consider for measurement (MyCustomer, 2015).

- **Revenues or sales:** how much money you made in total.
- **Conversion rates:** what percentage of people an affiliate encouraged to visit your website who subsequently purchased goods or services.
- **Cost per sale:** how much you had to spend to make each sale happen.
- **Return on advertising spend:** how much money you spent on a campaign and what your subsequent margin was.
- **Average order value:** how much an average order is worth.
- **Affiliate behaviour:** understanding how many affiliates you have, how active they are and how much revenue each one generates.
- **Average earnings per click:** this figure can be calculated by dividing the total commission an affiliate earned by the number of clicks they generated to help you see whether they are providing value for money.

CUSTOMER LIFETIME VALUE

You can also choose to measure CLV, which we've previously discussed. You'll want to measure it if you're interested in increasing the value of your existing customer base, to set it as a metric to work towards. It can prove difficult to pull together data from the affiliate network, your own sales data, and post-sales data, as they are likely to be stored on different systems. However, collating this data may be extremely worthwhile in the long run.

ATTRIBUTION

To measure attribution, you can determine which affiliates are driving the company's sales. Attribution enables you to ask questions like, 'Would you have got these sales anyway through SEO or would you have lost them because this site ranks higher?'

CUSTOMER INSIGHTS

Another option is to use an affiliate network, like CJ Affiliate, to take all of your raw data and plot them as customer insights. Basically, networks like CJ Affiliate go beyond the clicks to see who is doing the clicking (CJ.com, 2021). This in-depth look at your customer base will allow you to craft a more detailed consumer profile and optimize your marketing strategy. You can also follow this model to automate your own insight programme.

References

Affiliate Insider (2021) Why brand protection is key for your affiliate program, available at: https://affiliateinsider.com/featured-story/why-brand-protection-is-key-for-your-affiliate-program/

AffiliateWP (2016) Best practices for affiliate creatives and banners, and brand assets, available at: https://docs.affiliatewp.com/article/1071-best-practices-for-affiliate-creatives-banners-and-brand-assets (archived at https://perma.cc/5ELM-KYX5)

AM Navigator LLC (2021) Sample affiliate program agreement, available at: https://www.amnavigator.com/wm/ (archived at https://perma.cc/QAH3-E3LK)

Awin (2020) Awin, Dorothy Perkins and the Groupon reach network: Perking up your winter wardrobe, available at: https://www.awin.com/gb/advertisers/case-studies/dorothy-perkins (archived at https://perma.cc/VP7S-RAYF)

BigCommerce (2021) A beginner's guide to performance marketing, available at: https://www.bigcommerce.com/blog/performance-marketing/#what-are-the-most-common-uses-of-the-term-performance-marketing (archived at https://perma.cc/6FTZ-WQ2D)

CJ.com (2021) Dare to think big, available at: https://www.cj.com (archived at https://perma.cc/4CFB-8R2K)

Crazy Egg (2016) How to start an affiliate program that's actually successful, available at: https://www.crazyegg.com/blog/how-to-start-an-affiliate-program/ (archived at https://perma.cc/VA9C-MMGE)

Marketing Terms (2021) Super affiliate, available at: https://www.marketingterms.com/dictionary/super_affiliate/ (archived at https://perma.cc/U7QZ-GKPS)

MyCustomer (2015) How to measure the ROI of your affiliate marketing, available at: https://www.mycustomer.com/marketing/strategy/how-to-measure-the-roi-of-your-affiliate-marketing (archived at https://perma.cc/E44A-V3WG)

07

Creating content that excites, informs and converts

The Content Marketing Institute (CMI, 2021, 1) defines content marketing as 'a strategic marketing technique to attract and acquire a clearly defined audience through the creation and distribution of valuable, relevant, and consistent content with the objective of driving profitable customer action.'

Even though content marketing and content might seem identical and the terms are sometimes used interchangeably, they are not quite the same thing, although they overlap to some extent. Put simply, the difference between content marketing and content is the aim of the former – to drive users through the funnel and become customers. Content does not have an explicit aim. Content marketing exists to attract an audience, accumulate a following and drive sales.

Why invest in content marketing?

According to expert Neil Patel, content marketing is a long-term strategy that focuses on developing a strong relationship with your target audience by consistently providing them with useful, relevant, quality content. Unlike one-time advertising, content marketing demonstrates that you genuinely care about your clients. It's particularly useful for B2B or in-depth subjects where it's necessary to show expertise to win a customer.

Benefits of content marketing include:

- Increasing brand awareness and loyalty. Engaging content can help a newly established brand develop trust. You may simply begin to create trust within your online space if your audience finds the information you're sharing or creating intriguing, entertaining or useful.

- Conversion boosts. How can you transform interesting content into conversions? The following statistics from LYFE Marketing (2020) illustrate the conversion power of content marketing.
  - Content marketing has enhanced the quantity and quality of marketing leads for 74 per cent of the organizations surveyed.
  - Content marketing generates three times the number of leads as traditional marketing while costing 62 per cent less (Income Beetle, 2021).
  - Small and medium-size businesses that make use of content marketing generate 126 per cent more leads than those that don't (HubSpot, 2015).
  - Around 61 per cent of all online purchases directly result from a customer reading a blog (CMI, 2017, 1).
  - Businesses that produce 16 or more blog articles per month receive 3.5 times the amount of traffic than those that write four or fewer posts per month (Hubspot, 2020).
- It is relatively low cost.
  - In comparison with other forms of marketing, content marketing comes out at a low cost, even if article writing is outsourced.
- It can demonstrate your expertise and establish your brand as an authority – crucial during the consideration stage of the customer funnel.

TOP TIP

Planning ahead

The way brands and their audiences connect has changed dramatically in the digital age. With the rise of social media, marketers now have more tools than ever to build immediate interactive relationships. However, that doesn't mean they discard standard strategies that involve planning ahead. A combination of planned strategy and ad-hoc, responsive action is optimal.

- **Ad-hoc campaigns**
  This type of procedure can be seen in responsive social media efforts. They offer plenty of one-to-one communication between the company and the customer, making it easier to engage with and influence stakeholders across a variety of channels.

- **Planning ahead**
  Long-term campaigns, on the other hand, are meticulously researched, designed and implemented. These plans entail well-thought-out, detail-oriented creative efforts frequently presented to a specific target for advertising or PR purposes.

Planning is crucial to ensure you're addressing every stage of the customer journey, and giving people enough information and impetus to become aware of your brand, begin to trust it, purchase from you and become a repeat customer and advocate.

Step one: Set multiple goals

Look at the customer journey

First and foremost, the primary objective of a marketer is to anticipate and influence people's behaviour toward purchase. And there's no better way to achieve it than to consider the customer journey when creating goals.

AWARENESS

At the awareness stage, your responsibility is to grab attention. A conversion at this point isn't a sale; it's an email subscription, a page like, or maybe a return visit. Because your visitors aren't interested in the features of your product or service or even considering a purchase at this time, focus on solving problems and highlighting benefits. With informative content and excellent copy, you may manage to get hold of email addresses in exchange for a lead magnet. This may be an e-book, an email course, a video course, webinar or any other type of download that the visitor would find useful.

CONSIDERATION

At this time, your subscribers/blog readers/social media followers aren't ready to make a purchase. They are merely interested in your brand. They recognize that it can benefit them, but they aren't convinced. They require additional details to build trust, respect and buying intent. At this stage the key word is 'nurture', which means content that talks deeply about their problems and how to address them. Showcasing expertize and care for the customer at this stage is crucial.

CONVERSION

Here, you're overcoming objections and ensuring the sale is closed. It's important to prompt sales with a call-to-action at this stage, but you may also need to provide more personalized or segmented forms of content to get people over the line.

LOYALTY

Consumers today, more than ever, want to know that you care about them and share their values. Behind the scenes content, shareable value-based content and aftercare-based content works really well here.

Set SMART goals

Your marketing objectives specify where you want to go and what you're doing now to achieve them. Every marketing effort should be motivated by your marketing objectives.

SMART is a well-known framework for developing goals that make sense: Specific, Measurable, Attainable, Realistic and Timely. We'll quickly look at those in turn.

- **Specific** marketing goals: Set revenue and brand goals for yourself.
  - A non-specific marketing goal is 'gain more blog readers'. A specific marketing goal would be 'increase blog interactions with the 18–25 student demographic in the UK'. Specificity could be linked to:
    - demographics;
    - platform;
    - financial objectives;
    - particular segments;
    - particular products or services.
- **Measurable** marketing goals: It's critical to define success early on in order to track your progress. What criteria or key performance indicators (KPIs) will you employ to demonstrate your success?
  - It's important not to focus on vanity metrics here like 'likes', unless you are specifically aiming for this.
  - An example of a KPI could be 'increased leads by 50 per cent on student-related articles'.
- **Attainable** marketing goals: Examine your abilities to achieve your objectives. Setting marketing objectives is the simple part. You don't want to

create goals that are either impossible to achieve or so simple that they weren't worth setting in the first place. For example, if you know you have three hours per week to write content and can write 500 words per hour, it makes no sense to aim to churn out 10 articles per week.

- **Realistic** marketing goals: Make sure what you're proposing is feasible. This step allows you to discuss with your team whether your goals are realistic.
- **Timely** marketing goals: Set short-term and long-term marketing objectives. How long will it take you to achieve your objectives? Time frames should be matched to your objectives. Early on, talk about the realities of how long it will take to achieve your objectives. This will result in a far more relaxing integrated marketing experience.

CASE STUDY: CITIBANK – DOWNLOADABLE INVESTMENT GUIDE

The challenge

A financial services institution was looking to attract clients with very high net worth. These clients were difficult to find and didn't respond well to simple advertising.

The solution

The bank decided to create content that could add real value to their audience in order to demonstrate expertise, gain trust and, hopefully, attract new leads. They started by reviewing internal data and customer surveys to find pain points. From here they developed a series of PDF guides that solved these issues for their clients.

These guides were then promoted on LinkedIn to a highly targeted high-net-worth audience.

The results

The results were far beyond expectations, with over $100 million of business created in the first six months and a new set of prospects developed that were worth over $1 billion.

Step two: Determine your KPIs

Key performance indicators in content marketing may include the following, depending on the brand goals you've set:

- reduction in the funnel abandonment rate;
- boost in visitor loyalty;
- boost in revenue;
- boost in form submissions;

- surge in goal completions;
- rise in micro conversions;
- growth in page depth;
- reduction in bounce rate;
- increase in new site visitors;
- rise in the overall percentage of SEO-sourced traffic, both branded and non-branded;
- increase in content shares;
- surge in applause, amplification and conversation (on your social media handles and blog).

Matching brand KPIs to your particular objectives will make it much easier to track your progress and assess if your content marketing efforts needs tweaking. (See Table 7.1.)

Remember too that communicating outcomes properly is just as crucial as identifying them in the first place. Reporting on both brand KPIs and revenue can help you present the big picture of your efforts and show how they affect the whole brand. Having KPIs set from the beginning helps you provide an accurate picture of content marketing progress.

Existing content audit

If you're not sure what a good baseline or benchmark for your KPIs is, a good start is to audit your existing content and track back to various results

TABLE 7.1 Content goals and their related KPIs

Smart goal	Related KPI
Strategic partners	backlinks, mentions, new partnerships
Rapport and Trust	mentions, followers, promoters, returning customers
Customer Engagement	competitive price trends, linked shipping rate trends, shopping cart abandonment rate, conversion rate
Brand Loyalty	referrals, product reviews, promotors, returning customers
Conversions	competitive price trends, linked shipping rate trends, shopping cart abandonment rate, conversion rate
Revenue	website traffic, daily sales
Brand Awareness	subscription sign ups, social media followers, mentions (by partners and customers), website traffic

as if you had set KPIs at that time. That way you can get a numerical result per post or per content piece, or over a specific time period. This can act as your KPI baseline, which you're aiming to beat with your new content campaign.

We will discuss how to conduct a content audit later in this chapter.

Step three: Define your personas or avatars

Creating buyer personas or avatars helps in the development of your marketing strategy by revealing who the customers are, the situations they encounter and, most importantly, the objectives they seek to achieve. The personas you create for marketing should be an integral part of your strategy and help you make improved decisions.

Marketing personalities can differ dramatically from one industry vertical to the next, from B2B to B2C, and from one country to the next. Because there are so many elements that might form a persona, it all comes down to how a company tracks and stores data for a targeted consumer.

Asking questions

The idea of developing personas is to understand how a particular 'group' or 'segment' interacts and behaves with the app/website in order to spot crucial trends. These trends may overlap, allowing you to put them together to form a larger group based on their behaviour.

You want to find out the following information about each segment:

- where to reach them;
- what content interests them;
- what problems can you address for them;
- where in the buying cycle they are;
- what tone they most respond to;
- what format of content they most respond to;
- what topics they most respond to;
- how to get maximum engagement from them.

The questions you should be asking are:

- Who is engaging with you on existing social media?
- Demographics:
  - Who is engaging with your competitors?
  - What are the demographics of your typical blog reader?
  - What are the demographics of your typical customer?
  - Identify segments.
  - Take into account locations and languages.
- How much disposable income does your audience have? How much of a dent is a purchase with you going to make?
- What stage of life are your audience in and how does this affect how they consume information?
- Where does your audience spend most of their time online?
- What are the major pain points each of your products and services can solve and for which demographics?
- What tone of content does your target customer consume – such as educational, humorous?
- Who reads your emails/newsletter?
- When are they most engaged – days, times?
- Are your audience sharing your content and/or commenting (UGC)? If so, on what types of content?
- What word and phrases do they use – for example slang, insider lingo?

If you have a B2B business, the same questions apply, as business people are humans! However, you'll also want to explore:

- What is their business budget?
- Do they normally spend on these types of products or services or are you trying to do something disruptive, solve a problem in a novel way?
- What sizes of businesses buy from you?
- Who would be making these purchasing decisions?
- Who would be able to influence the people with purchasing decisions?

Gathering data

Let's take a look at some helpful hints for creating marketing personas using a combination of qualitative and quantitative research methods.

ANALYSE YOUR HISTORICAL DATA

Your historical sales data contain a wealth of quantitative information about your clients. These are customers who have already purchased from you, and it's important to understand why they did so. Look for the following characteristics or activities:

- **Set low, medium and high spend levels.** This can help you cross-sell and upsell if you have the opportunity. It can also assist you in rewarding more lavish spenders or incentivizing lower spenders through offers and discounts.
- **Geographical location.** Do people belonging to particular places spend more than others, and do they prefer some particular products?
- **Age and gender.** It's a widely used tactic for Gen Z, millennials and baby boomers because people from the same generation tend to shop in similar ways.
- **Weekdays.** It's always amazing how many individuals purchase on a certain weekday. It's no surprise that more people shop on weekends, but what about between the hours of 8 and 12 on a Monday morning?
- **Typical customer journey through your products/services.** What is customer LTV for various segments? What is their typical journey through your products/services?

LEAD SCORE

Lead scoring is the process of assigning a point value to a website action based on how valuable it is to you as a business (Chawla, 2021). This begins with a simple excel spreadsheet that assigns scores to various actions. These activities could include:

- downloading a file;
- filling out a form that tracks a particular field;
- looking at a webpage;

- viewing a video;
- signing up for a newsletter.

You can assign a score that leads to thresholds once you've established the actions you wish to score on the site. Typically, these are divided into the following scenarios:

- **Cold lead** (fewer than 100 points): This individual isn't interested yet and may have been browsing casually at the time.
- **Warm lead** (100–200 points): Interested and on the verge of making a purchase, it may require a little more time or just a nudge in the right way.
- **Hot lead** (more than 200 points): Ready to buy and should be contacted by the sales staff.

These steps and principles will assist you in defining your marketing personas significantly, in terms of how they move through the customer journey and by what means.

INTERVIEW CUSTOMERS

Find out why customers bought from you and what helped them make their decision by interviewing former or existing customers (feedback forms), customers on the website (live polls, chat and so on).

If you have a sales team, interview them. These employees are the ones who are closest to your clients and know who they speak with on a daily basis. They talk to customers and listen to their demands, understand shopping habits and hear common reasons for purchasing, and so on. They'll be able to tell you who the most common clients are and what trends they've noticed among the groups we described above, probably without even looking.

You can also get data from:

- social listening;
- competitor analysis;
- existing content marketing responses, comments and reactions;
- social media analytics;
- email analytics for content-based emails.

Step four: Understand content types and what they can achieve

What comes to your mind when you hear the term 'content marketing'? Most people instantly think blogging and social media. Even though blogging can be highly effective and profitable, there are many other sorts of material you can – and should – incorporate into your content marketing arsenal. In this step, we'll look at some of the most common forms of content and how to leverage them to generate new leads and revenue.

> TOP TIP
>
> Lead generation is critical for any company's success, and content marketing is one of the most effective ways to do it.
>
> Effective marketers understand that generating good content is the most effective approach to acquire leads. Content marketing generates three times the number of leads as other forms of marketing (Demand Metric, 2020).
>
> Lead generation can be done in numerous ways in content marketing. Of course, one of the most popular and effective is offering a lead magnet in exchange for contact details – this might be a cheat-sheet, free trial, downloadable PDF or e-book, free online course, webinar, report, or even a physical book sent through the post. There are other ways to generate leads, including making people enter their emails on a quote form, having them complete a test or quiz that requires their email address, and gated content.
>
> These are all highly valuable in marketing terms because they create an email list. And 'your subscriber list is your own golden egg-laying goose' (Dooley, 2020).

There are numerous types of content you can use within content marketing.

Blog posts

Blogs and articles are a fantastic resource for increasing traffic to your website. They improve the number of indexable pages on your domain while also adding value to your readers. They're also excellent for sending visitors to your landing or sales page.

Video content

Another excellent approach to increase traffic to your website is to use videos. According to 72 per cent of firms surveyed, video content helps ensure a fantastic ROI and enhances conversions considerably as well (LYFE Marketing, 2020). To boost the number of shares your video receives, make it intriguing and audience focused. Make full use of YouTube as well: it is the second most popular search engine. Creating optimized videos for the platform can drive a lot of traffic to your website. Video types can include:

- interviews;
- behind-the-scenes films;
- product demos;
- success stories;
- teasers;
- how-to videos;
- 'did you know' educational videos;
- values-based videos.

Social media posts

There are 3.78 billion social media users on the planet right now (Statista, 2021) and 54 per cent of shoppers use social media for research (GWI, 2018). You should take advantage of this and share posts on social media for increased awareness and engagement. This entails optimizing your social profiles, interacting with other users, and taking advantage of the potential of targeted social media marketing.

Podcasts

Podcasting is one of the most recent types of content generation that is rapidly gaining popularity. Podcasts can help you connect with your audience on a more personal level while also increasing traffic to your website.

Infographics

Infographics can boost your website's traffic by 12 per cent and generate 650 per cent more engagement than regular guest posts (Demand Gen Report, 2014). Infographics should be shareable for best results.

Other content types

- ebooks;
- toolkits;
- case studies;
- success stories;
- emails.

Take a moment to map out your entire customer journey, from them not being aware of your brand to becoming an enthusiastic advocate and repeat customer, through content alone. Identify multiple pieces of content for each stage of the customer journey.

Step five: Choose your content channels

It's not a case of guessing when it comes to selecting the correct channels for your content marketing. To work out what channels will be most effective, you must adopt a strategic approach. Revisit your goals and your audience avatar information about where your target audience spends time online.

You're looking at answering the following questions:

- Where will you share your content?
- Where will it live and be shared from?
- What are the benefits of paid media channels?
- What types of content channels are available?
- What mix of content channels can best support the entire customer journey?

Fit in the content marketing assets you identified in the previous step into channels, so you have a plan for each content channel.

There are three types of content channel, each with its own benefits and drawbacks.

Owned

These are the channels that your company solely owns:

- social media handles of the company;
- newsletter;

- blog;
- website.

There are two huge benefits of creating content on your owned content channels: 1) you don't have to pay to do it, and 2) you have total creative freedom. The downside, though, is that unless content is highly shareable, you're not necessarily reaching new audiences. Rather, you're speaking to the audience you already have. In this way, it's perfect for the Consideration, Conversion and Loyalty stages of the customer journey, but not necessarily Awareness.

Earned

This is the third-party organic distribution that you don't have to pay for – basically free promotion:

- directories;
- coverage in a reputed magazine or publication;
- customers, influencers or loyal fans sharing your content on their social media handles.

The three main benefits of earned channels are: 1) they're free, 2) they expose you to new audiences, and 3) they build credibility for your brand, either through appearing in a publication or being recommended by another customer or fan. This means this form of content channel is perfect for both the Awareness stage (expanding reach) and the Consideration stage (looking like a credible option). The downside to this is that you do not have total creative freedom.

Paid

These are the distributions on which you spend your money:

- paid editorial in publications;
- partnerships (brand collaborations, social media influencers and so on);
- sponsored social media campaigns (ads, content and so on);
- others (digital, radio, TV, print and so on).

The obvious downside to paid channels is that you have to pay to distribute content through them. However, they're excellent in order to reach new audiences (Awareness), and you can have more creative freedom than you would with earned channels.

Use this information to lay your content plan out over various different channels.

Step six: Keyword research and topic selection

Keywords aren't the be-all and end-all technique for developing content. If there's one thing that experts recommend, it's that you should always put your reader first. Otherwise, it would be impossible to stand out from the crowd with your material.

Through proper implementation of keywords, though, you can gain more traffic and reach your target audiences, either through ads promoting your content or through organic search.

List your main content topics

It's not enough just to write about a topic that is believed to be of interest to the website visitors. Take a step back and consider the larger picture first.

What do you want your business to be recognized for? What are the strengths of your company? What are the problems you solve? The topics acquired after answering these questions will most likely be broad generalized terms, but they would definitely steer you in the right direction. It may look like this for B2B enterprises in a range of industries:

- call centre quality assurance;
- outsourced marketing;
- digital transformation;
- automated storage and retrieval systems.

Begin by identifying the most important service you offer, and discovering keywords around that.

This initial step is vital, since every piece of content you develop for your social media platforms, blog or website must be a well-thought-out brick that strengthens your topic's structure. And, to increase organic traffic, one of the most effective strategies is to establish yourself as an authority on your topics with well-targeted and supporting content.

Subdivide your topic into supporting terms

After you've decided on a topic, you'll need to break it down into its constituent parts and variations. Consider your supporting terms to be the underlying beams that hold your main topic together because there's probably going to be a lot of competition around your main topic.

The chances of ranking for your main topic term are limited unless you're a mega-site or you operate in a very small niche. So, to attract qualified traffic, you should look for low-hanging fruit alternatives: keywords that are slightly more unusual and around the periphery of your main topic.

Make use of online tools

Now, open up a Google sheet and assign a tab to every single one of these supporting terms. This is where we are going to store all of our research, categorized by supporting terms.

Here are some great keyword suggestion tools:

- Answer the Public;
- Keyword Tool;
- SEMrush;
- Moz Keyword Explorer;
- Keyword Planner.

When you type in your initial keyword ideas, you'll be able to find data on how competitive they are, the search volumes and more relevant information. It's advised to choose keywords that have lower competition and higher search volumes. This is usually achieved with long-tail keywords.

You'll also be provided with suggestions for keywords you may not have considered. A single keyword can generate anything from 20 to thousands of proposed terms.

Many keyword tools also show the amount of social media engagements around particular keywords. This can help you evaluate and select topics that may garner higher levels of engagement.

Also, don't underestimate the potential of using Google to find suggested terms. If you're short on time or money, this is a great strategy. Begin by going to Google and typing in your term. What ideas do you get from the drop-down menu?

TOP TIP

Time to innovate

A smart content marketer is continuously trying new things, keeping up with the latest trends, and working to stay ahead of the curve. That way, they'll be able to create the most outstanding content for their brand's voice and image. One of the most effective methods to do so is to look at what other companies are doing and evaluate what works and what doesn't.

Here are some of the most important lessons to take away from the companies that are rocking the content marketing arena:

- Make the experience unique whenever and wherever possible.
- Make something original, even if it's only a new take on something old (CMI, 2017, 2).
- Make content that others want to share, whether it's humorous, powerful, entertaining, or newsworthy.

Step seven: Set up your content marketing calendar

What is a content marketing calendar?

A content marketing calendar is a tool that assists in planning and executing content marketing strategies in a timely and efficient manner. A content calendar will show how the material will be organized over a set period.

Consider it a road map for what you want to publish and in what sequence.

What should it look like?

In this section, we'll discuss what a content marketing calendar should like (F.I.T.S., 2021). The importance of layout for the sake of organization cannot be stressed enough. To plan your material, utilize an Excel spreadsheet or a Google Sheet. A dynamic platform like Google Sheets will be the most advantageous for you if you have a large staff working on content. A Sheets content marketing calendar can be simply worked on, changed and shared by a group of people. They're fantastic for teamwork!

Depending on how much data you want to put in your calendar, there are a variety of layout options. Some people like to organize their information on a traditional calendar so that they can view everything at once. Others prefer a linear layout with dates on the far left and content rows on the right.

If you intend to share the same or comparable content across several platforms, create distinct columns for each platform to accommodate any different modifications of the content you'll require.

Spreadsheets also allow you to establish various tabs for different types of material, such as website content, email content and social media content.

As a result, all of your content platforms may be grouped together on a single calendar for easy access (as in Table 7.2).

There are a few steps you should follow each time you start a new content marketing calendar, regardless of how you choose to organize it.

To begin, merely mark off the days on which you want to post content. Of course, it is not necessary for everyone to post content every day. On the other hand, some business owners publish new content several times per day. It all depends on the demands of your audience and the sector you're in. Whether it's once a week, three times a week or every weekday, aim to have a consistent content posting schedule.

When it comes to content marketing, consistency is crucial. You can more easily track patterns if you upload on a regular basis. It's nearly impossible to track patterns if you don't distribute your content on a set schedule effectively.

TABLE 7.2 Multi-channel content calendar for a week

	Monday	Tuesday	Wednesday	Thursday	Friday
Facebook	Monday motivation quote	link to latest blog post	behind-the-scenes photo	fill-in-the blank	update on weekend specials
LinkedIn	N/A	link to latest blog post	N/A	industry news	N/A
Twitter	behind-the-scenes photo	N/A	N/A	N/A	link to latest blog post

Consider industry standards and available resources when determining a content publishing frequency that works for you and your company. You don't want to overburden your content writers or proofreaders; otherwise, you risk producing low-quality content.

How far in advance should you be planning your content?

The longer you plan ahead in the area of content marketing, the better.

We recommend organizing your content at least a month ahead of time so you can develop a whole month's worth of content at once.

Weekly, quarterly or bi-monthly content calendars may be preferable depending on how frequently you publish material, but monthly calendars are usually the best option.

If you plan too far ahead, you may find yourself having to make changes as your plans alter.

Step eight: Create and post the content

Repurpose what you already have

As Income Beetle (2021) explains:

> When you reuse content, you're repurposing something you spent a lot of effort creating and translating it into different formats so it may be consumed more widely. Consider it as a form of recycling. You'd like to spend less time developing content and more time getting it in front of your target audience.

Try to think of all the numerous ways you could reuse that information that would be as effective as if you created it in one format.

Content audit

A content audit involves looking over all content previously created, and working out where it might fit in with the new content strategy. Some content may need to be rewritten or repurposed in a new way. You'll also begin to see gaps in content that need to be filled in order to appeal to the target audience and their stage in the buying journey.

To conduct a content audit, the best approach is as follows:

1. Include links to all of your content pieces on a spreadsheet.
2. Create columns for the following:
    - target keywords;
    - segments and personas;
    - buyer's journey stage;
    - format of content – video, text and so on;
    - topic.
3. Create columns for metrics:
    - interactions;
    - shares;
    - views;
    - total score (attribute a higher score to interactions and shares than to views).
4. Sort the spreadsheet according to the total score. This will show you which posts are performing the best, and which the worst, which can guide future content and assist in decisions on how to best repurpose content.

Beginning from scratch

Remember that buyer persona you made? You're crafting content for an audience with similar personas. So, ensure that the format in which you create content is enjoyable and keeps the audience glued to their screens.

FORMAT

A blog post, video, SlideShare, image, e-book, white paper, podcast, or whatever else your creative mind can think of could be a potential format.

Answer the following questions to choose an efficient format:

- Which format are you most comfortable with?
- Can you create content in this format regularly?
- Would you be able to maintain the quality levels with this format?
- What stage of the buyer's journey is this for?

After choosing a format, the next steps include the following.

CONTENT IDEAS BASED ON YOUR KEYWORDS

I advise using the content pillar strategy here.

According to HubSpot research (2017), the ideal approach to arranging content is to use topic clusters, which entails creating a long-form, comprehensive pillar page centred on a keyword that links to content on relevant subtopics (think blog posts).

This allows you to have both long-form and short-form content and makes it easy for you to categorize and organize your content.

ENTERTAIN, EDUCATE OR CONVINCE

Understanding that content marketing is similar to publishing, and that great content is the key, is a smart place to start. However, the next natural step is to consider what types of appeals will be effective for your target demographic.

In this stage, we'll go through three effective methods for creating valuable content that gets results. Exceptional content should perform one or more of the three tasks listed below: educate, entertain or convince/persuade.

Appeal 1: Educate While the majority of us may not remember our academic days fondly, practically everyone appreciates learning new things.

Fortunately, you already have a good understanding of how your target consumer thinks and feels, as well as their interests. The two most important tasks when looking to educate are to find prospective areas of interest for your audience and then come up with engaging, useful ways to educate your audience about those topics. This allows you to home in on their problems and show that you have means and methods to help them solve them.

Appeal 2: Entertain It's difficult to disagree that everyone enjoys being entertained. However, entertaining is probably the most challenging task on this list, and it's not always evident how to turn goodwill generated through entertainment into consumer engagement.

That said, it can make your content more likely to hold viral potential and share-appeal, which can significantly boost your reach and brand awareness.

Appeal 3: Convince This final appeal appears to be the most straightforward sales pitch, yet successful content that employs this strategy will aim for a much higher goal than selling one product. It's more about sharing your world view and touching something wider and deeper than your products. This helps the audience to bond with you as they sense shared values, and even come to see the world in a new way through your marketing.

Creative guidelines

HOW TO CREATE A GREAT INFOGRAPHIC

A graphic that is used to transmit complicated information is known as an infographic. Great infographics should be helpful to an audience, as well as visually appealing. Efficient infographics use storytelling to help the audience interpret data or contextualize it.

Research, statistics of some kind, descriptions of connecting elements, in-depth details, and step-by-step instructions could all be included in an infographic.

HOW TO WRITE A GREAT BLOG POST

Know who you are targeting Before jumping on the bandwagon of writing blog posts, it is important to understand your target audience and identify what they're searching for. Conduct thorough research and use the findings of that research instead of randomly guessing what your audience needs or wants to read.

Come up with juicy and intriguing headlines Your blog post is more than likely to fail to attract your targeted audience if it doesn't contain an intriguing headline. There is a lot of information online, and the headline is the quick signal viewers will look for to decide whether to spend their time reading the article.

Use subheadings frequently and shorten the paragraphs Formatting plays an important role in blog posts. Nothing frustrates the reader more than reading a blog post that contains a never-ending paragraph. Since most visitors tend to skim through the information before actually reading it, it is always advisable to use subheadings as much as possible. Including plenty of white space is also advised. Anything you can do to make your article reader-friendly will go a long way in increasing engagement and conversions.

SEO matters One aspect that's particularly challenging in the blogging industry is SEO. You have to perfectly balance the smooth experience of your users with your SEO. The truth is that organic Google searches account for a significant portion of most websites' traffic. Therefore, it is strongly advised to optimize your blog posts for vital SEO ranking elements to improve your SEO rating. Avoid keyword-stuffing as it can work against you, both in terms of SEO rankings and reader experience.

HOW TO CREATE A GREAT PODCAST EPISODE OR INTERVIEW

Be clear on your podcast format You can't host a successful interview unless you know exactly how you want it to go. And don't misinterpret it: we are not suggesting you produce the same type of show or host the same type of events as everyone else. However, being specific about the types of questions you'll ask, the pace and duration of the show, and possibly one or two questions you'll ask every guest will help you be more prepared, and it will also make it easier for your listeners to binge since they'll know what to anticipate.

Send a questionnaire prior to the interview Even if you think you know your guests deeply, delivering a pre-show questionnaire for them to complete is beneficial to everyone. It allows your guest to get a sense of the kind of questions you prefer to ask, and it assists you in gathering material that is specifically related to your programme, rather than public information obtained through the internet or casual discussions.

Research your visitors Other than demanding the pre-show form, make sure you conduct your research. Google will be your best friend while researching. LinkedIn can also supply a lot of relevant work information if it's a professional podcast. However, don't forget about old blog entries, other podcast interviews, social media updates and personal news.

HOW TO CREATE A GREAT VLOGS AND VIDEOS

Content Make a list of topics that fit with your brand and the ones that the target audience will find intriguing and engaging. Ensure to narrow down your topic, conduct thorough research and jot down crucial elements for your video.

Vlogs and videos do not have to be about your product or service at all. They should, however, be in line with your brand.

Story Plan a general beginning, middle and end for your vlog or video to keep it engaging. A good story usually has multiple scenes or moments where there are movements between 'positive' and 'negative' events or moods, even at a micro level. This helps keep attention.

Audio Assess your surroundings for any sounds and avoid filming in a noisy place to ensure viewers can actually hear you. You may want to use a special microphone or optimal sound quality.

Lighting Lighting is crucial, so make sure you have plenty of it. The quality of lighting is important as it effects video quality. If you're filming a static video, for example, talking in front of the camera, you may want to use professional lighting. You can use daylight and window light as a cost-free lighting alternative, but it doesn't always look as professional.

Background Consider where you are going to film the vlog or video. Will it be in front of a green screen or at the office or on location somewhere? If you're filming a talking-head video, consider using an engaging background and transitions to ensure it doesn't appear boring.

Camera The kind of vlog or video that you are looking to replicate should clearly be reflected in the type of accessories or camera you utilize. If you're looking to make a simple and straightforward vlog, you can use a webcam. A much smoother experience can be achieved with a DSLR camera on a tripod. It depends whether your brand image is more rough and ready, or smooth and polished. You may even find yourself using a GoPro underwater or up the side of a mountain!

HOW TO CREATE A GREAT E-BOOK

Pick a relevant or trending subject Keep in mind that the goal of your e-book is to generate leads, so pick a subject that would enable potential buyers to smoothly transition from downloading your e-book to speaking with your sales team.

Develop an outline The introduction to your e-book should both set the tone for the rest of the book and entice the reader to continue reading. Use your customer avatars and all existing customer information you have about their desires, pain points and what problems they're looking to solve, in order to create a solid outline that really speaks to your target audience.

Include visuals Depending on your industry, your e-book may look more like a professional report, or like a fashion magazine. Either way, it's important to include visuals that evoke the kind of feelings and associations you want to tie with your brand.

Build authority You can build authority with quotes, statistics, graphics of previous clients, recommendations from influential people in your niche, and case studies.

Include a call-to-action at the end Remember, the key reason to write an e-book is to generate leads. This does not mean it should be one long sales pitch – it must provide value – however, you musn't neglect to include a call-to-action at the end so leads are prompted to contact you or to buy. This can be even more effective if it's visual (a button with accompanying graphics) and hyperlinked. Because your e-book readers have most likely converted to leads, you can leverage the CTAs in your e-book to reconvert them and move them further down your marketing funnel (Hubspot, 2021).

Make a landing page specifically for your e-book Your e-book should be downloadable from a landing page on your website. A landing page is a web page that promotes/describes your service and has a form that visitors must complete with their contact information in order to get your e-book. This is how you can turn your website visitors into sales leads, which your sales team can then follow up on.

HOW TO CREATE A CASE STUDY OR SUCCESS STORY

Locate the ideal client Before you begin, obtain the client's permission and inquire about their willingness to participate in a case study. You can motivate them by publishing the case study on social media, tagging their company on all social media sites, and including a link to their website at the conclusion.

Use a standard outline to tell the story Storytelling is an extremely powerful marketing tool, and you can utilize it here to great effect. To tell a captivating customer success story, you don't need to employ fancy jargon – in fact, it's better if you don't. Instead, you'll want to make it as obvious as possible for the reader to comprehend how your organization helped a client solve a problem.

HOW TO CREATE A GREAT WHITE PAPER

Be professional and descriptive Writing a white paper differs from writing a blog post. You should write in a business-like tone and be fairly descriptive. To make your case, you'll most likely need to write at least 10 pages.

Emphasize the value you'll bring to the table Your white paper is an opportunity to project an image of expertise and insight that will benefit your readers, not a billboard for your company. In exchange, they may purchase from you in the future. But first and foremost, you must provide them with something of value, which you can only do by including plenty of insights and suggestions.

First write, then edit Once you've completed your plan, jot down your thoughts while they're still fresh in your mind. Simply begin writing. Don't start editing until you've finished the first draft. After that, you'll have no trouble going back and making things flow smoothly.

Follow up on how you can assist Make sure to mention it at the end if you're marketing a product or service that will benefit your readers. Unfortunately, you can't promote your product or service in the body of the white paper, but what you can do is include a catchy phrase while summarizing it.

WHAT TO WATCH

Monitoring comments

Comments are an important type of social media and blog-post interaction. When marketers look at the metrics on various social media platforms, engagements are often at the top of the list. Comments boosts SEO for blog post pages.

However, make sure to check your comments regularly. You may have spam comments, offensive comments or disparaging comments.

Consider a scenario in which one of your posts receives a large number of clicks, and the number of engagements skyrockets! Even if this is one of your most popular pieces, it could severely affect your business if the comments on it are unpleasant. Your post could have been controversial, or a nasty comment could have a snowball effect, portraying your material and your company in a negative light. Therefore, it's never a good idea to assume that all remarks are positive.

You'll have to decide whether or not your company needs to respond. This should be done on a case-by-case basis. Take a minute to consider whether or not the comments require a response, and then proceed with caution when writing one.

If you choose to answer, take your time crafting your message, as these comments will most likely be viewed by other potential buyers that visit your page. Remember to analyse the situation's significance and use caution before speaking. Whatever you do, don't get into arguments or write responses when you're feeling defensive.

Step nine: Analyse and measure results

Content marketing is a strategy utilized over a wide range of sectors to enlighten the audiences and spread awareness; however, the majority of the companies are still struggling with measuring success accurately.

According to the Content Marketing Institute's 2020 research, a good 80 per cent of respondents use metrics to measure performance, but when asked if they use KPIs to measure performance, that number drops to 65 per cent, and even lower when asked if they measure content marketing ROI: 43 per cent (CMI, 2021, 2).

Marketing teams will have to justify the resources required to develop high-quality content that genuinely moves the needle, so having those analytics and the ability to test against pre-determined KPIs is critical. In this step, we'll go over a few metrics that can assist your team in demonstrating the benefits of content marketing and illustrate why goal planning is such an essential part of the process.

User behaviour

User behaviour measurements don't tell you much on their own. However, they can give marketers directional knowledge regarding reader engagement and content performance when combined with other data (such as traffic performance).

Experts recommend keeping an eye on the following things in Google Analytics:

- new/returning visitors;
- pages/session;

- bounce rate;
- time on page.

CTR and impressions

In Google Search Console, it is advisable to track impressions and click-through rate in addition to traffic and user behaviour. This will illustrate whether the keywords for which your content is ranking in organic search truly translate to impressions and clicks.

How to find it: Performance > Search Results > Queries.

Tools to use: Google Search Console.

Keyword rankings

Ensure to thoroughly monitor ranking and keep a watch on primary keywords regularly. Of course, this necessitates keyword research in order to define priority keyword objectives. We advise tracking keywords with SEMRush, but several other alternatives could be used as well.

How to find it: (SEMrush) Search by URL & (GSC) Performance > Search Results > Queries

Tools to use: SEMrush, Google Search Console

Measuring against goals and KPIs

All of your digital marketing KPIs will be time-bound if you use the SMART approach, so you'll know what you need to accomplish and by when. You'll also be able to see how far you've come before the KPI is actually due. If you don't think you'll be able to meet your KPI, keep the other party informed on a frequent basis, so they don't get any unpleasant shocks. Keeping track of your accomplishments is especially crucial during a recession because market changes can significantly influence your finances.

Planning for the future

Your team can examine a hundred different metrics relating to your most recent blog post, new landing page, or email campaign, but none of them would matter until you have goals against which to compare success.

The most critical aspect of goal-setting for your content marketing programme is to set realistic expectations. For example, is it possible to reach 10,000 organic visitors without increasing your expenditure in 2022 if you had 1,000 organic visits in 2021? Of course, nothing is impossible, but let's be honest, it's highly unlikely.

Concentrate on historical data to determine whether goals are feasible given your budget and team's capacity. Even better, define or discuss these objectives with your executive team to ensure that everyone is on the same page. This way, there will be no shocks when the time comes for quarterly or annual reporting.

References

Chawla, Bhoomi (2021) How to create personas for marketing in 2021, available at: https://www.linkedin.com/pulse/how-create-personas-marketing-2021-bhoomi-chawla/ (archived at https://perma.cc/X3LG-B245)

CMI (2017) (1) 9 stats that will make you want to invest in content marketing, available at: https://contentmarketinginstitute.com/2017/10/stats-invest-content-marketing/ (archived at https://perma.cc/W2TH-CMCX)

CMI (2017) (2) Why you need content strategy before editorial planning, available at: https://contentmarketinginstitute.com/2017/03/content-strategy-editorial-planning/ (archived at https://perma.cc/9XBY-Y6JW)

CMI (2021) (1) What is content marketing?, available at: https://contentmarketinginstitute.com/what-is-content-marketing/ (archived at https://perma.cc/D3LH-4LW3)

CMI (2021) (2) B2B content marketing 2020, available at: https://contentmarketinginstitute.com/wp-content/uploads/2019/10/2020_B2B_Research_Final.pdf (archived at https://perma.cc/NY34-7PUU)

Demand Gen Report (2014) The power of visual content, available at: https://www.demandgenreport.com/industry-topics/rich-media/2906-the-power-of-visual-content-infographic.html#.VKtkmIc9-7m (archived at https://perma.cc/2DRT-3CET)

Demand Metric (2020) Content marketing infographic, available at: https://www.demandmetric.com/content/content-marketing-infographic (archived at https://perma.cc/68VB-PXJV)

Dooley, R (2020) Email marketing is your golden goose – don't kill it, available at: https://www.forbes.com/sites/rogerdooley/2020/05/04/email-marketing/?sh=df818f43711e (archived at https://perma.cc/82XY-TSXU)

Flash IT Solutions (FITS) (2021) How to create a content marketing calendar your followers will love, available at: https://www.flashitsolutions.com/create-content-marketing-calendar-followers-will-love/ (archived at https://perma.cc/XP98-EHTX)

GWI (2018) Social browsers engage with brands, available at: https://blog.gwi.com/chart-of-the-day/social-browsers-brand/ (archived at https://perma.cc/9HVL-TAAL)

HubSpot (2015) Blogging businesses experience 126% higher lead growth than non-blogging businesses, available at: https://blog.hubspot.com/blog/tabid/6307/bid/5519/blogging-businesses-experience-126-higher-lead-growth-than-non-blogging-businesses.aspx (archived at https://perma.cc/J3Y2-7ZQJ)

HubSpot (2017) Topic clusters: The next evolution of SEO, available at: https://research.hubspot.com/topic-clusters-seo (archived at https://perma.cc/YK5K-48MP)

HubSpot (2020) How often should you (or your company) blog?, available at: https://blog.hubspot.com/marketing/blogging-frequency-benchmarks (archived at https://perma.cc/7NYQ-QGNF)

HubSpot (2021) How to create an ebook from start to finish, available at: https://blog.hubspot.com/marketing/how-to-create-an-ebook-free-templates (archived at https://perma.cc/JN72-3BG2)

Income Beetle (2021) Content creation: The ultimate guide to content creation (no longer available)

LYFE Marketing (2020) Why is content marketing important?, available at: https://www.lyfemarketing.com/blog/why-is-content-marketing-important/#targetText=Quality%20content%20marketing%20can%20significantly,educate%20your%20leads%20and%20customer (archived at https://perma.cc/E9LV-47H7)

Statista (2021) Number of social network users worldwide 2017 to 2025, available at: https://www.statista.com/statistics/278414/number-of-worldwide-social-network-users/ (archived at https://perma.cc/K2QR-NDMA)

Bibliography

Andrews, J / LinkedIn (2021) How to create a buyer persona and use it to guide your marketing, available at: https://www.linkedin.com/pulse/how-create-buyer-persona-use-guide-your-marketing-jennifer/ (archived at https://perma.cc/NK6R-S4CZ)

AnswerThePublic (2021) Search listening tool for market, customer and content research, available at: https://answerthepublic.com/ (archived at https://perma.cc/3Q5T-3HXQ)

Brafton (2018) The evolution of content marketing and SEO, available at: https://www.brafton.com/blog/content-marketing/the-evolution-of-content-marketing-and-seo-infographic/ (archived at https://perma.cc/894B-3REK)

Edgecomb, C (2016) Blogging statistics: 52 reasons your company blog is worth the time and effort, available at: https://www.impactplus.com/blogging-statistics-55-reasons-blogging-creates-55-more-traffic (archived at https://perma.cc/S8ZT-YDUB)

Google (2021) Google Sheets: Free online spreadsheets for personal use, available at: https://www.google.com/sheets/about/ (archived at https://perma.cc/TYB6-ZXNF)

Grammarly (2021) Write your best with Grammarly, available at: https://www.grammarly.com/ (archived at https://perma.cc/6CHZ-Q6JJ)

Gregoire, R / CMI (2017) How to infuse 'know,' 'like' and 'trust' into your content, available at: https://contentmarketinginstitute.com/2017/10/know-like-trust-content/ (archived at https://perma.cc/6ZEF-HT46)

Hemingwayapp.com (2021) Hemingway Editor, available at: https://hemingwayapp.com/ (archived at https://perma.cc/66TN-6749)

Johnston, M / Moz (2016) Keyword Explorer, available at: https://moz.com/mozpro/lander/keyword-research (archived at https://perma.cc/AAU9-Z7SY)

Keywordtool.io (2021) Keyword Planner Alternative #1 for Google AdWords PPC and SEO, available at: https://keywordtool.io/ (archived at https://perma.cc/B4XF-MXVP)

Patel, N (2021) Content marketing made simple: A step-by-step guide, available at: https://neilpatel.com/what-is-content-marketing/ (archived at https://perma.cc/F5ZM-C58J)

Semrush (2021) SEMrush Keyword Magic, available at: https://www.semrush.com/lp/keyword-magic-see/en (archived at https://perma.cc/FT8G-YZ3X)

Wainwright, C (2021) How to map lead nurturing content to each stage in the sales cycle, available at: https://blog.hubspot.com/blog/tabid/6307/bid/31406/How-to-Map-Lead-Nurturing-Content-to-Each-Stage-in-the-Sales-Cycle.aspx (archived at https://perma.cc/3RPV-U6N7)

08

Delivering organic and paid social media that grows your brand

Social media marketing is increasingly becoming a dominant method for brands and businesses to promote their goods and services. The rise of social media in the past decade has created never-before-seen opportunities for digital advertising. You will rarely come across a business – from small local businesses to giant multinational corporations – that's not actively trying to stay relevant and in touch with its customer base through social media.

Why? The impact of social media marketing is undeniable. Whether it's through influencers, paid display ads, organic opportunities or other methods, using social media for marketing purposes has never been easier.

What makes social media marketing so powerful is the nature of social media itself. The sheer number of people using social media creates a huge audience, and businesses are quick to capitalize on that. Many smartphones and tablets come pre-installed with Facebook, Instagram, WhatsApp, and other social media platforms. This makes social media an entry point to the internet for many people around the globe. Recent reports (DataReportal, 2021) show that in 2021 4.33 billion people, or over half the world's population, use social media. The annual growth rate of social media users is 13.7 per cent on average. This means that every second, 16.5 new people sign up to a social media platform. The year-to-year increase in access to cheaper technologies like smartphones is a major driving force behind the increase in users.

Another reason marketers flock to social media is that the sense of personalization and direct contact that customers can experience with brands on social media platforms is unrivalled. Good social media marketing practices build brand loyalty, create new audiences and reinforce existing customer bases.

Organic and paid marketing

When it comes to social media marketing, there are two major ways to reach customers – organic and paid.

Organic reach is your activities on social media that are visible to your followers, that you don't pay the platform to promote. Think of posts about your products, pictures of your business and so on that are disseminated through the official social media channels of your brand.

Paid reach is when you put money into advertising on social media. This can be done in many ways, like sponsoring your posts, paying social media influencers to promote your products, running display ads, and more.

Organic social media marketing success is achievable if you post consistently and know how to keep your followers engaged. However, with some networks it can get tricky to have good organic reach, so you will have to get creative. This chapter will cover some of the tips and tricks that can help you garner organic reach. We will go over some of the key aspects of social media marketing, such as strategy, influencers, best practices and the significance of visuals. Then we will explore some of the most popular social media platforms one by one, and how to get the most out of them both organically and paid.

Social media best practices

Understanding your audience

The audience is the most important part of the social media puzzle to understand. Before delving into social media marketing, either organic or paid, you need to understand your audience well.

Understanding your consumers and their demands can help your business flourish on social media. Of course, there are many other factors, such as the quality of your content, timing and more. However, since social media is driven by people, one of the most important aspects of social media marketing is to understand who you're targeting. No matter how much money you spend, you will not be getting satisfying results if you're targeting the wrong audiences.

Factors to consider include:

- Understanding your audience is intricately intertwined with your brand identity. In order to know who your consumer base is, you must know well what you're offering and the different segments that can make use of it. You may have existing customer avatars. Use them, and/or build new ones.
- Once you have established your target audience, you should double down on your activity on social media platforms that they use the most. For example, if your target audience is younger people, you should consider using Instagram, TikTok and Snapchat to reach them. Older people are more likely to be on Facebook.
- If your target audience is women, you should consider advertising on Pinterest, where 78 per cent of users are female, by far the largest gender gap in social media users on any platform (Sprout Social, 2021, 1).
- Timing is everything on social media. You should aim to post your content or advertise at a time when your target audience is most likely to be online. For example, if you're targeting young professionals, they're more likely to check their socials in the morning with a cup of coffee or breakfast.
- Another aspect to consider is how people behave on social media. There are many nuances to where content ends up on social media – there are posts, chats, stories and so on. Knowing what your target audience is most likely to look at can help you in creating content.
- While analysing your potential audiences, look at their behaviour, and how they interact with brands and products. Always be on the lookout for existing user-generated content (UGC), and consider ways to generate more UGC. Many delighted customers are eager to share their opinions online on social media. This can act as social proof for your brand and gives you more content to share.
- If you know your target audience well, you know what types of media they're most likely to consume. This way, you can plan your social media campaign and apply all the insights you have about your target group to create content that they'll be interested in and engage with.

TOP TIP

Two-way marketing

Social media is all about engaging with the audience. It creates an opportunity for businesses to listen to the wants and needs of their consumers like never before, and to speak to their customers on a personal, more intimate level than was previously possible.

You should take advantage of this opportunity and spark discussions and dialogue with your audience.

Two-way marketing on social media also encourages users to generate content for you. By posting your products and talking about them with their followers, your audience can create valuable UGC for your brand – an excellent organic marketing strategy.

CASE STUDY

Social media is, at its heart, about being social. It's not simply about posting content, but about engaging and interacting. The best social media accounts to follow are those that do this well.

In 2021 we've seen some great examples of big brands interacting with each other and all credit to their social media managers for being able to walk the difficult line of maintaining their brand voice, adding humour and being interesting without causing controversy. Two great examples are:

1. When McDonalds defended Mayor McCheese when he was accused of being a corrupt politician because he had been mayor for over 30 years.
2. When Kitkat challenged Oreo to a Noughts and Crosses tournament using two KitKat segments to create the cross. Rather than responding with an Oreo to create a nought, Oreo sent back an image where they'd eaten the KitKat.

Creating the human touch

The whole premise of social media is built upon the desire of people to connect and interact with each other. This is also a crucial aspect to consider in social media marketing. Staying relatable and natural is the key to driving high engagement with your audiences. Capitalizing on the human need to connect on social media can create amazing success on social media.

Some substantial ways to create the human touch on social media include:

- Always keep in mind that people want to interact with each other, and provide opportunities to do so.
- Creating a personal page along with your business page can drive organic reach, particularly on platforms where organic reach for business pages is severely restricted.
- Build trust with your audience by showing your personal side and an insider view into your company.
- Create content that feels natural, frank and directed at real people, from real people. This can also apply in B2B – while you want to show you're professional, knowledgeable and credible, you also want to show you're the kind of people business buyers want to work with. At the end of the day, business buyers are also people.

TOP TIP

Be human

Giving a human face to your business can drive high engagement.

Showing how you work behind the scenes, creating vlogs with your staff, giving out tips and tricks related to your business, starting discussions around topics that are not just business-related, and just generally showing that you're real people living real lives, can all help your social media presence.

Displaying a good working atmosphere where individuals are friendly with one another and joke around can make your audiences feel like they're a part of your team, increasing your social media reach. You can use live streams and stories for such content.

Strategy and analytics

Social media strategy is included in any successful company's digital marketing strategy. Creating, executing, maintaining and optimizing a well thought-out strategy can help you create tangible deliverables that can indicate how well your company is doing on social media.

Consistency

As with almost anything, being consistent in social media marketing pays off. Remember:

- Being consistent is key to building and maintaining a strong following. If you don't post often, your following can quickly wither away.
- Strengthen your posts by creating a content calendar, and schedule when to post what. It's also smart to keep up with relevant public holidays and ongoing events to stay relevant.
- If your budget allows, hire a professional social media manager to get the most out of your company's socials.

Track analytics to guide strategy

Keep track of social media analytics to know what works well and what needs improvement. Virtually all social media platforms offer great statistics about your audiences and how they're interacting with your content.

Always remember the customer funnel as we've previously discussed (Awareness, Consideration, Conversion, Loyalty). All the buying stages can be targeted on social media by both organic and paid means.

Some social media platforms have better analytics dashboards than others. Luckily, there are many options allowing you to have one, integrated dashboard to manage all your social media presence using a single interface.

There are various social media metrics, but here are a few of the most significant ones to keep track of how your business is performing on social media:

- Engagement – measures how involved your audience is. Usually includes likes, shares and comments.
- Impressions – usually measures how often a post appears on the screen. Different social media might define impressions slightly differently, so keep that in mind.
- Social conversions – much like in traditional digital marketing, conversions are when a customer completes a purchase on your website. Social conversions happen after a customer ends up on your website through social media.

When analysing your social media statistics, also keep in mind the customer funnel. Different indicators can give you an idea of each of the stages in the funnel, as in Table 8.1.

TABLE 8.1 Social media metrics

Buyer stage	Type of metric	Specific metric
Awareness	Reach	Views of video
		Likes
		Page/profile visits
		Impressions
Consideration	Engagement	Comments, shares, likes
	Becoming a lead	Downloading lead magnet
		Sending a message to enquire about services
Conversion	Purchase	Purchase made on website/in-platform
	Intent to purchase	Add to cart
Loyalty	Being a brand ambassador	Shares
		Comments
		Generate UGC
	Repeat purchases	Purchase made on website/in-platform

Create different KPIs for organic and paid to know where you need to be putting more of your resources. When calculating ROI, consider the time, effort, labour and resources put into creating content, not just ad spend.

Integrate with other marketing strategy

Your social media presence should be smoothly integrated into your overall digital marketing strategy. Knowing your brand and being consistent in what you offer on social media, your website and in real life are essential for a successful social media presence.

You should use social media to send people to your landing page that:

- matches branding on social media and ads;
- is easy to navigate;
- requests contact details (newsletter subscription, and so on);
- shows benefits of committing to your business (for example, offer a complimentary gift, free shipping and so on with the first purchase).

Content creative guidelines

A variety of media

There are many types of content that you can use to create and grow your social media presence. Written text posts and blogs, images, videos, lives, infographics and much more can be utilized to get your point across to your target audiences.

The type of content you use can depend on which social media you're using. For example, it is more likely for written blogs to go over well with LinkedIn and Facebook users, since these platforms allow comfortable reading options on the feed. However, large texts aren't suitable for Instagram, which is more visual-driven social media.

VISUALS AND VIDEO FOR THE WIN

According to a recent survey (Sprout Social, 2021, 2), when asked what sort of content people prefer to engage with, 68 per cent chose photos, 50 per cent videos, and only 30 per cent showed a preference for text-based content. This shows that on social media, visuals are the driving force behind high engagement.

Some important things you should consider when creating visuals for social media are:

- Be mindful of copyrighted materials.
- Use a consistent and complementary colour scheme.
- Be strategic with text – don't overcrowd pictures with too much text.
- Consider the image sizing.

Every social media has different sizes for photos. It is vital to nail the correct size, otherwise your image might be stretched, pixelated or even cut off – failing to deliver your message as intended. Some of the most common sizes include square photos on Instagram at 1080 × 1080 pixels; 1200 × 630 for Facebook landscape pictures, and more.

Stories are unique in a way that their sizing generally remains the same across different platforms, making it easy to cross-post the same content on different social media. Stories on Instagram, Facebook, Twitter and LinkedIn are all 1080 × 1920 pixels.

Videos on social media have shown to raise conversions by as much as 86 per cent (WebFX, 2020). Remember:

- Keep your videos interesting for your target audience.
- Use your products, services and inside info to engage with viewers.
- Make sure to open a video with a catchy, interesting intro to grab attention right away.

COPYWRITING

As discussed in Chapter 5, copywriting is a huge subject that we cannot adequately cover here. It is important, though, to note that copywriting is an extremely important skill when it comes to social media. I'll remind you of the AIDA acronym here, which you should follow when crafting copy: Attention, Interest, Desire and Action.

You want to grab the Attention of the reader right away, Interest them with what you have to offer, play into their Desire to use your products and, finally, urge them to take Action, like signing up for your newsletter or visiting your website.

Many people hire professional copywriters to ensure their copy is optimized for conversion.

Split testing

Finally, you must analyse how posts are going over with your audiences, whether that's in terms of paid ads that are leading to conversions, or organic posts that you're using to grow reach.

Split testing is always a good idea when it comes to social media ads and digital ads in general. It gives you the opportunity to see what you can tweak to make your ads even better.

Split testing, or A/B testing, is where you create multiple versions of an ad, but changing only one element at a time. For example, you keep the image and body text the same, but change the headline. Then you run those two ads simultaneously, with the same budget and same target audience. The ad that gets the lowest cost-per-click is the winner, and that headline is selected while the other is discarded. For best results, split-testing can be an ongoing process where cost-per-click is continually optimized.

Influencer marketing

The influencer marketing industry has flourished in recent years. Many companies are spending a great deal of money to get exposure from influencers. The market was estimated to reach $13.8 billion in 2021, a $4.1 billion rise from the previous year (Startup Bonsai, 2021).

Influencers usually take up a special niche that closely correlates with their interests and/or lifestyle. They post consistently on their social media platforms and have a devout following. Many companies have jumped on the influencer bandwagon, paying large sums of money to these people to promote their products.

Cost of influencer marketing

The rates in the influencer marketing industry vary drastically. How much you're going to pay an influencer depends heavily on their following and, well, their level of influence.

A sponsored post from a smaller influencer with a modest number of followers can cost anything from $100 to $1000. Being featured by influencers with millions of followers, on the other hand, may cost you tens of thousands of dollars, or even into six figures. The rates depend on the niche, the location, the extent of the partnership and much more.

Locating influencers

To find the right influencer for your business, you have to know your target audience exceptionally well. Influencers are mostly followed by younger people, millennials and generation Z. If this is your target demographic, you can narrow it down by your specific niche. To find the right influencer for you, search through hashtags of topics related to your business and look up influencer videos on YouTube related to your niche.

Once you have found the right person, you can reach out to them using their email, which can often be found in the 'bio' section of their social media. You should tell them a little bit about your company and why you're interested in working with them. It is more likely for influencers to accept your offer if what you do/sell relates to their interests and they like your terms. You may have to be prepared to negotiate.

You can also join platforms that are designed to help brands and influencers connect and make mutually beneficial deals and arrangements.

WHAT TO WATCH

Brand damage

When operating with influencers and UGC, you can run the risk of brand damage.

It is not so rare for influencers to get in hot water for their comments or actions online. If your company is closely related to certain influencers and they promote your products often, their tarnished reputation can also affect yours.

Therefore, always be careful when choosing influencers and make sure their core values are closely related to your company's guiding principles. To avoid such unfortunate circumstances, you may negotiate in advance with influencers on the types of content in which you want your brand to appear.

Facebook

With almost 3 billion monthly active users, Facebook is the largest social media platform worldwide. It is also one of the biggest venues for digital advertising, making $70.7 billion in revenue in 2020 (Marketing Dive, 2020).

Facebook has a broad user base across the world, but the 25–34 age group is by far the most active on this social networking platform. Out of all Facebook users, 18.9% are male and 12.6% are female in the 25–34 age group. Overall, 72.6 per cent of users are between 18 and 44 years old (Statista, 2021, 1).

Paid opportunities

There are many paid opportunities for your posts and ads on Facebook. Once you set up a business page for your brand, you can start running ads. Using Facebook's Ads Manager, you can control your ad campaigns on Messenger, Instagram and even some third-party apps using Facebook's Audience Network feature. Ads Manager is a great way to track your ad campaigns and know what works well with your target audiences.

There are many opportunities to promote on Facebook:

- **Page:** You can promote your business page to garner more likes and potential customers.

- **Individual posts (boosted posts):** You can use Facebook to advertise certain stories and posts. You can include photos, videos, and text.
- **Actions you want a user to take:** You can promote certain actions, for example liking your page, visiting your website and so on.
- **Your website:** Facebook can help boost traffic on your website. Facebook has one of the highest CTRs across all platforms – make sure to take advantage of that. Aim for 0.1 per cent CTR. The average is 0.04 per cent.

Facebook offers many ad formats to choose from. When deciding on which layouts work best for you, consider that the vast majority of Facebook users – close to 99% (Statista, 2021, 2) – use their phones to access the social network.

When designing your ads on your PC make sure to check how they will look on different sized mobile devices. Ad formats on Facebook include:

- **Image Ads:** As we've noted over and over, visuals are very important to social media advertising. Make sure to use high-quality images to promote your business.
- **Video Ads:** Using videos can be even more powerful – you can entice potential or existing customers by showcasing your products using a combination of visuals, sound and motion.
- **Carousel Ads:** With this format, you can display up to 10 visuals (photo or video) using a single ad. You can add separate links to them. This is a great format to show off several of your products or different features of the same product.
- **Collection Ads:** This feature uses Facebook's immaculate algorithm and data for customization.

Facebook offers amazing targeting opportunities. You can utilize this by choosing to target very particular groups of people. Because of the way this social network works, Facebook has huge amounts of data on users, including:

- **Location:** If you're a local business, you can only target people that live close to your business.
- **Language:** Filtering out people who might not understand the language in which you operate can lead to even more customers who are sure to be interested in your products.
- **Age, gender and other demographics:** You can use this option to target specific demographic audiences.

- **Profile information:** Using this option, you can target people who work at a certain company or go to a certain university, and much more.
- **Interests:** Arguably the most powerful of options, you can target people whose interests are closely related to your products.

Using Facebook Pixel, an analytics tool, you can target Lookalike Audiences – people who have similar parameters as your target audience or customer base.

Organic opportunities

When it comes to organic opportunities, unfortunately a business page on Facebook will struggle to deliver any organic reach. Even if you amass a high number of followers, they won't be likely to see most of your posts. Data shows that posts organically reach only around 6.4 per cent of your followers (Social Media Today, 2019).

If you want organic reach on Facebook, you should consider personal profile posting. You could ask your employees about posting on certain news or products your company offers from their personal pages. However, this can cause problems, as employees might see it as an infringement of their privacy, and the content of their personal posts may not be a match with your brand. If, however, an employee does not have a Facebook account already, they may be willing to set one up solely for organic Facebook marketing for the brand. I'd advise you tread carefully, however.

THE ALGORITHM

The ease with which content on social media was presented to consumers chronologically is long gone. It has been replaced by a complicated algorithm that controls the order of posts and ads based on individual interests and habits.

There are several ways in which you can try to urge the algorithm to show your content to more users. If you post highly shareable content, that will increase reach. Additionally, you can time your posts based on the time of the day your target audience is most likely to use Facebook.

FACEBOOK GROUPS

Facebook groups are a great way to grow your audience and create individual connections with them. You can use groups to get feedback from loyal customers, offer sneak peeks to your future products to them, and much more.

- **Interact with people in large groups:** Look for groups with lots of members in it that might be interested in your products, and try to engage with them in the group posts.
- **Create your own group:** This can either be for existing customers to build loyalty, or a group for potential new customers, or it could incorporate both. You can provide members with valuable content, and then ask for a sale. It is recommended for every one post to promote your products, you create four posts that are providing value.
- When you have a Facebook group with a high level of activity and engagement, the algorithm displays posts to members in their newsfeed.
- You can request the email addresses of users as a prerequisite for joining your group, to help you build up an email list and conduct email marketing. This may be offputting to many people, however, so you might consider offering your lead magnet in exchange for emails within the group, instead.

FACEBOOK WATCH

When advertising and trying to grow your audience on Facebook, you should keep in mind the importance of Facebook Watch, where users watch videos. A recent study shows that over 15 per cent of all content on Facebook is video and that is likely to raise even more moving forward (Socialinsider, 2021). The data also points at the higher CTR rate for videos compared with other types of posts.

Because of the importance of videos on Facebook, you should have a dedicated video strategy:

- People are more likely to watch shorter videos that get straight to the point.
- Try to have original content in videos.
- Encourage users to spark discussions in the comments section.

Instagram

Instagram is another popular social media app under Facebook's ownership. It has over 1 billion active users each month.

Compared with Facebook, where the user base spans across all age groups, Instagram is mostly popular with teenagers and younger adults.

Over half of Instagram users are 34 or younger (Statista, 2021, 3). When creating a strategy for Instagram, you should keep in mind the younger demographic and target them with appropriate content and ads.

There are many great opportunities on Instagram for businesses. Driven by visual media and, increasingly, short video content, Instagram offers its users multiple ways to view photos and videos. There are regular posts, stories, IGTV and reels. Additionally, Instagram has a dedicated shop section, where you can showcase your products for easier access for customers.

Paid opportunities

There are numerous paid opportunities on Instagram. As noted, you can use Facebook Ads Manager to control your campaign on Instagram. You can create separate ads for Facebook and Instagram, or run the same ones on both platforms.

When creating ads, you can choose where they will show up. You can promote your posts that showcase your products, create stories and promote them, or create generic ads that will show up on different platforms.

When creating a profile for your brand on Instagram you must decide to make it a business or personal profile:

- A business account offers insights into your audience, reach and much more.
- Personal profiles can be made private, creating a sense of exclusivity for potential customers requesting to follow your brand.
- Personal profiles of your employees posting about your brand can make you more relatable and interesting for your customers.
- You can have the main brand account as a business profile and keep additional ones private.
- With a business profile you can add information to your account, such as location, opening hours and more.

There are many ad types on Instagram. Choosing the right one for your business can be crucial in getting clicks and conversions.

- **Image and Video Ads**: You can promote your business using visual posts and boosting them. These will show up on the main feed on Instagram. You can include links to your website or purchase options.

- **Stories Ads**: These are shown in between stories. You can add the 'swipe up' function to direct customers to your website. Stories Ads can be customized to your liking, adding various interactive elements, such as polls, stickers, tags and more.
- **Reels Ads**: Similar to Stories, Reels Ads will show up on the Reels page in-between users' videos.
- **Carousel and Collection Ads**: These work in the same way as on Facebook. You can include several different images and videos in one post. For Collection Ads, the algorithm will determine the products from your catalogues to show to specific customers.
- **Shopping Ads**: These show users your products that can be purchased directly on Instagram, without ever having to leave the app. This recent addition has helped grow many e-commerce businesses on the platform.

INFLUENCERS

Instagram, along with YouTube and TikTok, is one of the best social media networks for influencers. You can take advantage of this and get in touch with Instagram influencers whose interests are related to your business.

You can pay influencers to feature your product in their posts, stories, reels and more. You can use Instagram to reach new audiences using influencers, grow your following on the app and ultimately get high ROI by reaching conversions.

Organic opportunities

Organic reach opportunities on Instagram are a little better compared with Facebook. Instagram allows you to have a more personal connection with your followers, even from business accounts.

Organic best practices for Instagram include:

- Be consistent in your content – always post using all the different options (posts, stories, reels and so on).
- Use stories to promote your business – prompt followers to engage with your content.
- Create a personal touch by responding to the DM (direct message) inquiries from users. This can boost your sales by making potential customers feel important and valued.

- Have fun with your followers. Post quizzes, questions and other prompts to spark discussions.
- Run giveaways for your followers. You can ask your followers to invite their friends for the opportunity to win prizes, for example.
- Use hashtags.

On Facebook, there's a chance your posts will end up on people's feeds even if they don't follow you. This is not the case for Instagram. Otherwise, the Instagram algorithm acts the same way as Facebook's – filtering and adjusting the posts and showing at the top what users are most likely to be interested in.

When you have a high number of followers on Instagram, your posts are more likely to appear on more feeds. Because of this, the number of followers on Instagram can be even more important than on Facebook. It is best to grow your Instagram following as fast as you can. Ads and influencers can help you in garnering followers, but to keep them, you have to be consistent in your content.

Consistency entails both the right and steady timing, as well as the style of your posts. You can decide if you want to post exclusively pictures of your products, graphic design posters, behind-the-scenes of your work, or a combination of all of these. Just make sure that your Instagram profile looks cohesive at the first glance.

WhatsApp, Snapchat and Messenger

Messaging apps can be a great way to engage with your customers, provide support and even promote your business using ads. They are great for building trust and personal relationships with your customers. If you're a small business, you can take inquiries, complaints, or any sort of feedback through these messaging apps.

WhatsApp and Messenger are both owned by Facebook. WhatsApp had over 2 billion active users a month in 2020, with Messenger slightly behind at 1.3 billion users (Statista, 2021, 4).

Even big brands are starting to use messaging to communicate with customers. This creates a personalized experience for users, leading to higher conversion rates.

Remember:

- Messaging builds personal connection and trust.
- With business accounts you can send rich content to customers, including pictures, videos, GIFs and so on.
- Messaging apps can add on to your social media strategy, but can't be substitutes to active social media presence.

Since Messenger and WhatsApp are relatively similar, let's go over some of the organic and paid opportunities that they offer.

WhatsApp

WhatsApp doesn't offer paid ads on the app, but you can still use it for marketing purposes by contacting your customers via direct messages. Some companies also use group chats.

You can use broadcast in order to send your message to numerous customers, without them knowing the message was sent to others as well as them. This is free, when email marketing broadcasts are not, and the average open rate of WhatsApp messages is 70 per cent (Search Engine Journal, 2016) compared with just 21.33 per cent for email (Mailchimp, 2019). Could messaging marketing become the new email marketing?

Messenger

Facebook Messenger offers small ad spaces within the app. You can use this opportunity to include messenger ads in your campaign. It will require different dimensions than full-scale Facebook and Instagram posts, but it may serve as a fantastic reminder for potential consumers of your business and products.

In terms of organic options, marketers have been using chatbots on Messenger to act as both sales and customer service agents, which could help within the Consideration and Loyalty stages of the customer journey respectively. These are usually activated when a Facebook user decides to get in touch with the brand through their company page. While chatbots are too complex a subject to get into here at length, you may find them useful for your business.

Snapchat

Snapchat is an interesting platform for marketing. If you're targeting teens and young adults, this platform is perfect to promote your business. Over half of internet users between ages 15 and 25 use Snapchat. It is the most popular social network among younger people, with Instagram and TikTok close behind. The country with the largest Snapchat users is the USA, with 108 million. In fact, 69 per cent of US teens report using Snapchat. On average, Snapchat has 293 million daily users (Omnicore, 2021, 1).

Starting out with disappearing images and videos in direct messages, Snapchat has evolved to include various types of media on its platform, offering numerous great opportunities for marketing. In order to get the most out of Snapchat, you have to understand its capabilities and what its users expect from you:

- Originally a simple messaging app, Snapchat has grown into a well-rounded social network.
- You can utilize Snapchat's AR (augmented reality) features by creating interactive filters that consumers can use on their faces and surroundings.
- Most users expect brand Snapchats to provide behind-the-scenes content that can't be found elsewhere.

Capitalizing on the younger audience of Snapchat can get you a high ROI. There are many paid opportunities on Snapchat to grow your business.

With mostly young people using the app, Snapchatters are 60 per cent more likely to make impulse purchases (Hootsuite, 2020, 1). This statistic, combined with excellent targeting tools and various ways to advertise, makes Snapchat one of the best social media for advertising your business.

For organic reach, you can increase your following by offering exclusive photos, videos and insider info about your business and products. This gives Snapchat users a sense of exclusivity and builds trust.

Snapchat, as a messaging app first and foremost also offers the same perks that other similar apps offer. You can get in touch with customers directly, get feedback from them and create impactful connections that will lead to conversions.

TikTok

Another social media app popular with young people, TikTok had its start in China in 2016. Since then, it became the most downloaded app in 2020 with 115 million downloads in March 2020 alone (The Fact Site, 2021). In total, the app has been downloaded 2 billion times (Hootsuite, 2021, 1).

The popularity of the app was accelerated by the Covid-19 pandemic. With more people spending time indoors, it became one of the ways people spent their days quarantining and easing the isolation by watching videos.

The sudden popularity of TikTok has prompted other companies to introduce features similar to the Chinese social media platform. YouTube has their version of TikTok videos called Shorts, Instagram has Reels and even Snapchat jumped on the bandwagon, introducing Spotlight. However, other apps offering similar formats of video haven't hurt TikTok and it continues to rise in popularity worldwide.

As for the demographics of the app, 50 per cent of global users represent people aged under 34, with 32.5% being between 10 and 19 (Hootsuite, 2021, 1).

There are many opportunities on TikTok for both paid and organic reach. Whichever you use, it's important to know that putting your message in the first three to five seconds of an ad can increase CTR by as much as 63 per cent.

Paid opportunities

TikTok offers different paid options, including ads, sponsored videos and more. To get the most out of TikTok, your brand account should be actively posting new videos on a regular basis. To enhance the exposure of your brand, you can ask employees to make additional content and post on their accounts to spread the word about your company.

TikTok offers numerous paid opportunities for advertising:

- **In-Feed Video Ads:** The most popular type of ad on the platform, these videos appear on a user's For You page, along with native TikToks, offering a seamless integration into the feed.
- **Branded Hashtag Challenge:** This option capitalizes on the viral nature of 'trends' on TikTok. Here, you can ask users to record themselves performing a dance or a challenge and post it using a hashtag that will appear on the Discover page.

- **Brand Takeover:** These ads appear when a user opens the app. They are short videos, typically under five seconds. They take up the whole screen and can be customized with hashtags, links to your website and more.
- **TopView Ads:** These are also full-display ads, but can be longer than Brand Takeovers, up to 60 seconds. However, they don't show up as soon as the app opens, rather they appear randomly while using the app.
- **Branded Effects:** Similar to Snapchat and Instagram, you can use your branded filters to promote your business. They can include AR features, music and much more.

Organic opportunities

TikTok, while massively popular, is still behind in user numbers compared with major players like Facebook and Instagram. This makes organic reach a little bit easier to accomplish. The key to a successful organic reach on TikTok, as with many other apps, is consistency. Posting every day or even several times a day can increase the chances of going viral and ending up on many For You pages.

Many popular TikTok videos are informative in nature. The easy customizing options on TikTok and addictive nature of short, easy-to-digest videos, make this platform perfect for brands to gain new customers.

Targeting people in the Awareness stage in the funnel can happen organically on TikTok. By being consistent with your content and engaging with your audiences, you can win over many people.

Whether you decide to invest in ads or create consistent, high-quality content for your brand's TikTok page, you should keep in mind that the audience on the app is young. Making relatable content that can be easily shared with friends is the key to successful TikTok marketing.

Twitter

Twitter, like Facebook, isn't heavy on only one segment of the age demographic. People of all ages use Twitter for different purposes. In recent years, Twitter has become a go-to place for many public figures, politicians and celebrities to share their thoughts, news and announcements with the world. This is reflected in people worldwide using the platform as a news source (12 per cent of all users).

There's an interesting gender divide in global Twitter users, with only 30 per cent being female (Omnicore, 2021, 2). Twitter is most popular in the US, closely followed by Japan and UK. In the US, 21 per cent of adults are active on Twitter.

As a brand, you can use Twitter to target different segments of society. Statistics point out that Twitter users are on average more educated and wealthier compared with those on other social media platforms, with as high as 77 per cent of Americans earning $75,000 or more using the platform.

Twitter is often used for light-hearted memes and videos, as well as official announcements from government officials from all over the world. Therefore, while using the platform, it is important to strike the balance of staying relatable yet keeping things professional.

Paid opportunities

Twitter offers several different paid advertising options that you can choose from, based on your goals and strategy.

- **Promoted Tweets:** Like boosted posts on Facebook, you can promote individual tweets from your account. They will show up to your target audience that might not be following you.
- **Promoted Accounts:** You can promote the whole account using this option, rather than opting for a single tweet. If you're looking to gain new followers, this is an excellent way to do that.
- **Promoted Trends:** Twitter displays trending topics. These are the subjects that people tweet about the most in real time. With Promoted Trends, you can include your brand on the list, making it interactable in the same way as any other trend.
- **Promoted Moments:** This option allows you to extend your story and not be limited to only 280 characters. It can display several Tweets that tell a cohesive story.
- **Automated Ads:** If you don't know which of the above options is the best for your brand, you can choose Automated Ads. This option lets Twitter promote your profile and tweets with your chosen target audiences.

Organic opportunities

While Twitter offers numerous paid reach options, you can also utilize organic reach to explore new audiences and interact with your followers.

- Unlike other social media we've discussed, Twitter users can choose from Top Tweets and Recent Tweets. Top Tweets will act the same way as Facebook and Instagram algorithms, choosing the tweets the user is most likely to be interested in. While Recent Tweets will show Tweets from the people the user follows chronologically.
- Tweeting consistently is the key to increasing your organic reach. The more you tweet, the more likely it is for your tweets to end up on as many people's feeds as possible.
- Use photos, videos and GIFs. Visuals are also important on Twitter. Your tweet is more likely to get Likes and Retweets if it includes some form of media. According to Twitter's official stats, tweets with GIFs receive 55 per cent more engagement compared with those without them. As for the videos, they see as much as 10 times more engagement (Hootsuite, 2020, 2).
- Spark discussions and conversations. Twitter is a great platform to have a discussion with other users. You can encourage such acts by asking questions, creating polls and so on.

Finally, keep in mind that both paid and organic reach can be very individual, based on specific users. In order to get the most out of Twitter, make sure to keep track of analytics. Once you see what works well with your target audience, you can tweak your campaigns, tweeting patterns and more to fit the interests of your customers.

YouTube

YouTube, a social video platform, is the second most-visited website worldwide, only falling behind its parent company Google. YouTube has been a go-to place for videos for over a decade and the Covid-19 pandemic has only increased its success.

Popular among all age groups, people watch over a billion hours of YouTube videos every day. With the number of logged-in users at 2 billion,

YouTube only falls behind Facebook in this regard (Hootsuite, 2021, 2). However, it's important to keep in mind that many users might not even log into an account and still enjoy content on YouTube without ever registering on the platform.

The viewership of YouTube is evenly distributed over age demographics, while the gender ratio is a bit skewed towards males, with 56 per cent. Data shows that, on average, viewers aged 18 and over consume media on YouTube for 41.9 minutes daily. While there are many users who access YouTube on a wide range of devices, such as desktops, laptops and TVs, 40.9 per cent of viewers use mobile to watch videos (Hootsuite, 2021, 2).

As with Google, YouTube offers advertisers and content creators numerous ways to earn and spend money on the platform. Many creators use YouTube as the main platform for their content. Creators get paid in ad revenue based on views, as well as sponsorship deals with numerous brands.

Paid opportunities

YouTube offers excellent ad services. Since the platform is owned by Google, it is integrated with the Google Ads service, making it easy to include YouTube in your digital marketing strategy.

When consuming media on YouTube, users can get different types of ads. Some of them are only available on certain devices, such as overlay ads that are only on desktop.

- Ads can be placed within a video at different times, including before the video starts, during the video and after the video has ended.
- Skippable video ads: These allow users to skip after five seconds of watching. With this type of ad, it's important to make an impression within that five seconds to keep people.
- Non-skippable videos: These must be viewed by a user before accessing a video. They're usually between 10 and 20 seconds.
- Bumper ads: These are short videos lasting no longer than six seconds and can't be skipped. They should be watched in order for a user to view their desired video.
- Overlay ads: As noted, these are only available on desktop. They appear on the lower 20 per cent of the video, much like banners.

Thanks to Google's powerful targeting tools, YouTube ads can be personalized to specific users, leading to more conversions.

Organic opportunities

Ads aren't the only way to get ROI on YouTube. You can reach people organically if you create high-quality content and dedicate enough time and resources to perfecting your videos.

- If your company channel garners a large number of views, you can monetize your content and make additional income from YouTube videos.
- Consider investing in influencers. YouTubers are some of the oldest content creators on the internet. They know well how to sell products to their viewers. Consider partnering with YouTube personalities to raise awareness of your brand.
- Create content related to your products, or closely linked to your niche. For example, if you own a pet salon, you can create content giving out tips and tricks of grooming. This is likely to get you more customers who would want to entrust you with their pet.
- Be open about your practice. Showing off what you do behind the scenes on YouTube can be a great way to engage more people.
- Try to end videos with an open question to spark discussions in the comments. This will increase engagement and make your content recommended to more users.

Combining your general digital ads strategy with YouTube can prove to be beneficial to reach new customers and gain more conversions. Maintaining a regular upload schedule and creating content related to your brand can make people interested in your products and trust your company more.

Pinterest

Pinterest is often overlooked by marketers, but there's a great potential in advertising on this platform and it should definitely be on your radar. Since its inception over 11 years ago, users have saved over 240 billion pins on the platform.

Compared with other social networks where people mostly go to keep up with friends, world news, and so on, over 90 per cent of Pinterest users mainly log onto the platform to look for shopping inspiration.

It has a reputation of being only of use for marketers who are targeting mothers and other women between the ages of 35 and 65. This is slowly changing. While 80 per cent of US mothers are on Pinterest and 78 per cent of all users are female, the number of millennials and men of all ages is growing on the platform by the day (Sprout Social, 2021, 1), opening it up for other marketers.

- If a consumer is already looking to buy something, it is much easier to target them with your products, especially if you offer a wide range of items in your catalogue.
- Pinterest makes bold claims, stating that compared with ads on social media, their platform offers '2.3× more efficient cost per conversion' and '2× higher return on ad spend for retail brands' (Pinterest, 2021).
- You can target consumers on every step of the funnel on Pinterest.
- You can promote your products directly on the website using Shoppable Ads.

Organic reach can also be achieved on Pinterest.

- To garner more followers, use as many keywords as possible related to your brand and products in order to rank highly on search engines.
- Create boards filled with your products and inspirations, and communicate your brand values through them.
- Create Rich Pins. These are pins that include extra information, such as a link to an article or product. You will have to go through a validation process in order to create such pins, but once you do, you can create as many as you'd like.
- In order to catch the eye of customers, make your pins stand out. Use your logo, tag line, text and images to create enticing pins that are both attention-grabbing and interesting.
- Try to keep up with the current trends and inspirations. For example, during autumn, try to lean into creating boards that are related to the seasonal celebrations.

Finally, analyse the data provided by Pinterest to know where you can improve your ads and pins and what works best with the unique Pinterest audience.

LinkedIn

LinkedIn has over 700 million active users. What started out as a networking website for professionals has evolved into a robust social media platform. Many people use LinkedIn to advertise their brands, market themselves in order to land a dream job and keep in touch with colleagues in the same industry.

The demographic on LinkedIn is mostly professionals looking to advance their careers and stay on top of the cutting-edge discoveries in their field. This makes LinkedIn an excellent platform to advertise. Research has shown that over 50 per cent of internet users making over $75,000 use LinkedIn (HubSpot, 2021).

With the steady growth of users, advertising opportunities have also increased on LinkedIn. The platform's professional nature makes it one of the top contenders for B2B marketing. Most of LinkedIn's users have their interests defined well and are ready to spend money on what they like. It shouldn't come as a surprise that the conversion rate on the platform is much higher than on Twitter and Facebook.

Paid opportunities

LinkedIn offers objective-based advertising, meaning that you can easily target audiences in the specific funnel phase that you desire. LinkedIn offers Awareness, Consideration and Conversion ads, making it easy for you to choose which one suits your current goals best.

As for the types of ads, there are quite a few to choose from.

- **Sponsored Content:** These are native ads that will pop up on your target audience's feed. You can use them to share inspiring stories from your business practice and interest more people in your brand and what you offer.
- **Sponsored Messaging:** This option sends your ads directly to a user's inbox.
- **Text Ads:** These show up on the desktop version of the website and can be used for building strong leads with your target audiences.
- **Dynamic Ads:** These ads use personalization by showing users some of the basic information on their profile, along with their picture, followed by an ad prompting them to take action.

Organic opportunities

When it comes to organic reach on LinkedIn, many of the same tips apply as on other platforms. However, there are some key aspects that you should consider.

- Professionals have started using LinkedIn not only to share their experiences and résumés with the rest of the world, but as a platform to share their ideas and creations. You can use your brand page, as well as your employees' professional accounts to create content that includes interesting stories, tips and tricks related to your sector.

- LinkedIn has slowly introduced numerous options for native content, such as photos, videos, documents and more. Try your best to utilize these options and capitalize on your content.
- Use testimonials and UGC to appeal to professional audiences on LinkedIn. While reviews and UGC are great for any social media platform, LinkedIn audiences will value the input of others more.

Keep the posts and ads on LinkedIn professional and don't shy away from sharing your valuable experience and insights to other professionals. This will create trust between you and potential customers and can create excellent opportunities for B2B.

Reddit and Quora

Both Quora and Reddit aim to increase user-to-user communication with their platforms. However, the way they approach this is different.

Quora is a question and answer-based website, providing people with information about topics they want to learn more about directly from people most specialized in the field. Reddit is mainly a news aggregation and discussion website, with many communities finding a place on the website using its unique structure of subreddits.

Reddit is one of the top 10 social media websites in the US, having 52 million daily active users worldwide. The user base on Reddit is diverse, but the most recent stats show that the largest age group on the platform is 25 to 29 (Oberlo, 2021). There are close to 3 million subreddits dedicated to niche topics. As with many other platforms, videos rank highest in engagement on Reddit.

- For paid reach on Reddit, you have to create a well-thought-out strategy, identifying subreddits (communities) that are related to your products and where your target audience is most likely to be.
- Promote your posts on subreddits that you have identified and make sure to include information on your brand and what to offer.
- When trying to get organic reach, try to include interesting links and media with your posts that will spark discussions.

- The most you can get from Reddit without paying for ads is to use it as a research tool to see what your target audiences are up to and how their interests are shifting. This will allow you to evolve your brand in the right direction without losing touch with your target audiences.

Quora hosts over 300 million active users monthly. The female-to-male ratio on the website is 43/57 (Foundation Marketing, 2021). Compared with other social media, Quora ads mainly (60 per cent) target B2B.

- Quora offers paid reach options using different types of ads. The website offers highly personalized ads based on users' interests.
- If you have specialized knowledge in a certain field, you can utilize that to answer the questions of people looking into the issues you know the most about. This will grow your organic reach on Quora. You can mention your company, but your answer should not look like an ad – it should be thoughtful and useful. This is more likely to win you conversions.

The key to successful paid and organic reach on Reddit and Quora is finding and identifying the right communities and users that will be interested in what you have to offer.

Chinese social media networks

The social media landscape in China is unique. Because of the high demand, there are many different players coming and going from the field on a year-to-year basis. If you're looking to advertise on Chinese social media networks, it can be difficult to keep up with the fast-shifting trends. That said, many marketers consider the effort more than worth it, especially when it comes to driving purchases and partnering with influencers.

The *South China Morning Post* reported that, with more than 70 per cent of Chinese Gen Z consumers preferring to buy products directly via social media, the key opinion leaders (KOL) economy is now valued at US$8.6 billion (Yuzu Kyodai, 2020). (KOL is the term used for influencers in China.)

WeChat is one of the most popular apps in China. It started out as a simple messaging app, but has evolved into much more, allowing its users to perform a myriad of actions, such as buying tickets, ordering food and more.

2020 saw WeChat's highest number of monthly active users, with an average of 1.2 billion (Marketing to China, 2021).

- There are numerous ways to generate paid and organic reach on WeChat. First, you must create an official account for your brand, through which you can update customers on news, promotions and so on.
- WeChat users are unique, with high rates of sharing useful information with their peers. Posting content that will engage audiences can strengthen your brand image and gain you trust among users.

Douyin is a Chinese name for TikTok, therefore many of the same tips apply here. However, when trying to advertise on Douyin, make sure to utilize influencers as much as possible. Chinese consumers are even more likely to trust people they have followed for a long time.

Kuaishou is another social media platform, mainly focused on short videos. Its popularity is on the rise with 20 billion uploads and 300 million daily users in 2020.

QQ is one of the oldest social media platforms, which started out as a messaging website in 1999. Since then, it has evolved to meet the ever-changing demands of the Chinese market. QQ falls behind only WeChat in monthly active users. However, most of QQ's user base is people under 30. It's also used as a platform within the workplace. Due to its ability to transfer large files, it's often used instead of email. If you're targeting young professionals in China, QQ is a perfect fit for your goals.

General good practice

- Most of the Chinese social media platforms offer some form of paid advertising.
- The key to successfully taking up space on the Chinese social media market is knowing who your target audience is.
- To strive for organic reach, you will have to invest significant time and effort in creating content that will be interesting for consumers, who will in turn share your products with peers.

The oversaturation of the Chinese market with many social media apps can be intimidating at first. However, after you've determined who you're targeting and what motivates them to generate conversions for you, you can confidently select which platforms best suit your objectives.

References

DataReportal (2021) Global Social Media Stats, available at: https://datareportal.com/social-media-users (archived at https://perma.cc/MY5S-6SV6)

The Fact Site (2021) 10 tip-top facts about TikTok, available at: https://www.thefactsite.com/tiktok-facts/ (archived at https://perma.cc/2C36-FXLS)

Foundation Marketing (2021) 21 Quora statistics marketers need to know for 2021, available at: https://foundationinc.co/lab/quora-statistics/ (archived at https://perma.cc/4FNZ-9TSH)

Hootsuite (2020) (1) 21 Snapchat stats that matter to social media marketers, available at: https://blog.hootsuite.com/snapchat-statistics-for-business/ (archived at https://perma.cc/YME5-76VH)

Hootsuite (2020) (2) How the Twitter algorithm works in 2020 and how to make it work for you, available at: https://blog.hootsuite.com/twitter-algorithm/ (archived at https://perma.cc/A75J-VA9E)

Hootsuite (2021) (1) 23 Important TikTok stats marketers need to know in 2021, available at: https://blog.hootsuite.com/tiktok-stats/ (archived at https://perma.cc/4586-NDWK)

Hootsuite (2021) (2) 25 YouTube statistics that may surprise you: 2021 edition, available at: https://blog.hootsuite.com/youtube-stats-marketers/ (archived at https://perma.cc/FGR5-WEJS)

HubSpot (2021) 31 LinkedIn stats that marketers need to know in 2021, available at: https://blog.hubspot.com/marketing/linkedin-stats (archived at https://perma.cc/6HD4-44NF)

Mailchimp (2019) Email marketing benchmarks and statistics by industry, available at: https://mailchimp.com/resources/email-marketing-benchmarks/ (archived at https://perma.cc/S8TA-PKLP)

Marketing Dive (2020) Facebook's ad revenue rises 25% to record $20.7b, available at: https://www.marketingdive.com/news/facebooks-ad-revenue-rises-25-to-record-207b/571404/ (archived at https://perma.cc/2J2N-6RNL)

Marketing to China (2021) Top 10 Chinese social media for marketing (updated 2021), available at: https://marketingtochina.com/top-10-social-media-in-china-for-marketing/ (archived at https://perma.cc/GF6Z-BTRU)

Oberlo (2021) 10 Reddit statistics you should know in 2021, available at: https://www.oberlo.com/blog/reddit-statistics (archived at https://perma.cc/3EB2-A4EV)

Omnicore (2021) (1) Snapchat by the numbers: Stats, demographics and fun facts, available at: https://www.omnicoreagency.com/snapchat-statistics/ (archived at https://perma.cc/7R9H-5P3Q)

Omnicore (2021) (2) Twitter by the numbers: Stats, demographics and fun facts, available at: https://www.omnicoreagency.com/twitter-statistics/ (archived at https://perma.cc/5CRC-SKAP)

Pinterest (2021) Advertising on Pinterest, available at: https://business.pinterest.com/en/advertise/ (archived at https://perma.cc/2YNZ-CYCC)

Search Engine Journal (2021) Dominating your WhatsApp marketing strategy, available at: https://www.searchenginejournal.com/the-ultimate-guide-to-whatsapp-marketing/161221/ (archived at https://perma.cc/VE24-EYT5)

Socialinsider (2021) What 3,977,410 video posts tell us about Facebook video strategy in 2021, available at: https://www.socialinsider.io/blog/facebook-video-study/#keyfindings (archived at https://perma.cc/MCP4-9XXE)

Social Media Today (2019) 10 need to know Facebook marketing stats for 2019, available at: https://www.socialmediatoday.com/news/10-need-to-know-facebook-marketing-stats-for-2019/547488/ (archived at https://perma.cc/WP64-H74S)

Sprout Social (2021) (1) 23 Pinterest stats and facts marketers must know in 2021, available at: https://sproutsocial.com/insights/pinterest-statistics/ (archived at https://perma.cc/5EZ7-39UH)

Sprout Social (2021) (2) 36 essential social media marketing statistics to know for 2021, available at: https://sproutsocial.com/insights/social-media-statistics/ (archived at https://perma.cc/7NDS-7QJU)

Startup Bonsai (2021) 29 influencer marketing statistics to inform your strategy, available at: https://startupbonsai.com/influencer-marketing-statistics / (archived at https://perma.cc/P4X5-YBL2)

Statista (2021) (1) Facebook: users by age and gender, available at: https://www.statista.com/statistics/376128/facebook-global-user-age-distribution (archived at https://perma.cc/UT7Q-VUGZ)

Statista (2021) (2) Facebook users reach by device 2021, available at: https://www.statista.com/statistics/377808/distribution-of-facebook-users-by-device/ (archived at https://perma.cc/NHE4-QK6S)

Statista (2021) (3) Instagram: age and gender demographics, available at: https://www.statista.com/statistics/248769/age-distribution-of-worldwide-instagram-users/ (archived at https://perma.cc/MU78-8VZR)

Statista (2021) (4) Most popular messaging apps, available at: https://www.statista.com/statistics/258749/most-popular-global-mobile-messenger-apps/ (archived at https://perma.cc/EML3-XFAZ)

WebFX (2020) Social media marketing videos [+5 best practices], available at: https://www.webfx.com/blog/social-media/social-media-marketing-videos/ (archived at https://perma.cc/E3YW-C6JL)

Yuzu Kyodai (2020) Cornering the market in consumer trust: Chinese online influencers, available at: http://www.yuzukyodai.com/2020/07/14/cornering-the-market-in-consumer-trust/ (archived at https://perma.cc/NF3K-JBLR)

Bibliography

Forbusiness.snapchat.com (2021) Why advertise on Snapchat?, available at: https://forbusiness.snapchat.com/advertising/why-snapchat-ads?utm_source=GoogleSEM&utm_medium=PAIDB2B&utm_campaign=G_Search_Brand_CA_Gamma%7CSnap_Business&utm_term=CA&utm_content=Forbusiness (archived at https://perma.cc/3GCN-5WMR)

Sprout Social (2021) Social media demographics to inform your brand's strategy in 2021, available at: https://sproutsocial.com/insights/new-social-media-demographics/ (archived at https://perma.cc/RCL6-MXFC)

09

Using analytics to interpret and optimize your results to maximize performance

Analytics is a term for the computational analysis of data. Analytics helps us to identify, understand and communicate significant patterns and trends in data. It provides valuable insights that we may not otherwise see – and it's crucial that you use analytics to your advantage for digital marketing. Analytics is your insight into the growth and future of your business.

Using analytics helps us to answer the following key questions:

- How is the market responding to us?
- How well are we retaining existing customers and finding new ones?
- Which campaign strategies are working? Which are not working?
- How should we spend our ad budget?
- What can we do next to get the most for our money and time?

Companies use analytics to uncover insights to help them develop business strategy, make better decisions and offer better goods, services and personalized online experiences.

There are three types of analytics techniques: descriptive, predictive and prescriptive. Combining these methods is invaluable for company survival and growth.

Seventy-eight per cent of B2B marketing professionals actively monitor the influence of their marketing initiatives on profitability. It is apparent that more organizations, even if they were initially sceptical, are embracing marketing analytics (B2B International, 2021).

This chapter will look at how to use analytics to analyse and optimize your results to maximize performance.

Step one: Before you start

Setting yourself up for success

Marketing analytics let you evaluate the ROI of advertising campaigns as a whole, and of specific elements such as calls-to-action (CTAs), blog posts, channel performance or thought leadership pieces.

Setting goals and committing to the process is the first step in your marketing analytics journey. The key steps include:

- **Plan and design:** Before you begin, establish goals and targets to ensure that you are not simply reporting for the sake of reporting.
- **Execute:** Your marketing measurement programme's effectiveness depends on how successfully you implement it, just like any other business change.
- **Create an analytics culture:** Hiring the right individuals is only the beginning – you also need to integrate analytics into conversations, operations and reviews.

To set yourself up for success, you need to undergo the following stages:

1. TAG SPECIFIC ACTIONS AND TRACK THEM

Let's start by reviewing how to add tags to your sites and apps, and track them. Header code tags help search engines to validate your site and identify you as the site's proprietor. To add tags:

1. Go to the HTML Website Builder.
2. Click settings, then SEO Google, and then advanced SEO Settings.
3. Various third-party services support header code tags.
4. Using Google Webmaster tools, enter your URL in the provided space, and click 'add a site'.
5. In the next window, select the Alternate Method tab, and select the HTML Tag option.
6. Copy the Meta tag generated, copy from the third-party service, and paste it into the advanced SEO tab area in the previous window.

7 Click 'Apply'.
8 Make sure to publish your site and finish the verification procedure with the third-party service.

Your website now has a header code meta tag.

2. GO PRIVATE – RECENT CHANGES TO COOKIE TRACKING, AND PRIVACY CONSIDERATIONS

It's difficult to imagine modern media — with material on every topic, in every language, at the fingertips of billions— without advertisements as its economic backbone. Targeted advertising has led to companies collecting masses of individual user data, typically via third-party sources. As a result, consumers have lost trust.

In a survey by Pew Research Center, 72 per cent of respondents felt that almost everything they do online is being monitored by advertising, technology firms or other groups. And 81 per cent said the risks of data collection outweighed the benefits (Auxier *et al*, 2019).

In 2021, David Temkin, head of advertising products and privacy at Google, said:

> If digital advertising doesn't evolve to address the growing concerns people have about their privacy and how their personal identity is being used, we risk the future of the free and open web.

As a result, Google announced in June 2021 that 'it will stop the use of third-party cookies in Chrome by the end of 2023, joining a growing list of browsers ditching the notorious tracking technology' (Cookiebot, 2021).

Tracking may be made private by implementing creative privacy measures such as prohibiting third-party cookies and any other tech that violates user privacy.

3. SET UP A PROPER DASHBOARD

A project management dashboard shows metrics, figures, and insights for a project or plan. A dashboard is ideal for different departments wanting to track the performance of their initiatives and programmes, identify previous and present patterns and contribute to making the company more innovative.

Because of its ease of use and flexibility, project dashboard technology is also helpful for interdepartmental cooperation.

An effective marketing dashboard should:

- make it clear what you want to accomplish;
- show all the metrics you need to see;
- demonstrate the importance of various metrics using size and position;
- provide context for your numbers;
- sort your metrics by relevance;
- maintain consistency and use clear labelling for your audience;
- allow you to add new metrics, sources and large sets of data;
- be secure from data leakage.

The value of appropriate dashboard design should not be underestimated. Poorly designed dashboards may fail to transmit necessary information and insights, and any inaccuracy this causes could harm more than help.

The type of dashboard you need to use depends on:

- what questions need to be answered;
- who is reading your dashboard;
- how many sources are connected to your dashboard;
- project scope (time and budget).

It is vital to combine all dashboards into a single management display, just like Google Data Studio and Tableau. This lets you compare strategies, forms of communication and so on, to determine what is creating the best results. It is also more convenient. We will explore dashboards in more detail shortly.

4. USE CRM SYSTEMS

The last stage in setting yourself up for success relates to customer relationship management (CRM) and automation systems. CRM software collects and stores customer information that can be used for lead generation. These systems help you communicate your dashboards to your suggested clients.

Review your goals and objectives

Objectives and goals allow you to assess how well your web application achieves your desired outcomes. A goal indicates an accomplished action, known as a conversion, that adds to your company's success.

The amount of data provided to you in analytics might be daunting. To prevent being overwhelmed, recall your goals and stay focused.

First, you need to establish key performance indicators (KPIs) which you will measure. Later, you may experiment with different types of data to obtain more insight.

Know your measurements

At any moment, we may be engaged in various initiatives to increase the income and exposure of our sites. To understand which activities generate outcomes, we must find out how our users arrive at, interact with, browse through and convert on our site.

You can use insights on KPIs for various purposes, such as enhancing user experience, boosting resources for failing areas, and detecting possible difficulties customers may have when using your site.

A marketer may need to track several KPIs, depending on the type of business and marketing goals. Table 9.1 is a useful guide to the core KPIs used to measure each channel.

OVERALL WEBSITE TRAFFIC

Traffic refers to the number of website visitors. A few factors affect the number of individuals who visit a website, such as their purpose and personal goals and how they encountered the website.

Traffic is a key indicator of an internet business's brand presence. Any decrease in your site traffic indicates that your material is insufficient, your links may be faulty, or your approach is unsuccessful.

TABLE 9.1 KPIs for marketing performance by channel

	Main indicator	Primary KPI	Secondary KPI	Tertiary KPI
PPC	impressions	cost per acquisition	conversions	click-through rate
Email	delivery rate	conversion rate	click-through rate	cpen rate
Social	followers	conversions	site visits	engagement
SEO	impressions	revenue	conversions	site visits
Content	content views	conversions	shares	bounce rates
Referrals	referrals gained	revenue	conversions	site visits

Optimizing all pages on your website with relevant keywords is one approach to boost total website traffic. Publish in-depth reports often and market your material on social media networks. Using targeted ads leading to a homepage is another way to capture clients' attention.

TRAFFIC BY SOURCE

The Web Traffic Sources statistic detects and compares the channels that lead visitors to your website. Even though they may come via banner ads or sponsored search initiatives, the four primary traffic sources are: direct, referral, organic and social.

Direct users are those who typed your URL directly into the address bar or bookmarked it and revisited the site. A referral is when customers are sent to your website via a link on another website. An organic search is when a visitor clicks your link in a search result. In other words, they do not end up on your site due to paid ads. Social may also be organic, when people visit your website via your social media presence or content updates.

NEW VISITORS VERSUS RETURNING VISITORS

One of the most fundamental forms of user segmentation is new versus returning visitors. New users are those who have never visited your website, app or another platform before and are interacting for the first time. Returning users are individuals who have previously visited the site. They return for the helpful content.

There are several methods for increasing the number of repeat visits to your website. One way is to create and publish quality information that can be accessed through search engines. You may also promote blog posts on Twitter by using one or two relevant hashtags. One of the most popular strategies to persuade your visitors to return to your website is to email your subscribers when new content is released.

SESSIONS

A session refers to the time a user spends on your website and the activities they engage in within that time. A session may include page views, transactions and social interactions. Multiple sessions may occur within a day, week or month. There may be multiple site visits within a session.

AVERAGE SESSION DURATION

Web Analytics calculates average session duration by dividing the total time of all visits (in seconds) for a particular period by the total number of sessions for the same period. According to research, the average session length is the fourth-most-tracked Google Analytics statistic (Databox, 2021). Users that have a long average session length are the most likely to be relevant to your business.

There is one drawback that makes average session length a problematic measure to calculate. The user must take action when they visit for Analytics to calculate the amount of time spent on that web page. Examples of actions that trigger this measurement include playing a video, clicking a link and filling out a form.

PAGE VIEWS

A page view is the act of loading (or reloading) a page in a browser. The page views statistic represents the total number of pages seen. When analysing traffic to individual web pages, this is a crucial measurement.

MOST VISITED PAGES

The most visited page on a website is the page the user gives the most attention. In 2021, the top three most-visited websites have around 152 billion monthly visitors, outnumbering 47 websites combined.

EXIT PAGE

The exit page is the final page a user views on a website before leaving or before the session expires. By evaluating from which page your visitors most frequently leave your site, you may enhance these pages to keep users on your site and increase conversions.

BOUNCE RATE

Bounce rate measures the percentage of site visits that are single-page sessions, with the visitor leaving without viewing a second page. It is commonly used to assess the overall engagement of a website.

There are several reasons why a user may leave your website. There are two primary reasons: the site took too long to load, or the user could not find what they were looking for. Other factors include issues with page loading or visitors not feeling motivated to continue forward.

Lower your bounce rate by reducing the time it takes for your page to load, including internal links in your page copy, carefully using images or other graphics in your content, and adding an engaging CTA.

CONVERSION RATE

Any desired action that you want the user to take can be referred to as a conversion, from button clicks to making a purchase and becoming a client.

Many websites and applications have numerous conversion goals, for example a legitimate sale, gaining a subscriber, finishing a download and acquiring a lead entry. To improve conversion rate, you need to discover how to develop the perfect call-to-action that will fascinate and educate, and improve your conversions.

IMPRESSIONS

The impression is a KPI that measures how frequently your ad is seen. Impressions are the number of times your material is displayed, regardless of whether or not it is clicked. One impression is collected for each time your ad shows on a search result page or another site in the Google Network, or any other network.

SOCIAL REACH

Think of 'reach' as the number of unique individuals who see your material. A piece of content must first be sent to a feed (impression), and then a user must engage with the platform to view the piece of material in their feed (reach).

Increase your reach by completely branding all of your social media pages, consistently providing curated and unique content and engaging with the community.

SOCIAL ENGAGEMENT

When assessing social media performance, engagement is perhaps the most essential of the three metrics to consider. That is because engagement is the only one of the three that directly involves the user. It's one thing to have someone view your material, but to engage them and move them to take action is another.

When your content motivates a consumer to take action, they advance rapidly through your brand's 'funnel of awareness'. Viewers that interact with your material are significantly more likely to become prospective sales leads. Clicking, sharing, liking, retweeting and commenting are ways to engage on a specific post or page.

EMAIL OPEN RATE

The open rate of an email is the proportion of your total number of subscribers who open a specific email. You may examine your open email rate to see how practical your email marketing approach is. Open rates vary greatly and are affected by a range of factors, such as:

- the email sender's industry;
- subject line;
- day of the week;
- time of day.

Regardless of the difference in open rates, a decent open rate is generally 20–40 per cent. If your email open rate is extremely low, you may have failed to capture the attention of your subscribers with your subject line or have not chosen the best time to send your email.

CLICK-THROUGH RATE

The click-through rate (CTR) is the proportion of people who click on an item they have been exposed to. CTR is a statistic used to assess the effectiveness of emails, websites and online advertising (Google, Bing, Yahoo and so on). CTR is commonly used to evaluate the performance of marketing campaigns. It may be assessed in a variety of contexts, including:

- a link in an email that prompts the recipient to take action (CTA);
- a link on a landing page;
- a pay-per-click (PPC) ad on a Google search results page;
- an advertisement on a social networking platform such as LinkedIn or Facebook.

The higher the click-through rate, the more influential the ad is in creating interest.

COST PER CLICK

CPC stands for cost per click. Its's the amount you spend for each click in your pay-per-click (PPC) ad campaigns. Your maximum bid, quality score, and the ad rank of other advertisers competing for the same keyword all impact your cost per click.

Your CPC is an important metric to monitor since visits and charges add up rapidly. If your CPC is too high, you will not recoup your advertising costs (ROI).

COST PER CONVERSION

Cost per conversion (CPC or CPCon) shows how much it costs to attract a client who will successfully convert. A conversion can include completing a purchase, signing up for something or watching a video, depending on the goal of the advertising.

CPC shows how successful an ad is in reaching its goal, based on the entire cost of the ad. This is essential knowledge for managing your budget and deciding on the best strategies for promotion. You may reduce your CPC by boosting your conversion rate.

COST PER ACQUISITION

CPA assesses the total cost of obtaining one paying client at the campaign or channel level. CPA is an essential marketing success statistic that is distinguished from the cost of acquiring a customer (CAC) by the granularity with which it is used. It is a financial statistic that is used to determine the direct revenue effect of marketing initiatives. CPA gives a commercial viewpoint for measuring campaign success.

Cost per acquisition is employed in the following paid marketing channels:

- PPC;
- affiliate;
- display;
- content marketing on social media.

It may also be utilized for e-commerce SEO, email and other platforms that do not require direct advertising but still incur costs.

OVERALL ROI

Whether you're using ads to boost sales, create leads or drive other proper customer behaviour, it's a good idea to track your return on investment. Knowing your ROI allows you to determine whether the money you're spending on ads is producing healthy earnings for your company.

The return on investment is the ratio of your net profit to your costs. It's usually the essential metric for an advertiser, since it's focused on your unique advertising goals and demonstrates the true impact of your advertising efforts on your business.

The aims of your campaign determine the technique you choose to calculate ROI. You may work out how much money you've made through Google ads by calculating your ROI. ROI may also be used to assist you in determining how to allocate your budget. ROI data may also be used to enhance the performance of less successful initiatives.

Step two: Get to grips with your dashboards

Track your metrics using dashboards

A digital marketing dashboard is a tool that visualizes essential marketing KPIs. A dashboard should offer a range of reports that track data over a specified period. Analysing this data gives insight into your marketing strategies, allowing you to adjust them as needed and enhance future advertisements.

The finest data dashboards provide answers to critical business issues. Dashboards, as opposed to complex business intelligence technologies, are intended for fast analysis and informational awareness. The general guideline is that no more than seven metrics should be presented on a dashboard, since it serves as a quick-glance depiction of the status of a goal.

MARKETING PERFORMANCE DASHBOARD

A marketing dashboard is a monitoring platform that displays marketing statistics, KPIs and metrics through data visualization. Marketing dashboards are designed to provide teams with a real-time picture of their marketing performance.

At its core, this dashboard answers the question, 'How are we functioning right now?' They are meant for ongoing monitoring and widespread distribution.

ATTRIBUTION

Customers may interact with several ads from the same advertiser on the route to conversion. You may select how much credit each ad interaction receives for your conversions using attribution models. Attribution models may help you optimize across conversion pathways by providing a more profound knowledge of your advertising work.

Attribution design offers you a more significant say over how much compensation each advertising engagement receives for conversions. That enables you to:

- find ways to influence customers earlier in the purchase cycle;
- match your company – use a model that best fits how consumers look for what you have to offer;
- increase your bidding – improve your bids based on a deeper knowledge of how your advertising is doing.

Attribution analytics determine which routes and content had the most influence on converting or taking the targeted future action.

Marketers now employ various attribution methods, including multi-touch attribution, lift studies, time decay and so on. These models' insights on how, where and when a customer engages with brand messaging enable marketing teams to change and customize campaigns to match the particular wants of individual consumers, therefore boosting marketing ROI.

To effectively understand the true value of each of your marketing channels, it is essential to use attribution models that best fit your products and/or brand. If you have long consideration journeys, understanding how consumers move between paid search, display, organic search and email, for example, is essential.

SEO ANALYTICS DASHBOARD

SEO metrics and KPIs are values that marketing teams use to evaluate their website's success in search engine results. Any marketing team's primary function is search engine optimization.

Teams must analyse SEO KPIs and follow improvements month after month to truly understand their search marketing effectiveness. This study can assist in determining top-performing pages, top converting keywords, and parts of your website that require search optimization.

An SEO dashboard holds all of your web analytics data and serves as a central point for all of these data sources, allowing digital marketers to gain a comprehensive knowledge of SEO performance through analytics.

E-COMMERCE MARKETING DASHBOARD

Your goals for the data will ultimately determine anything you measure on your e-commerce marketing dashboard. If you want to measure the outcomes of a single campaign, you should construct a separate dashboard. For day-to-day activity, you should track a combination of social media, sales and site traffic.

Brand discovery is critical to identifying marketing possibilities, and traffic sources are vital for monitoring an e-commerce marketing dashboard. Other KPIs to watch on the e-commerce dashboard are:

- return on marketing investment (ROI);
- sales by contact method;
- web traffic sources;
- goal completion rate;
- cost per lead;
- end action rate.

AMAZON MARKETING DASHBOARD

According to Amazon (advertising.amazon.com), 'Amazon Attribution is an advertising and analytics measurement solution that gives marketers insight into how their non-Amazon marketing channels across search, social, video, display, and email impact shopping activity and sales performance on Amazon.' You may discover new ways to develop your Amazon business by using this data to improve experiences outside Amazon.

Amazon sellers may utilize the Amazon marketing dashboard, and the same configuration can be used to create a dashboard for Shopify and other similar platforms. This dashboard is now available to professional sellers who are Amazon Brand Registry members, merchants, and agencies with clients who sell Amazon products.

You may analyse, optimize and plan which of your approaches maximizes return on investment and boosts profits in order to build future marketing plans on Amazon.

WEB ANALYTICS DASHBOARD

A web analytics dashboard lets you assess the performance of your website by measuring data such as visitors, page views and online conversions. This dashboard can be used in various contexts, such as digital marketing, social media, SEO, UX and e-commerce.

Each of these use-cases takes a distinct approach to the performance of the website. A web analytics dashboard has the advantage of allowing your entire team to monitor the website's performance.

Typical KPIs measured on a web analytics dashboard

- % conversion rate;
- # page views;
- % new versus returning visitors;
- # new or unique visitors;
- # page views per visitor (pages/sessions);
- % referral traffic;
- % sources for incoming traffic;
- # website visitors;
- # email leads created (goal conversions);
- % bounce rate.

SOCIAL MEDIA DASHBOARD

A social media dashboard is a social content management system that enables individuals or companies to manage their social media presence across many channels or accounts through a shared database.

Some dashboard applications are intended to handle numerous accounts on the same platform. TweetDeck, for example, is exclusively available for Twitter.

Most social media dashboards incorporate features designed to improve the efficiency, standardization and effectiveness of social media publishing. Content scheduling, collaboration tools that make it simple to add team members to the content production process, and permissions control over who may approve postings are all possible features. A few KPIs for this dashboard are:

- social interactions;
- goal fulfilment rate;
- traffic sources.

YOUTUBE ADS DASHBOARD

The YouTube dashboard provides a comprehensive picture of the performance of your YouTube channel. Connect your YouTube channel quickly and efficiently to track views on your videos, average viewing length, and the number of new subscribers you've gained. Visualize overall channel performance to understand where your viewers are coming from and which videos are performing well. This dashboard helps you to:

- monitor the performance of your YouTube channel at a glance;
- visualize your video performance based on key performance indicators, such as views and average view time length;
- highlight the activity and trends of your channel subscribers.

Three YouTube dashboard examples are:

1. Video performance dashboard.
2. Channel performance dashboard.
3. YouTube KPI dashboard.

A few key metrics to visualize YouTube channel performance are views, average time duration and average view percentage.

GOOGLE ADWORDS CAMPAIGN STUDIO

The Google AdWords Campaign Studio dashboard allows you to track the metrics of a Google ads campaign and the ROI. It provides a deeper knowledge of which subjects and keywords should be prioritized in your approach. This dashboard helps you to see your:

- performance overview;
- account performance;
- campaign performance;
- ad group performance;
- device and geo (country/territory) performance;
- auction insights performance.

EMAIL MARKETING DASHBOARD

An email marketing dashboard provides essential, real-time data showing the ROI of your email campaigns. Email marketing is a successful digital marketing approach as it allows you to target specific prospects and consumers. Its objective is to convert prospects into customers, and existing customers into loyal users.

A dashboard for email marketing provides you with a high-level overview of your email campaign. You'll also be able to track important metrics and performance indicators to measure your email marketing activities.

CMO MARKETING DASHBOARD

The dashboard for the chief marketing officer overviews all marketing services, including social media, email, online performance and lead generation. The dashboard provides an instant answer to the inquiry, 'How well are we doing?' It brings together analytics from many sources to give a comprehensive picture about your marketing effectiveness.

By presenting this information on a CMO dashboard, you provide executives with the option of checking in on daily performance. They can change campaigns as they are carried out, if necessary, rather than giving a campaign overview after it's too late to change the outcome.

A few essential metrics every CMO Dashboard should have are:

- cost;
- revenue;
- profit;
- return on ad spend (ROAs);
- cost per acquisition (CPA);
- conversions.

ONLINE MARKETING DASHBOARD

This dashboard is designed to provide a high-level overview of six essential marketing channels:

- website performance;
- digital advertising;
- inbound lead generation;
- social media;
- email marketing;
- revenue generation.

One of the most critical metrics this dashboard tracks is the conversion rates of leads in the funnel. Website visitors must be converted into leads and, eventually, new customers. This number is supported by the monthly revenue metric, which allows the marketing team to assess how their efforts have impacted profitability.

An online marketing performance dashboard usually displays the following KPIs:

- ROI on capital investments;
- completion rate target;
- traffic sources;
- the purchase funnel.

Step three: Turn insights into action

Analytics lay the groundwork for a unique customer experience and deeper engagement – from targeting and selling to retaining, engaging and serving. Using analytics to derive insight from data is the first step toward finding and owning the most significant customers – engaging their loyalty, increasing results while lowering costs, and maximizing your organization's efficiency (Deloitte, 2017).

Analytics should not be the end objective, but, rather, a strategic facilitator. Begin with the most pressing concerns, then sift through the available data to see how it might inform you about those difficulties.

Other queries should be framed around data that isn't currently available, and you should discover where to acquire it. Unexpected sources of knowledge can lead to unforeseen decisions that put you ahead of the competition. No organization sets out to make choices without first gaining as much knowledge as possible.

It is not enough to collect and report data. Marketers must take action to improve their future outcomes. Marketers have access to an unlimited amount of data, but effective marketers use the data to modify their decisions and enhance their tactics.

CASE STUDY: NISSAN'S GOOGLE ANALYTICS

A great case study that is featured in my book *Digital Marketing Strategy* (Kingsnorth, 2019) is Nissan's use of Google Analytics.

Nissan run a number of websites around the world that aid consumers in their decision around their vehicle purchase. Visitors to these sites are able to look at Nissan's products, download promotional materials and book a test drive. These are therefore clearly not e-commerce sites, but Nissan wanted to do much more than tracking simple goals. They also wanted to understand visitor preferences such as car model and colour.

Nissan therefore implemented Google Analytics and used the e-commerce functionality in an innovative way to capture this information and gain the understanding. The approach was simply that a visitor requesting a test drive or brochure was asked to complete a form which, as well as asking for contact details, also requested information on the vehicle they were interested in, such as model and colour. This information was captured via the simple addition of an e-commerce tag that was added to the 'thank you' page that appeared after the form completion.

Nissan were then able to analyse the data and understand which vehicles were regularly generating interest and therefore tailor their marketing strategies appropriately in each market.

Google Analytics is of course just one of many platforms available but the key for your strategy is to understand that gathering detailed data can inform commercial decision-making and the shape of your digital strategy, so, using analytics tags in innovative ways to gain this data can be hugely valuable.

WHAT TO WATCH

Insight, not data

Data, analytics and insights are all critical. These terms are frequently used interchangeably, although they do not signify the same thing.

Measuring minor amounts of data is restrictive and can be deceptive. Small data sets may represent chance rather than a trend. For example, if campaign A receives 10 clicks and 2 orders and campaign B receives 15 clicks and 1 order, we cannot claim that campaign A is superior since the data sample is too small.

To confirm a prejudice, data might be distorted. Sometimes we see what we want to see and present findings that demonstrate what we want to see. That is known as data selection bias. Confirmation bias is the use of incorrect facts to confirm an assumption.

Data and analytics complement each other to provide a comprehensive knowledge of your user base. Insights give critical information about your customers and indicate steps you can take to enhance your business. These insights, however, cannot be acquired without analytics, and analytics are meaningless without data.

STEP BY STEP

Knowing your customers

1 Gather data.
2 Use analytics.
3 Analyse insights.

Everything a company needs to prosper is already in its data. Its actionable insights give the advice that the firm requires to expand gradually. Businesses cannot hope to thrive in today's unpredictable economy unless they have strong analytics abilities.

The problem for most organizations is not obtaining data, but, rather, putting it to use. Being insight-driven means consolidating all recorded data into a single source, to produce a complete picture of how each internal and external aspect affects the organization. It means using insights to decide on the next course of action, considering all possibilities.

It's important to be aware of causation versus correlation. A correlation between variables does not imply that a change in one variable is the cause of a change in the values of the other variable. Causation denotes that one event is the outcome of the other event's occurrence; that is, there is a causal link between the two circumstances.

When sunscreen sales rise, so do ice cream sales; but higher sunscreen sales are not the *source* of increased ice-cream sales. However, they are correlated. Of course, the weather is to credit for both increases in sales. Similarly, to comprehend the facts, you must first understand the context. An analyst will be unable to explain why a result occurred if they do not grasp the context from which it came.

Lack of insight results in a lack of engagement. Today's mobile engagement issue is a direct result of organizations operating in the dark, where far too many brands have failed to use the data at their disposal, missing out on critical insights. The insights provided by data and analytics enable a company to gain a deep understanding of its customers, empowering it to develop significant interaction possibilities.

Don't pass up the opportunity to fully understand your consumers — use your data, analytics and resultant insight to build your business!

References

Auxier, B, Rainie, L, Anderson, M, Perrin, A, Kumar, M, and Turner, E (2019) Americans and privacy: Concerned, confused and feeling lack of control over their personal information, Pew Research Center, available at: https://www.pewresearch.org/internet/2019/11/15/americans-and-privacy-concerned-confused-and-feeling-lack-of-control-over-their-personal-information/ (archived at https://perma.cc/G9AZ-8J4X)

B2B International (2021) B2B marketing: A guide – 10 key differences from consumer marketing, available at: https://www.b2binternational.com/publications/b2b-marketing/ (archived at https://perma.cc/UFW5-TSDB)

Cookiebot (2021) Google ending third-party cookies in Chrome, available at: https://www.cookiebot.com/en/google-third-party-cookies/ (archived at https://perma.cc/PHP3-YM6A)

Databox (2021) The 10 most-tracked Google Analytics metrics, available at: https://databox.com/the-most-tracked-google-analytics-metrics (archived at https://perma.cc/8763-72WH)

Deloitte (2017) Analytics to improve outcomes and reduce cost, available at: https://www2.deloitte.com/content/dam/Deloitte/us/Documents/life-sciences-health-care/us-lshc-analytics-to-improve-outcomes-and-reduce-cost.pdf (archived at https://perma.cc/DUT7-UPYE)

Kingsnorth, S (2019) *Digital Marketing Strategy: An Integrated Approach to Online Marketing* 2nd edition, Kogan Page, London

Temkin, D (2021) Charting a course towards more privacy – first web, Google, available at https://blog.google/products/ads-commerce/a-more-privacy-first-web/ (archived at https://perma.cc/5E5A-R7UR)

Bibliography

YouTube (2021) How YouTube works – Product features, responsibility, and impact, available at: https://www.youtube.com/intl/en-GB/about/press/ (archived at https://perma.cc/FN6P-7CZR)

Villanova University (2020) How marketers use data analytics to reach new and existing customers, available at: https://taxandbusinessonline.villanova.edu/blog/how-marketers-use-data-analytics-to-reach-customers/ (archived at https://perma.cc/9GAF-45M5)

10

Automating your email and CRM plans to deliver compelling digital communications

Email automation is a method of delivering automatic marketing to the right individuals with the right message at the right time – without having to do the work – thanks to marketing automation platforms. Customer relationship management (CRM) platforms have a tool to maintain customer data and manage contact strategies.

These two platform types are interlinked, and there are many powerful tools available to manage all of your email, social media, advertising, customer data web analytics and much more in one place, so you can gain true marketing insights and automate marketing actions.

In this chapter, we'll look at both platforms and how they can be used with a focus on email.

Advantages of CRM and marketing automation

- By integrating CRM with marketing automation, marketing teams can give individuals the most relevant content and information at the most appropriate point in their customer journey. This can reduce the sales cycle by half, and give potential customers a better experience during the sales process.
- In a 2014 survey, 74 per cent of users claimed their CRM system gave them better access to client data and the capacity to provide excellent service (Software Advice, 2014).

- Despite social media's vast readership, in 2014, email was more than 40 times more effective at attracting new clients than Facebook and Twitter combined (McKinsey, 2014).
- Marketing automation software helps four out of five users improve their leads, and 70 per cent have experienced an increase in conversions (Demand Gen Report, 2018).

Marketing automation feeds your sales pipeline from the top to the bottom of the funnel, while email allows you to communicate with customers at any time during the process.

The value of automated email campaigns, and effective strategies

Marketers benefit from automated emails because they reduce the time-consuming job of creating, sending and managing email workflows.

Still on the fence about it? These statistics don't lie (Emma, 2019):

Benefits of automated email marketing

- Compared with traditional emails, automated emails have had 70.5 per cent higher open rates and 152 per cent greater click-through rates.
- Personalized emails bring about six times the income of non-personalized emails.
- Nurtured leads are 47 per cent more likely to make a purchase.

Step one: Data migration

Define key business processes

The procedures that have the greatest impact on your customers, staff and bottom line are known as key business processes. In a nutshell, your main processes provide an answer to the question, 'How does our company generate value?'

In addition, you'll know exactly where to spend your investments and energy after you understand your critical business procedures. Given the financial and mental hardship of Covid-19, it's more critical than ever to pinpoint the processes that actually matter.

Key processes are often operational processes that fall under one of the following categories:

- handling customer service;
- providing services;
- marketing and selling services and products;
- creating and managing services and products;
- developing a vision and a strategy.

Each of the above is a big-picture category. Identifying important processes necessitates a deep dive into each area to determine where you have a competitive advantage to maintain and where you need to improve.

Use the following questions to understand your core business processes better:

- How does your business collect new leads?
- How does your sales process work?
- How does fulfilment work once a lead is converted into a customer?

List services you currently use to manage customer data

The days of using spreadsheets to store client information are long gone. Instead, businesses that care about maintaining their clients' confidentiality store their clients' data in a secure CRM database, which must be GDPR compliant.

These tools are intended to make organizing and collecting critical information safe and straightforward. They can also provide data-driven segmented customer insights, which is a terrific method to spot areas for improvement.

Service integration

While CRM software is effective in itself, combining it with different technologies in your sales stack makes your job much easier. It is recommended that your CRM must operate as the hub for all of your sales activity, and integrations should act as the supporting block that helps make your central software even more powerful.

Let's take a look at some different types of commonly used applications that can be integrated into your CRM to enhance its functionalities:

- Gmail, Outlook – business email;
- Mailchimp – marketing email;
- Outlook or Google Calendar – appointment management;
- QuickBooks – finance management;
- PayPal – payment processing;
- Facebook, Twitter, LinkedIn and so on – social media.

Utilizing the new functions of your CRM, and common mistakes during migration

If you're thinking about switching to a new CRM for your company, there are a few things you should consider before you go ahead and make the switch.

UNDERESTIMATING THE AMOUNT OF EFFORT REQUIRED

Migrating to a new CRM is no different in terms of difficulty, and it should be treated as such. You're moving digitally, which means you'll need to prepare ahead and execute as planned.

PUTTING INTO ACTION BEFORE DEFINING

While this is especially true for automation, transferring any process into a new CRM necessitates a full grasp of what is currently being done.

DIPPING ONE TOE INTO THE WATER

This is by far the biggest dream-killer of all the problems described above. Even if you make both of the aforementioned errors, you can still succeed. However, if you handle the first two but fail to deliver on this one, your failure is virtually assured. You must commit to a comprehensive migration and consistent use of a new CRM on a daily basis. Failing to comply with this would cause severe consequences.

Step two: CRM automation

Evaluate needs and budget

You must first know your current marketing processes and understand how to measure success before taking the necessary steps to select an automation platform. Furthermore, determining where you need to improve can assist you in deciding which marketing automation technology is best for your company.

This section highlights the four-step process for selecting the best marketing automation for your company.

1. DETERMINE WHETHER YOU NEED A MARKETING AUTOMATION PLATFORM

Assessing your organization's needs, financial resources, managerial support and personnel capabilities will demonstrate whether an automation platform is required.

In addition, you could use the following questions as a guide to assess whether the answer is yes or no to an automation platform.

- Have you outgrown your current marketing system?
- What marketing automation capabilities are most critical to your business?
- What kind of marketing platform do you need?

2. LOCATE AND CONTACT APPROPRIATE PLATFORMS

Spend time examining each platform's features once you've established that your firm needs a marketing automation tool. First, make a list of all the automation skills you currently possess, as well as those you would like to acquire. Once you've compiled a list, conduct thorough research and contact those that suit you.

3. ARRANGE A DEMO

To stay relevant and be able to make solid comparisons, schedule demos with your list of vendors within a limited time frame. Ensure all possible internal users are on the demo call because they are the ones who will be utilizing the marketing automation software daily. When you're walking through the demos, keep an eye out for how simple and user-friendly the platform is. Your staff will be more efficient if it is user-friendly.

4. READ THE REVIEWS AND THOROUGHLY EXAMINE THE CONTRACT

Read platform reviews and even call out to companies like yours to check if they love the platform, just like you would if you were buying something online. Then, for an in-person deep dive into which platforms perform best and how they're being used, ask around at conferences and events.

When picking CRM software, there are a few things to keep in mind.

Identify your major CRM expenses

The primary factors that go into determining the cost of CRM are:

- migration;
- training;
- integration;
- storage.

These are, however, only the costs that are visible. In actuality, the costs are significantly higher. This is the reason why the majority of smaller businesses opt for an all-in-one platform with lower costs instead of the conventional CRM software.

CHECK OUT THE COST OF A CRM INVESTMENT

The main question is: how much will this action increase my revenue? Of course, the methods for determining this vary, and the best strategy to use depends on the situation.

Starting with the organization's or division's income, the CRM is likely to be only one aspect that determines that figure, so you'll need to go deeper. Most likely, you'll have to track success by looking at revenue per client, client securing costs, or transformation rate.

Since the revenue that a standard small business generates isn't as high, they struggle to budget for these highly expensive CRMs and other automation tools and, as a result, are forced to look for alternatives.

PICK A SPECIFIC MODEL AND STRUCTURE

The trend for CRMs is clearly toward distributed computing. In a recent poll (Oracle, 2017), 79 per cent of respondents said they were working on or planning a cloud project. Meanwhile, 33 per cent said they planned to spend more on cloud services in the coming year.

What do you want to achieve with automation?

Businesses that are new to marketing automation should define clear goals as to what they want to accomplish with email marketing automation. Setting goals and launching a marketing automation campaign should be done simultaneously.

Let's take a look at how to define objectives for your marketing automation campaigns.

- **Set SMART objectives.**
  This is fundamental. Any objective must be specific, measurable, attainable, relevant and time-bound.
- **Set goals using marketing automation.**
  Your marketing automation should assist you in defining goals. The key is knowing your gathered data and using it as a guide.
- **Align marketing and sales objectives.**
  Sales and marketing are two concepts that are deeply intertwined. You can't set goals for one without taking into account the other. So, while you're setting your goals, keep both demands in mind.
- **Create a marketing strategy that is easy to understand.**
  Through marketing automation, it's simpler to create smarter processes and workflows that use data and analytics to nurture leads down the sales funnel.
- **Examine the metrics.**
  Only by reviewing your metrics can you see the larger picture. Each metric is related to another, and it is one of those significantly crucial factors upon which your success depends.
- **Test. Analyse. Repeat.**
  Once you've determined all of your objectives and finalized your marketing automation methods, put them into action. You can't just sit back and wait for the results. To make necessary adjustments, you should test which strategies are working and which are not.

Choosing the right CRM and expanded CRM explanation

CRM solutions have a reputation for accelerating corporate growth. Businesses of all sizes are eyeing them for assistance in reaching new heights of success. But what many companies have failed to understand is that selecting CRM software includes a substantial degree of risk if proper planning is not done ahead of time. If you don't have a suitable road map in place, your implementation strategy is likely to fail, and you risk losing your investment.

Businesses fail to simplify procedures due to a lack of relevant information, leading to costly CRM installations, resulting in failure.

To assist you in dealing with this complex matter, we've compiled a list of the four most essential measures to take when selecting the best CRM solution for your company.

1. **Define your functional and business requirements.**
   First and foremost, it is necessary to determine the business's demands, which, in turn, will assist in determining the extent to which a CRM can help the company achieve its goals. The rule of thumb is to list the problems you'd like your CRM to answer and then define the key features you'd like in your CRM.
2. **Ensure everyone's on board.**
   CRM implementation is a significant change for any business. To achieve a smooth transition, it is critical to have everyone in the organization on board.
3. **Assess the options.**
   You must choose between a cloud CRM and an on-premises CRM, based on your business needs and available resources. Both have advantages and disadvantages.
4. **Select the best CRM software based on the evaluation results.**
   Because you will be investing a significant amount of time money, and human resources in purchasing a CRM, you deserve the best option available that will provide you with the desired return on investment.

An intelligent CRM system will streamline marketing operations and reduce the quantity of customer data collection required by a marketing team to follow up on leads.

TOP TIP

Data control

When it comes to data, today's magic word is 'control'. Data is the 'new gold', and gaining control of it is critical for any organization's success.

You can make better decisions regarding sales, marketing, hiring, investing and a thousand other concerns if you have more data at your disposal. Conversely, failing to obtain accurate data for these decisions can lead to catastrophic issues for businesses.

The key to maintaining data control is to ensure that the related metadata is appropriately maintained – that an organization can locate all of the data it requires, regardless of how it is labelled in databases and storage systems.

Metadata consistency is one of the most critical parts of data governance, but it's also one of the hardest to implement. The manual approaches employed by business intelligence teams to locate metadata are no match for the massive volume of data that must be combed through.

Automated systems that locate and analyse metadata allow businesses to learn what they really have, and these systems might just be the most efficient way to avoid the irritation associated with manual and semi-human search methods.

Step three: Automated marketing and email

Setting up an automated marketing system

The crux of marketing automation is email. So, when it comes to creating lead-nurturing workflows, most brands and marketers talk about using email as a marketing communication channel (particularly for B2B). This isn't unexpected, given that email still has the highest return on investment among all marketing channels.

Email automation software automatically sends marketing emails based on workflows, user data and online behavioural triggers. Thanks to the integration of consumer data platforms and email tools, this software dramatically reduces operational expenses and improves productivity. In addition, this makes reporting and obtaining information a breeze.

The abandoned-cart reminder is a popular automatic email that you will have seen. This message is sent to everyone who leaves the checkout page without buying. Although it may appear simple, abandoned-cart emails have three times the open rate of typical e-commerce emails (Moosend, 2021) and can convert at a rate of over 10 per cent (Campaign Monitor, 2019).

Any online business that wants to establish a profitable email list needs to automate its email marketing.

What is email automation and how does it work?

When an event occurs, an email is sent out using email automation (automatically sent). Your email marketing tool or your marketing automation tool sends the email.

Before we get started, let's familiarize ourselves with some of the most commonly used email marketing terms.

- trigger – an event that causes something to happen (such as those mentioned below);
- autoresponder – an email that is set to automatically respond to incoming triggers;
- sequence – a sequence of emails that begin due to a trigger;
- spam – unwanted email sent to someone who never opted in;
- opt-in/subscribe – when someone takes an action to receive emails from you;
- unsubscribe – when someone takes an action to stop receiving your emails;
- CTR – the clicks on the links within your email;
- bounce rate – undelivered emails. Soft bounces are temporary, such as out-of-office messages; hard bounces are permanent, for example if the email address no longer exists.

TOOLS FOR EMAIL MARKETING AUTOMATION

Functionality and price are the key differentiating factors between an email automation tool and a standard email marketing tool. Regular emails, like newsletters, are sent using an email marketing service. You may create automation around such emails utilizing a marketing automation solution.

A marketing automation tool may have the following functionalities:

- landing page builder;
- analytics;
- online behaviour tracking – email subscribers navigating your website;
- program management – handle marketing campaigns over various platforms;
- email sequence builder.

There are several marketing automation tools to pick from if you're seeking one. A few well-known examples are HubSpot, Salesforce and Marketo.

Email campaigns that you must have

1. THE WELCOME EMAIL

Consider the welcome email campaign to be a sequence of emails sent after a new subscriber joins your list. This campaign gives you an ideal chance to promote your brand, especially when readers are more receptive to it.

When used correctly, welcome emails can produce a lot of money. In terms of stats, these email campaigns are noted for having higher than normal click-to-open rates and CTRs.

2. THE PROMOTIONAL EMAIL

These emails, as the name implies, are usually used to promote a product and get it out there. They are often the most common transactional emails. However, a typical subscriber receives dozens of these per day, so yours may get lost amid the chaos.

Make your promotional emails stand out by being systematic and purposeful in your approach. Create a thoughtful set of emails that are interconnected and build on one another. Add a sense of humour, elicit strong emotions, pique curiosity and employ eye-catching designs and templates.

3. THE TRIGGERED EMAIL

Consider a triggered email campaign as a series of automated communications, where a user's activity might set off a chain of further personalized and relevant emails.

According to DMA research, triggered campaigns and campaigns that were not solely promotional produced over 75 per cent of email income (DMA, 2013).

Taking a survey, buying goods or services, adding an item to the basket and clicking links in an email are all examples of actions that can initiate a trigger.

4. THE NEWSLETTER

Newsletters continue indefinitely, so they may not be considered standard campaigns. Consider them as a way to keep in touch with your readers on a regular basis.

5. THE ABANDONED-CART EMAIL

This is a triggered email that appears when a customer adds an item to their basket but does not complete the purchase. Campaigns based on such circumstances are frequently timed and incentivized. This type of email marketing, like welcome emails, has higher than average open and conversion rates.

CASE STUDY: A B2B COMPANY

The challenge

A B2B company had done a good job of attracting potential new clients but was struggling to convert them. The sales team were reaching out but not always able to get through. Sometimes it was due to speed of response, sometimes due to incorrect contact information. They needed to find a way to encourage their prospects to get in touch with them.

The solution

The company used their marketing automation platform to create a sequence of emails designed to entice new prospects to get in touch and combined this with the sales cycle to maximize contact rates and conversion. It started with chasing the lead followed by promoting the product benefits and finally ending with an offer. The sequence was as follows:

1. New lead submitted.
2. Immediate email confirmation with benefits of purchasing.
3. Sales team call the prospect.
4. Email highlighting benefits.
5. Sales team call again.
6. Email highlighting more benefits.
7. Sales team call again.
8. Time-based offer email.
9. Sales team call again.

The results

Following the introduction of this approach, sales conversion immediately increased by 25 per cent with no cost to the business. As a result, the company started to introduce sequences into all of their internal processes with further positive results across the organization.

How do you go about creating an email automation sequence?

No matter what sequence you are looking to develop, the required steps will be the same.

1. **Determine who you'd like to attract.**
   Begin by looking at previous clients and determine their qualities and interests.
2. **Study the challenges that your current customers/audience are facing.**
   Research your customers'/audience's challenges regarding your products or services. This will assist you in developing compelling sales angles.
3. **Create your incentive using the information you've gathered.**
   Make use of the information gathered in the preceding steps to generate interest in the subject. Another option is to create a guide to capture email addresses. People will sign up to download the guide (or whatever the incentive is), then you can offer them a free trial.
4. **Instruct others to take the action you desire.**
   To plan ahead, you'll need to make a 'map' (you could use Lucidcharts). The first stage on the map is the welcome email. After that, you'll send follow-up emails with links to the incentive. What would happen after that?
   - The prospect might become a consumer, so you must move them to a consumer list.
   - In case they don't become consumers, you could add them to your newsletter list.
5. **Write the emails.**
   What relationship do you want to build with the subscriber? Keep this in mind while you draft the emails. Help them to feel like they're a member of the community by making them feel welcome, telling them about yourself and following through on your commitments (free trial, a guide and so on). Make sure you're creating a relationship as well as offering valuable material with each email you send.
6. **Create the email sequence.**
   You need to plan the email sequence, including when each email will go out to your subscribers. There are a few popular methods. Email sequences can involve just a few or many, many emails. The following example is a shorter version:
   a. Thank you for your enquiry – send immediately.
   b. We couldn't get hold of you – 2 days later.

   c Reminder of the benefits of working with us – 4 days later.
   d Here's an offer/discount if you buy now – 5 days later.
   e Don't forget the offer and benefits – 7 days later.
   f End sequence – add either to customer list or prospect list for future communications.

7 **Opt-in segmentation and deployment.**
Your marketing tool might have the necessary opt-ins, but specialized tools generally do a better job. Opt-ins can be based on various factors, including location, page visits and other actions. Some tools have split testing, which is always recommended. Segmenting your email list successfully will ensure that messages get in the correct inbox at the right time.

8 **Send traffic to the opt-ins.**
This could be organic traffic, referral traffic from other websites, or bought traffic from Google, Bing and Facebook Ads, among other sources.

9 **Examine and improve your results.**
Measure and improve what works. For example, change the language, the opt-in style, or the reward to increase your opt-in rate. You can do the same thing with your email sequence: if you discover that people aren't reading your emails, you could experiment with other subject lines. Keep in mind that the method of communicating with new email subscribers must be distinct from how you communicate with existing clients. You'll have to separate these two.

Remember, the most important rule of email marketing automation is prioritizing your users' experience; therefore, think outside the (in)box!

TOP TIP

Privacy

Cloud computing is no exception to the double-edged sword that is technology. Nevertheless, cloud services and hosted infrastructure have a slew of advantages.

For the interest of both the customer and the law, business owners must secure the confidentiality of their client's data, maintain data integrity and guarantee that information is readily available without jeopardizing security. The ethical principles of the legal community and associations must also be respected at all times.

If a hacker can breach a company network, whether this is cloud storage or apps on rented infrastructure, they can have complete access to all the private and confidential information. However, companies can easily prevent fraudsters from stealing documents and data by encrypting data at all times.

WHAT TO WATCH

Zoho, Hubspot and Salesforce CRM platforms review

Zoho CRM

Zoho CRM provides real-time customer reports and insights. Within your CRM, you may hold sales meetings and presentations, schedule webinars, and collaborate with your team. In addition, it has an AI-powered sales assistant that can make advanced deal predictions, send intelligent warnings and advise the optimal times to contact your leads.

Salesforce

Salesforce gives you a complete picture of your customer interactions. You can use Salesforce to manage customer accounts, track sales leads, track marketing activities and provide post-sale care. It assists in predicting which sales leads are most likely to convert, determining the optimal channel for engaging with clients, and personalizing the encounter depending on their actions.

HubSpot CRM

HubSpot CRM is a flexible platform that can be used by salespeople, marketers and customer support representatives in your company. It enables you to manage better, track and communicate with your consumers. For example, you can use the same platform to handle and reply to all of your customer inquiries.

Email design best practices

Email readers frequently scan over text and delete emails that don't provide value or do appear to be too content-heavy. Designing emails properly boosts engagement and prevents you from creating content that will put subscribers off.

Let's take a look at some of the best practices while designing your email:

- Write a compelling subject line.
- Create an eye-catching pre-header.

- Be succinct.
- Keep your email consistent with your brand.
- Consider your arrangement.
- Make each email unique.
- Include one-of-a-kind visual content.
- Add emojis.
- Use a responsive design.
- Include a call-to-action.
- Run an A/B test on your design.
- Create a signature for your emails.

Best copywriting practices

When reading online, people read words in a different way from when reading printed materials. Instead of reading from left to right and line by line, website visitors tend to scan the page for phrases or keywords that strike their eye.

So, what can you do to improve the readability of your email copy? First of all, format copy so that users can scan it – this includes including plenty of white space. If we know that consumers spend most of their time looking for specific information, the way you format your text can make a significant difference.

Here are a few best practices to remember:

- Make use of a lot of headlines.
- Use of bullet points.
- Keep paragraphs short.
- Place emphasis on important terminologies and phrases using bold or italic.
- Remove extraneous words.

As I've said throughout this book, copywriting is too wide a practice to discuss in full detail here. Many businesses employ expert copywriters to write sales copy that converts. Alternatively, you can look into learning various copywriting methods and applying them yourself. You should employ split testing for open rates on different subject lines, for example, and again on email body copy for clicks.

When to send

According to studies, prioritize your send days in the following order (CoSchedule, 2018):

1. **Tuesday:** According to the majority of the data from these researches, Tuesday is by far the best day to send emails.
2. **Thursday:** If you send two emails per week, Thursday is the best day to send at least one.
3. **Wednesday:** While no single survey has shown that Wednesday is the most popular, it has been ranked second on multiple occasions.

TOP TIP

Spam

According to one study, only 79 per cent of emails sent by legitimate email marketers make it to users' inboxes (Return Path, 2016).

How come? Well, even a minor mistake can drive an email from a trustworthy email marketer into the ninth circle of email marketing hell, resulting in catastrophic, almost irreversible harm to email deliverability and sender reputation. Therefore, it is crucial that the marketer is aware of the dos and don'ts of targeted email marketing. Below are some preventative measures so your emails can arrive where you intend them to – the inbox, not the spam folder.

What is spam and how can you avoid being treated like it?

Spam traps are an ISP's first line of protection against spammers. They're actually email addresses that were created with the sole purpose of detecting and tracking spammers.

If your triggered email is sent to such an address, your ISP will immediately mark you as a spammer. If this happens, your deliverability rates will suffer significantly, as your IP address and 'from domain' will be blocked. To become a 'good sender' once again may take up to a year.

Recycled spam traps are another issue to be concerned about. They are dormant email addresses that an ISP receives after a specific amount of time has passed with no activity. The implications of sending an email to such an address are less severe. Yours or your client's ESP will send you a bounce notification, advising that you're contacting a static address. If you continue to send emails to hard bounces, your ISP will eventually mark it as a spam-trap hit.

Here are some factors to keep in mind in order to avoid spam filters:

- Treat the unsubscribers with respect.
- Avoid using spam trigger words.
- Take good care of subject lines.
- Avoid media-rich content.
- Ask for the subscription twice.
- Use a well-known sender name.
- Take good care of the email body.
- Select a reputable ESP (email service provider).
- Acquire a third-party certificate.
- Check to see whether you've been blacklisted as a sender.
- Before sending your emails, make sure they are error-free.
- Keep on top of ISP practices, anti-spam law and spam filter technology.

Step four: Tracking and analysis

Each email marketing campaign is different but, regardless of the tools you use or the method you choose, you will almost certainly encounter stats at some point in the journey.

Metrics to track

OPEN RATE

Your open rate is the first and most basic measure you should keep track of. Although not every receiver will open every campaign you send, those who do will account for the majority of your open rate percentage. Don't be alarmed if your open rates look to be on the low side. Most email marketing campaigns tend to average around 30 per cent (Hubspot, 2021, 1).

Your title is the most crucial component that makes readers open your emails. Create an enticing, intriguing subject line to avoid being ignored or flagged as spam. You can use Mailchimp to track open rates once you've decided on an engaging headline.

CLICK-THROUGH RATE

This is the number of people who click on any links in your email. To get this number, we take the total number of views for a campaign and divide it by the percentage of visitors who went to another page after clicking.

Every well-designed email campaign should have a clear objective. You could have a variety of reasons, including increasing sales, providing relevant material to users and encouraging them to return to your site. Each objective should have one call-to-action – minimum. If your CTA is not getting clicks, the chances are that your copy, design or CTA itself is at fault.

CLICKS PER LINK

This metric lets you dig a little deeper and see which links people are clicking on. The benefit is that you can work out what kind of material your readers enjoy and use that data to develop future campaigns.

CONVERSION RATE

As we've mentioned, every innovative email campaign must have a purpose – whether that objective is to make a sale or simply to increase the number of clicks and visitors to your website. A user has converted when they've taken the desired action and the objective has been achieved. Therefore, the percentage of users you've managed to convert is tracked by your conversion rate.

The significance of this metric is self-evident. To track it, clearly define your objectives, then implement them with your email marketing software. Unfortunately, Mailchimp's free account does not feature goal tracking, but Google Analytics does. You could integrate the two platforms and then set up goal tracking in Google Analytics.

BOUNCE RATE

The bounce rate refers to the percentage of users who open your email and exit without engaging. They might have a quick scroll, but the key is that they take no action.

Users who bounce can be tracked in Mailchimp, and if the behaviour persists, they can be instantly removed from your list. If you don't want to use the latter option, Google Analytics has you covered with regular bounce-rate tracking.

UNSUBSCRIBES

Users will occasionally unsubscribe from your email list, which is a well-known email marketing indicator. Perhaps they didn't find your content relevant, or they were simply tired of getting too many emails. In any case, it's difficult to pinpoint the exact reason why consumers unsubscribe, but you can reduce the rate by improving the quality of your campaigns.

SPAM COMPLAINTS

One of the most hated aspects of running an email campaign is dealing with spam complaints. It's what happens when someone marks your email as spam. Your email marketing platform should track this and, if it happens too often, they may take action against your account. MailChimp devotes a whole area of its service to present you with the most up-to-date spam complaint reports.

The prime reason for spam complaints is pushy sales tactics. Quality and putting customers first are the best ways to prevent such complains.

FORWARDING RATE

When a user forwards your email campaign to another person, they contribute to your forwarding rate. It's calculated as the percentage of recipients who forwarded your email.

Your forwarding rate is an intriguing metric, since it indicates a degree of passion for your material that is above average. If someone chooses to share one of your campaigns, you can be confident that they find the information useful. Mailchimp has a handy way to track your forwarding rate. You can include a 'Forward to a Friend' link in your emails so you can later analyse how many people shared it.

TIME SPENT

This measure refers to the length of time a person spends looking at your campaign. Then, your email marketing software puts those times together to calculate an average of the time that people spend reading your emails.

Analyse your list health

An email list can only be called 'a healthy email list' if it contains few to no inactive recipients, bounces, spam complaints and unsubscribes. Consider list health to be a combination of several of the email marketing KPIs we've discussed thus far. You can say that your list is healthy if you can keep them at normal (or healthy) levels.

A/B testing

You can use A/B testing with email by sending one version of your campaign to a sample of your subscribers, and another version to a different sample. Compare the data to see which campaign will be most effective to use later on.

TRICKS AND TIPS FOR RUNNING A/B TESTS EFFECTIVELY

- **Come up with a hypothesis:** You need a strategic hypothesis about why one variation would perform better than the other to have the best chance of generating a positive boost in conversions from your A/B test. Ensure that you formulate a basic hypothesis for the test prior to starting.
- **Start prioritizing:** You'll probably have a lot of A/B test ideas between subject lines, button colours and copy modifications. Not all A/B tests will be valuable, so make sure you prioritize the ones that will provide the best information in the most efficient way.
- **Build on what you've learned so far:** Not every A/B test you perform will result in a good conversion boost. Some of your modifications will lower conversions, while others will have no effect at all.

The goal is to learn from each A/B test you run and apply what you've learned to produce more decisive campaigns in the future.

References

Campaign Monitor (2019) What is the average conversion rate for cart abandonment?, available at: https://www.campaignmonitor.com/resources/knowledge-base/what-is-the-average-conversion-rate-for-cart-abandonment/ (archived at https://perma.cc/F6UB-XYCH)

CoSchedule (2018) Best time to send email backed by 14 data-driven studies, available at: https://coschedule.com/blog/best-time-to-send-email (archived at https://perma.cc/N8HH-72PR)

Demand Gen Report (2018) The rise of marketing automation – statistics and trends, available at: https://www.demandgenreport.com/resources/infographics/the-rise-of-marketing-automation-statistics-and-trends (archived at https://perma.cc/5EYD-6CCK)

DMA (2013) National client email report 2013, available at: https://dma.org.uk/uploads/National%20Client%20Email%20Report%202013_53fdd7e6684de.pdf (archived at https://perma.cc/REX7-YBTT)

Emma (2019) 5 stats that reveal the state of email in 2019, available at: https://content.myemma.com/blog/5-stats-that-reveal-the-state-of-email-in-2019 (archived at https://perma.cc/PYR5-B8D2)

HubSpot (2021) (1) What's a good email open rate and click rate?, available at: https://blog.hubspot.com/marketing/email-open-click-rate-benchmark (archived at https://perma.cc/S3G8-V8YH)

McKinsey (2014) Why marketers should keep sending you e-mails, available at: https://www.mckinsey.com/business-functions/marketing-and-sales/our-insights/why-marketers-should-keep-sending-you-emails (archived at https://perma.cc/66CK-Z65E)

Moosend (2021) Shopping cart abandonment stats you'll need for 2021, available at: https://moosend.com/blog/cart-abandonment-stats/ (archived at https://perma.cc/U7KA-HJES)

Oracle (2017) Key learnings from Private Cloud Development, available at: Oracle-Pvt-Hybrid-Cloud-Tabulated.pdf

Return Path (2016), 2016 deliverability benchmark report, available at: https://returnpath.com/wp-content/uploads/2016/07/2016-Deliverability-Benchmark.pdf (archived at https://perma.cc/4Q2G-XXZT)

Software Advice (2014) CRM software userview, available at: http://www.softwareadvice.com/crm/userview/report-2014/ (archived at https://perma.cc/6LG3-TJZY)

Bibliography

Constant Contact (2021) available at: https://www.jeffbullas.com/go/constantcontact (archived at https://perma.cc/2PZ9-Z27Y)

European Commission (2021) What does the General Data Protection Regulation (GDPR) govern?, available at: https://ec.europa.eu/info/law/law-topic/data-protection/reform/what-does-general-data-protection-regulation-gdpr-govern_en (archived at https://perma.cc/UP9H-KQMW)

Google, Bounce rate – Analytics Help, available at: https://support.google.com/analytics/answer/1009409?hl=en (archived at https://perma.cc/SUY3-YYS6)

Google, Create, edit, and share goals – Analytics Help, available at: https://support.google.com/analytics/answer/1032415?hl=en (archived at https://perma.cc/6WK6-DXP6)

Hubspot (2021) (2) Inbound marketing, sales, and service software, available at: https://www.hubspot.com/ (archived at https://perma.cc/X97R-6UE9)

Infusionsoft (2021) Grow sales and save time with marketing automation, available at: https://www.infusionsoft.com/ (archived at https://perma.cc/R8SM-J7XH)

Jeff Bullas / Mihai, C (2017) The complete guide to email automation for beginners, available at: https://www.jeffbullas.com/complete-guide-email-automation-beginners/ (archived at https://perma.cc/W45G-BUCP)

Lucidchart (2021) Intelligent diagramming, available at: https://www.lucidcharts.com/ (archived at https://perma.cc/K7HU-92JS)

Mailchimp (2021) (1) Add the forward to a friend link, available at: https://mailchimp.com/help/add-the-forward-to-a-friend-link/ (archived at https://perma.cc/BXL4-J5CY)

Mailchimp (2021) (2) View abuse complaints, available at: http://kb.mailchimp.com/reports/view-abuse-complaints (archived at https://perma.cc/47Q7-YLGA)

Mailchimp (*nd*) (1) Integrate Google Analytics with Mailchimp, available at: http://kb.mailchimp.com/integrations/e-commerce/integrate-google-analytics-with-mailchimp (archived at https://perma.cc/L758-V56A)

Mailchimp (*nd*) (2) Use open tracking in emails, available at: https://mailchimp.com/help/about-open-tracking/ (archived at https://perma.cc/KR44-TBU5)

Mbsy (2021) #1 referral marketing software by Ambassador, available at: https://mbsy.co/convertkit/6164925 (archived at https://perma.cc/62T2-JLNA)

11

Using e-commerce and retail partners to scale your merchandizing

In this chapter, we will discuss how e-commerce and retail partnerships enhance your business's scalability. First, e-commerce is a digital industry worthy of your attention. In simple terms, e-commerce refers to the buying and selling of goods and/or services over the internet. E-commerce can work as a substitute for or a complement to 'bricks and mortar' stores.

This term may strike you as broad, but don't let that discourage you from considering e-commerce. Within the world of e-commerce, there are five important models to know:

1. **Business to Consumer** (B2C): 'go-between' businesses that connect buyers to sellers (such as Expedia, Trivago);
2. **Business to Business** (B2B): companies buying and selling from other companies (such as IBM);
3. **Direct to Consumer** (D2C): a manufacturer/producer that sells its good directly to consumers without a distributor or retailors (such as Glossier, Everlane Stitch Fix);
4. **Consumer to Consumer** (C2C): transactions between two private-end users via an online platform (for example eBay, Etsy);
5. **Consumer to Business** (C2B): consumers who provide services (reviews, referrals and so on) to companies.

Benefits of e-commerce

As you can see, the variety of e-commerce models allows you to pick the best strategy for your business. Why else should you choose e-commerce? This mode of merchandizing helps streamline and scale your business. To be specific, here are four benefits of choosing e-commerce:

1. **Low cost:** E-commerce opens up possibilities for effective online and social media marketing. These ads can direct potential consumers straight to your website through one click. You can also cut costs by replacing some employees with automated checkout, billing and other operational processes (The Balance Small Business, 2019).
2. **Easy to track stock and logistics:** Unlike physical stores, online stores can keep tabs on a customer's browsing and buying behaviour. You can then use that data to inform targeted (and retargeted) marketing (Marketing91, 2021).
3. **Expands consumer base:** E-commerce transcends geographical limitations without requiring you to maintain a physical store chain. When you move your business to the digital marketplace, you can more readily interact with consumers from all over the world, not just those in the physical location of your stores.
4. **Infinite space:** With an online store, you do not have to worry about running out of physical space for inventory, cashiers, product lines and so on (Oberlo, 2021).

Retail partnerships

Now that you have a brief overview of e-commerce, let's look at retail partnerships. In this approach, businesses team up with one another to sell their own products in a complementary, non-competitive agreement. These partnerships assume a number of forms, but I will draw your attention to six popular models (LEK Consulting, 2015):

1. **Traditional brand-retail partnerships:** One brand opens a 'store-in-a-store' space within a larger retail setting, like a department store.
2. **Retail-retail partnerships:** One retailer gains exclusive control of a category within another retailer's store (such as CVS Pharmacy in Target).

3 **Marketing partnerships:** Brands with a shared target audience co-develop marketing content.
4 **Loyalty partnerships:** Companies share incentives and data across loyalty programmes.
5 **Digital partnerships:** A smaller brand works with a larger e-commerce presence in the digital equivalent of a shopping centre.
6 **Events:** Two or more businesses co-host a digital/physical event with promotions, shared marketing and so on.

Like e-commerce, retail partnerships can bolster your business's viability. It is, simply put, a win-win situation; all involved businesses stand to profit greatly by joining forces in the marketplace. We will explore more of these benefits in step seven of this chapter.

All in all, both e-commerce and retail partnerships are worthwhile tactics to consider for your business. In the following steps, we will break down everything you need to know to make well-informed decisions about these areas. The steps are as follows:

1 Selecting the right product.
2 Setting up an e-commerce store.
3 Manufacturing, packaging and shipping the product.
4 E-commerce customer service.
5 Launching an e-commerce store.
6 Scaling your business.
7 Retail partnerships.

Step one: Selecting the right product

Before you leap into the world of e-commerce, you must decide on your product(s). Broadly speaking, your ideal product should meet a set of tried-and-trusted criteria:

- decent sales volume – a high number of units within a certain reporting period;
- low seasonality – sells consistently throughout the year instead of experiencing predictable peaks and valleys;

- low competition – not heavily associated with one brand name already;
- room for improvement – a product that you can adapt based on customer feedback;
- easily manufactured and shippable – should balance cost efficiency with value;
- follows trends – a product in an industry of mass commercial interest.

Furthermore, you should definitely avoid products with high shipping costs, any potential legal entanglements, or from sectors outside of your expertise.

Identify a unique value proposition (UVP)

You want to pick a product of high value in the market. Notably, value is distinct from price (which we will address later!). First, you need to identify and consider gaps in the market that only your business can fill. You should ask yourself: 'What niche desire will my product cater to?' As you research, you can also pinpoint your competitors' trendiest products and contemplate ways to provide an improved version of their product. The key to success here is creative and innovative thinking.

Test viability

Ahead of releasing your product to the market, it is important to test its viability. For an initial test, you can conduct Amazon category searches and peruse Google ads to gauge the demand for your product. Test keywords and earmark the most searched ones for your marketing strategies. Once you have cleared this test, you may consider creating a prototype to test on small groups matching your targeted audience. Their response to your prototype gives you an opportunity to anticipate your product's success and to integrate more improvements to the product.

Pricing strategies

While value and price are different metrics, you should consider both before launching your e-commerce store. Pricing requires a careful analysis. Your goal is to maximize profit margins by including *all* costs associated with the product, even marketing campaigns. To calculate price, you can opt for one of the following approaches (Oberlo, 2020):

- **Cost-based pricing:** This is the most straightforward method of determining price. For this calculation, you add the manufacturing cost, the shipping cost and your preferred margin.
- **Competition-based pricing:** Choose this method if you're interested in better understanding your competitors. Here, you analyse other brands with a similar product, perhaps with a price tracking tool, to identify a suitable price range for your product.
- **Value-based pricing:** This is best for long-term planning. You combine the cost-based (your baseline) and competition-based strategies (competition price) to create a range of potential prices. Then, you can scale your prices based on the success of your product.

CASE STUDY

The challenge

A major retailer was running e-commerce websites across the globe with local sites in each country. Every site was managed by its country team and so, while there were similarities, each country was different in its content and its approach to positioning its products. While that led to some strong localization, it also meant that learnings were not integrated consistently across the sites.

The solution

The company looked at how it could keep the localization while ensuring consistency. After researching technology options, they settled on a solution – to use a headless commerce system. After selecting a partner, they reviewed the product and content across the sites and found that over 85 per cent of it was the same. On this basis, they were able to quickly build the same templates, features and optimized journeys for all sites but still allow for localization.

The results

The company no longer needed to build hundreds of unique pages, but was able to build one structure and optimize it for the entire global network, saving thousands of hours of work and increasing conversion rates across every site in the portfolio.

Step two: Setting up an e-commerce store

After choosing your product(s), your next step is to organize your e-commerce store. This task requires you to transform a blank web page into a personalized online shopping experience for your customers. As you build your digital storefront, you will consider both practical and cosmetic considerations. Treat each of the following decisions with equal weight as you would with a bricks-and-mortar store.

Claiming a space

Every e-commerce store must have its own domain. You should secure a .com or .org link address with a short, memorable, intuitive domain name. When choosing your name, make sure no one uses your domain name (or something similar) on popular social media platforms like Twitter, Facebook and Instagram.

Once you have secured your domain, you should shift focus to your e-commerce store's infrastructure. The web pages must be easy to navigate and intuitive with drop-down menus and searchable categories. Here are a few must-have elements to include in your e-commerce store:

- **Story page** (or an **about page**): You should dedicate this web page to the history behind your business. Make it personable and really put a human face to your company.
- **Shipping and returns:** Online shoppers will always want to know estimated shipping times, domestic and international shipping rates and your return policy. This information should be as accessible as possible to put your customers at ease.
- **Customer service and contact:** Usually located at the bottom of every web page, include a customer service phone number, email, and – if you have the employee base – a chat box for your customers to ask questions or notify you of any glitches.
- **Frequently asked questions:** As your business grows, some questions will come up again and again. Once you learn of these common concerns, collate them on one web page for your customers to reference.
- **Call-to-actions:** These are snappy phrases to encourage customers to sign-up/subscribe to your business's mailing list or recurring service. CTAs usually appear as pop-up pages with two or three fields for the customer's name, email address and phone number or physical address.

- **Social 'proof' or testimonials:** Keep track of positive reviews and testimonials and disperse them through your e-commerce store to increase new customers' confidence in your product.
- **Product descriptions:** Since your customers cannot physically engage with your product, your descriptions must be as detailed as possible. Be sure to include all relevant information like colour options, sizes, potential uses, warranties and so on.
- **Visual merchandizing:** Your pictures of your product can make or break a sale. Carefully consider an appropriate style and colour scheme to create a visually appealing display.

Choosing an e-commerce platform

If these directives feel a bit overwhelming to you, never fear. You can also opt to set up your store through an existing e-commerce platform. Usually, this option requires monthly and/or transaction fees, but it will streamline your set-up process and expose you to e-commerce markets.

AMAZON

If you're looking for a simple, no-fuss approach, opt for Amazon. Through Amazon, you can set up a digital storefront connected to their infrastructure and branding. Amazon even offers an option for you to ship products via 'Fulfilled by Amazon' so that you do not have to worry about negotiating shipping rates. Amazon's drawbacks are its limited set of storefront templates and its mass of associated fees, but, perhaps the cost is a fair trade-off for the exposure to millions of potential customers.

SHOPIFY

Shopify works best if you have a bigger budget to take advantage of its perks. The platform comes with built-in SEO features, automated marketing and educational materials. What's more, Shopify has over 70 professional and free store themes. It also offers an expert marketplace, where you can hire a freelancer or agency to help you manage your online business. If you prefer to complete that work yourself, Shopify includes over 6,000 apps to help you track, manage and optimize your e-commerce store. You can test Shopify for 14 days before starting monthly payments.

ETSY

Owners of small businesses selling handmade and unique products should choose Etsy over the other options. Etsy has a host of special features, including statistics, beginner's guides and a seller handbook. You can customize your Etsy storefront with your brand and logo and optimize your shop for Etsy's internal search bar. Despite Etsy's assortment of listing, advertisement and transaction fees, you can save up to 30 per cent on shipping by purchasing labels from Etsy.

WOOCOMMERCE

This platform differs from the others on this list because it is a plug-in. In order to use WooCommerce, you must have a WordPress blog and a host website for your e-commerce store. Being a plug-in, WooCommerce has flexible costs. You can customize your cost based on your store's website host and your domain cost. WooCommerce provides a variety of features, including automated taxes, translation into 24 languages and a security package through Jetpack.

BIGCOMMERCE

If you have a passion for innovation, take a look at BigCommerce. Its state-of-the-art model allows you to integrate your e-commerce store with Amazon, eBay, Google and Facebook. As a forward-thinking, trendy platform, BigCommerce prioritizes convenience by allowing digital wallets (such as Apple Pay), accepting over 100 currencies, and offering 24/7 tech support. As with Shopify, you can experience a free trial before opting into a monthly subscription.

TOP TIP
Product listing

A product listing page presents a list of products based on a category or search query. This organization method enables your website to funnel consumers to relevant product detail pages. Rich with metadata and keywords, your product listing pages can influence SEO rankings and the internal structure of your e-commerce store.

Eight aspects of product listings

By investing in your product listings, you will promote product discovery, encourage user engagement, and decrease purchase time. Consider the following aspects to better enhance and streamline your consumers' experiences (AB Tasty, 2020):

1. **Headers**: Treat every web page header as a promotional space. Focus on keywords.
2. **List view vs grid view**: Choose which web page view suits your product. List view is better for products that require extensive info and specs (like tech). Grid view works better for products that rely on visual comparison.
3. **Products per page and per row**: Depending on the size of your images, the number of products, and the volume of product information, you can decide how to arrange your products on a web page without cluttering it.
4. **Product thumbnails**: These stylish, small pictures are especially important for visually driven industries.
5. **Navigation**: One of your top priorities is to craft the most intuitive website possible. Help your customers by providing ways to sort/rank products according to criteria (colour, type, shape, size and so on).
6. **Product info**: Provide background on each product. You can include star ratings, discounts, stock availability, an add to cart button and a short description of the product.
7. **Quick view**: You could include a miniature version of each product page with an embedded 'add to cart' button.
8. **SEO**: To boost your e-commerce store's visibility, be sure to make your product pages keyword rich, as product listing pages account for 50 per cent of all e-commerce traffic.

Step three: Manufacturing, packaging and shipping

Manufacturing, packaging and shipping are important logistical concerns to address before your e-commerce store goes live. These areas may feel like a low priority in comparison with what we have discussed thus far, but they are integral to your online business's success.

Manufacturing

Unless you plan to make your product in-house, you will need to secure a manufacturing partnership. Your manufacturer is in charge of bringing your product design to fruition. You want a manufacturer who both understands your goals and can provide the highest-quality product possible.

Location is another key factor in choosing your manufacturer. Perhaps, your brand emphasizes community, so you want to hire a local manufacturer. On the other hand, your brand may be all about globalism, and so working with an international manufacturer better reflects your goals. No matter your parameters, you will want to pursue a positive, long-term working relationship with your chosen manufacturer.

Packaging

A product's packaging is almost as important as the product itself. Your packaging should fit your carefully crafted branding while being of low cost and efficient. You may decide to imprint your logo on every package or to use customized shipping paper. Some companies, like Amazon, even offer a gift-wrapping option convenient for special events, birthdays and holidays. For additional ideas, research your competitors to see how they personalize their packaging.

Shipping

Once you have settled on a manufacturer and designed your packaging, you will need to work out the best shipping model for you. The previously mentioned e-commerce platforms offer a variety of shipping options, but you may also consider third parties if they provide simpler logistics or cheaper fees. If you plan to ship internationally, you will also want to consider customs regulations and calculate how those will impact your pricing. In the event that you decide to manufacture your products in-house, the most sensible option may be to ship from your place of business or from your workshop.

Distribution

To simplify this step in your e-commerce process, you can opt to work with a distributor. Distributors function as intermediary entities between the manufacturer and the retailer. They expedite the logistical process of getting manufactured goods in the hands of the consumer. With your distributor(s), you can construct one of three distribution strategies: intensive, exclusive or selective. For the intensive strategy, you will plan to sell your products in as many outlets as you can. Exclusive distribution requires you to limit distribution to one or very few outlets. Similarly, selective distribution involves selling your product at certain outlets in specific locations.

In business terminology, any relationship between manufacturers, retailers and their intermediaries is called a distribution channel or supply chain. Distribution channels come in two main forms: direct and indirect. Direct channels allow consumers to purchase products from the manufacturer; indirect channels allow consumers to purchase products from a wholesaler or retailer. Generally speaking, the more intermediaries in a distribution, the more a product's price will increase. Depending on your product, you may decide that having a distributor best ensures hassle-free experiences for your consumers. However, if you manufacture your own products, as an Etsy seller might, a direct-to-consumer model will make the most sense for your business.

Step four: E-commerce customer service

About 55 per cent of e-commerce stores fail because of poor customer retention. You can avoid this pitfall by providing quality customer service from day one. E-commerce stores with poor customer service lose consumers because they ineptly handle (or completely ignore!) reports of defective products, unfulfilled/incorrect orders, or lapsed refunds. By integrating customer service into your e-commerce infrastructure, you will ensure that these concerns do not slip through the cracks and that your valued customers feel heard. Here are six ways to enhance your e-commerce store's customer service:

1 **Automated customer support email:** Craft an automatic email for whenever a customer submits a report or query. This email should include the report's case number and an estimated response time. A small gesture, this automated email assures the customer that their concern has been received and will be acted upon.

2 **Email templates for common enquiries:** While you should encourage your customer service employees to be personable and patient, help them by providing a set of templates for frequently asked questions. The uniformity will increase your business's perceived professionalism.

3 **Website chat boxes or help desks:** Embed in your website live chat boxes or a help desk for customers to ask quick, simple questions as they shop. By including these immediate customer service channels, you help bring a customer closer to buying their chosen product or at least affirm their confidence in your business.
4 **Personalized customer service:** If you run a small business on Etsy or another platform, show your customers appreciation by including handwritten or signed thank-you notes with their purchases. A simple expression of gratitude goes a long way in building strong, positive relationships with your customers.
5 **Free items:** Offer first-time or loyal customers free items to go with their purchases. These can either be a surprise good hidden in the packaging or a perk shown at the customer's online checkout.
6 **FAQs:** As discussed in step four, you should include a web page dedicated to recurring customer service questions.

Step five: Launching an e-commerce store

After shoring up your infrastructure, it is time to launch your online business. Even though your ribbon-cutting will happen digitally, the grand opening of your digital store can be just as exciting as the launch for-a bricks and-mortar store. Follow this section carefully to ensure your grand opening proceeds without any hitches.

Choose the right launch time

Your optimal launch time will work for most or all of your target audience's time zones and not conflict with any major events or holidays. Most importantly, you will want to double-check that your stock is ready to go.

Create a landing page

Ahead of your launch, customers may search for your website, so craft a landing page to greet them. This page should include minimal text but showcase your brand and ethos. Keep it sleek and uncluttered and feature high-resolution photographs of your top products. You can also include social media widgets and empty fields to encourage interested customers onto a marketing mailing list.

Use social media

Generate buzz for your store's launch via social media platforms such as Instagram. Regular postings leading up to your grand opening can drive interest and keep your business at the front of people's minds. Through hashtags or paid campaigns, you can target your desired audience, sharing testimonials and alluring product sneak peeks.

Launch your store

The final step is the launch itself. Make sure to post reminders to your email list and to all of your social media platforms. You should also promote opening day/week sales and promotions to draw more traffic to your e-commerce grand opening.

Step six: Scaling your business

At this point, your business is up and running smoothly, which encourages you to set your sights on scalability and growth. Through a combination of tracking, automating and advertising tactics, you can work smarter (not harder) while growing your e-commerce store. Read on to learn about key performance indicators, hiring automation and e-commerce marketing.

Key performance indicators (KPIs)

Track the following KPIs in order to collate helpful data:

- **sales per month** – an intuitive KPI, simply comparing how many sales your business makes per month;
- **average order size/value** – how many items in an average order, or the worth of an average order
- **visitor conversion rates** – what percentage of visitors subsequently purchased goods or services;

- **cart abandonment rates** – what percentage of visitors who begin a cart do not complete their purchase;
- **site traffic** – how many distinct consumers visit your site on a given day/month/week/year;
- **sources of traffic** – whether consumers access your link via Google search, social media, advertisements, mailing lists or word of mouth;
- **average time** – how long a visitor spends on the site;
- **number of email subscribers** – how your number of email subscribers fluctuates throughout the fiscal year;
- **social media followers** – track and compare social media followers based on the platform.

Hiring

As your business grows, you should consider hiring employees to help keep your e-commerce store up to date and as efficient as possible. Here are a few departments where you may want extra assistance:

- **Graphic design and copywriting**
  Creating fresh, exciting content for your e-commerce store takes time, dedication and expertise. Hire designers and copywriters who can consistently provide quality content for all of your advertising campaigns, promotions and discounts. Designers may even help you retool your logo.
- **Social media**
  Some influencers use social media accounts as their main form of income, so it makes sense to treat social media management as a part- or full-time occupation. By delegating social media to your employees, you can feel assured that your brand will be consistently engaging with potential consumers all over the world.
- **Basic admin**
  You can also hire employees to run communications throughout your distribution channel and to handle any glitches on the website. These employees act as initial problem-solvers who treat small hiccups so that you can focus on bigger crises.
- **Customer service**
  Especially if you incorporate a chat box, virtual help desk or phone line, you should hire plenty of customer service employees to provide 24/7 assistance. These employees are public-facing representatives of your

brand. Conduct specific interviews to ensure your customer service employees reflect your goals and the quality experience you wish to provide.

Automation

With the advance of modern technology, you do not need to hire a person to complete every single task. You can easily automate and schedule marketing materials across your email lists and social media. Also, about 91 per cent of companies with more than 11 employees use a (CRM) system to automatically collect, track and analyse data (Nomalys, 2019).

Advertising

As your business grows, you want to enact strong, innovative advertisement tactics to both bring in new customers and retarget returning customers. Learn the different types of e-commerce marketing and best practices to keep your momentum.

TYPES OF E-COMMERCE MARKETING

E-commerce marketing relies on social media, digital content, search engines and more to promote products and service across the internet. To determine which strategies best suit your business, it is helpful to divide marketing into seven broad categories (HubSpot, 2020):

1. **Social media marketing**
   Create launch pages on the most popular social networks. On Instagram, specifically, you can create a mini-store within your Instagram profile. You (and other Instagram users) can also tag your products in timeline posts and stories. Instagram's capabilities streamline purchasing and encourage impulse buying, two great boosts to your conversation rates. Other forms of social media marketing include display and banner ads.
2. **Content marketing**
   Hire copywriters to produce articles, blog posts and videos about your products, or you can create content yourself. Producing content on a consistent basis will help improve your website's ranking within search engines. Importantly, this content also includes your product page copy. As we discussed in step two, your product listing pages must be rich in keywords and the product's name.

3 **Search engine marketing**
Research your keywords for search engine optimization (SEO) and invest in pay-per-click (PPC) and product-specific ad campaigns. PPC campaigns through Google guarantee to show your relevant web pages to potential buyers whenever they search keywords matching your campaign. If need be, you may want to register with Google Ads.

4 **Email marketing**
Set up automated email campaigns to your subscribers. These campaigns can take the form of monthly newsletters, post-purchase follow-ups, or even shopping cart reminders. In post-purchase follow-ups, consider asking your customers to leave a review. For shopping cart reminder emails, both encourage your customers to complete their purchase and recommend similar products.

5 **Influencer marketing**
Collaborate with Instagram influencers to generate sponsored posts tagging your business and showing your products. An influencer can be an 'ordinary' person, a celebrity, or a community managing an Instagram account. Micro-influencers, who have between 10,000 and 50,000 followers, are usually the most cost-effective partners as they tend to have a higher engagement rate.

6 **Affiliate marketing**
Work with people and businesses who will help to sell your product for a commission. See Chapter 6 for more details on affiliate marketing.

7 **Local marketing**
Use tracking cookies to find localities where you can offer discounts or focus marketing efforts.

No matter which marketing strategies you use, here are seven techniques to improve your advertising efforts (Instapage, 2020):

1 **Use Google Ads:** Peruse Adwords to identify product keywords that will appear on search results.

2 **Go mobile:** Top advisors estimate that 73 per cent of e-commerce will take place on a mobile device. Prioritize mobile marketing and make sure all graphics are compatible with mobile dimensions.

3 **Consider post-click optimization:** Not every advertisement's link should go to the home page. Personalize each ad to send consumers to the web page most relevant to that ad. This process may sound tedious, but there are automation tools to expedite page creation.

4 **Optimize your conversion rate:** Your conversation rate refers to the number of people who visit a webpage or view an advertisement compared to the number of people who fulfil the webpage or ad's goal (a purchase, email sign-up and so on). You can use A/B and multivariate testing to form and test out methods to improve your conversion rates.

5 **Incorporate omni-channels:** Track your customers' purchase habits in-store and online to inform which advertisements they will see online, either via Google search or social media. Your advertising efforts should use many channels, not just your online store and email list.

6 **Add chatbots:** Artificial intelligence can help encourage web page visitors to complete a purchase. You can code chatbots into your e-commerce store so that a little pop-up greets every visitor. For a well-developed example, consider Kayak's chatbot, which helps customers book a trip completely through artificial intelligence. While a new marketing strategy, it is worth a try since experts predict that chatbots will comprise a $1.3 billion market by 2024.

7 **Demographic targeting and retargeting on social media:** Use your customers' data to automate advertisements for similar products all over social media. 78 per cent of shoppers between 18 and 34 say that they found new products from Facebook, so be sure to invest in Facebook advertisement campaigns.

TOP TIP

Upselling and cross-selling

Upselling and cross-selling are two other advertising tactics. Upselling encourages customers to buy a better, more expensive version of a product. Perhaps the more expensive product has value-added features or changes to the old model. Cross-selling encourages customers to buy additional products to complete their purchase (*aka* bundling).

Sometimes upselling and cross-selling are seen as unethical practices to cheat the customer out of more money. I would like to encourage a mindset shift. These selling tactics expose customers to the best possible deal to fulfil their needs. Also, these strategies are proven to increase customer retention, average order value and lifetime value. Remember: you always want to prioritize customer retention. The probability of selling to an existing customer is 60–70 per cent as opposed to 5–20 per cent for selling to a new customer.

How to upsell and cross-sell

Like all business strategies, upselling and cross-selling's success depends on timing and execution. You should only upsell most reviewed and/or bestselling products. Products optimal for cross-selling are often at least 60 per cent cheaper than the customer's already chosen product. To make your up- or cross-sell attractive, try these methods:

- Narrow choices. Refrain from overwhelming your customer by offering too many choices! When upselling, gently offer one or two options to the customer. Do not pressure them with more options if they decline your initial upsell.
- Offer bundles. When cross-selling, eliminate choice all together by presenting the customer with a bundle of related products, which includes the product they already intend to purchase.
- Price anchor. A popular up sell method, use a dummy choice to make the superior choice look cheaper. For example, you may sell one book for $3, two books for $6 (dummy choice!), and three books for $7.
- Post-purchase. Cross-selling can occur after the customer has checked out. Use confirmation pages and other post-purchase confirmations to present the customer with more products, incentives and discounts.

Step seven: Retail partnerships

For our final step, let's revisit retail partnerships. As a reminder, retail partnerships involve two or more businesses collaborating for mutually beneficial purposes. This section will describe the types of partnerships in more detail, outline the benefits of this approach and provide tips for maintaining a successful retail partnership. Each partnership consists of the donor(s) and the host(s).

Types of partnership

TRADITIONAL BRAND-RETAIL PARTNERSHIPS

One brand (donor) opens a 'store-in-a-store' space within a larger retail setting (host). This model is most apparent in department stores, where clothing and cosmetic brands own outlets within a host department store (LEK Consulting, 2015).

RETAIL-RETAIL PARTNERSHIPS

One retailer (donor) gains exclusive control of a category within another retailer's store (host). For instance, CVS has acquired all of Target's pharmacies.

MARKETING PARTNERSHIPS

Two or more brands with a shared target audience co-develop marketing content. By collaborating on marketing, all brands lower their customer acquisition costs while seeing better returns on investment. In this partnership, the more experienced and established brand acts as the host.

LOYALTY PARTNERSHIPS

A partnership in which companies share incentives and data across loyalty programmes, this model is more popular in the UK and Canada than in the US. However, consider Sears' rewards programme, which is run by American Express. In this example, Sears acts as the host and American Express acts as the donor.

DIGITAL PARTNERSHIPS

A smaller brand (donor) works with a larger e-commerce presence (host) in the digital equivalent of a shopping centre. Explore this model if you are a small business looking to jump-start an online presence.

EVENTS

Two or more businesses co-host a digital or physical event with promotions, shared marketing and so on. Just as with marketing partnerships, the more established brand providing a physical/digital space acts as the host.

Benefits of partnerships

Since the host and donor business take on different roles, they also experience a different set of benefits. Effective retail partnerships should be beneficial to your business, regardless of your role in them.

HOST BENEFITS

- **Use of space**
  For physical businesses, hosts can personalize their shopping experience by incorporating donors into their real estate. In digital space, hosts can devote entire web pages to their donor's business. In both scenarios, this collaboration creates a more dynamic storefront and adds some novelty for existing customers.
- **More customer traffic**
  Like launching a new product line, introducing a donor will draw new consumers to the host retailer. The partnership will create opportunities for consumers to cross-shop, increasing their likelihood of engaging with both the host and donor retailers.
- **Improved customer experience**
  The retail partnership, if done well, will create fresh retail experiences for the host's customer base. The host may even choose their partnerships based on which retailers complement their inventory. For instance, a clothing retailer may partner with a lingerie retailer.
- **Increased competitiveness and profitability**
  The host retailer can choose a donor retailer with assets differing from their own to reap the benefits. For instance, the host may choose a donor with a wider inventory, more developed distributor channels, or greater knowledge of a specialized market.

DONOR BENEFITS

- **Reduced costs**
  For donors, partnering with a host will almost always be cheaper than breaking into the market on their own. By working with a host retailer, the donor benefits from the more established host's equity, spurring rapid growth.
- **Attracting new consumers**
  The donor's association with the host will validate their respectability, professionalism and quality. Whether the partnership revolves around co-marketing or a shared location, this endorsement of the donor will encourage new customers to at least peruse its retail offerings.
- **Gaining experience**
  Small donors can use their retail partnerships as a learning experience. While benefiting from the host's relative expertise, the donor can perfect a scalability model unique to their brand.

Dangers of partnerships

As you can see, retail partnerships offer plenty of perks for both the host and donor retailers. However, each partner must enter the partnership with caution, ensuring the partnership's parameters adhere to all parties' growth strategies. Here are a few common pitfalls to avoid:

WEAK STRATEGIC RATIONALE

Do not enter into a retail partnership for the sake of it. Instead, carefully consider your business's internal strategy and how exactly your partner factors into that strategy. To strengthen your strategic rationale, ask yourself a few questions:

- What benefits does my retail partner have to offer?
- Will these benefits enhance my retail goals?
- How will this partnership improve the customer's experience?

LOSS OF IDENTITY

Both hosts and donors should question whether or not the partnership aligns with their customers' expectations. Retail partnerships can reshape but should not override your existing brand.

UNHEALTHY PARTNERSHIPS

Be aware of your retail partner's potential weaknesses. While in a partnership, your business will be connected to any and all of your partner's developments – both good and bad. For example, a retailer at risk of going out of business would not make a healthy partner.

How to make a successful partnership

Now you know what to avoid. On the other hand, here are four positive traits to look for in a retail partner:

1. **Market overlap:** You want a retail partner with a similar, but not identical, customer base in order to expand your business's share of the market.
2. **Clear communication of expectations:** Your partner should know and communicate their goals and incentives from the outset. Knowing your partner's expectations helps you understand the nature of the partnership.

3 **Ample resources:** As a mutually beneficial relationship, your retail partner must offer some resources to make the partnership fruitful.

4 **Flexibility:** While having set goals is important, you should also look for a retail partner with the willingness to renegotiate the partnership as the relationship develops.

References

AB Tasty (2020) The definitive guide to creating perfect product listing pages in 2020, available at: https://www.abtasty.com/blog/product-listing-pages-optimization/ (archived at https://perma.cc/3SPC-XKDS)

The Balance Small Business (2019) Advantages and disadvantages of e-commerce, available at: https://www.thebalancesmb.com/ecommerce-pros-and-cons-1141609 (archived at https://perma.cc/T46D-42YQ)

HubSpot (2020) Everything you need to know about ecommerce marketing, available at: https://blog.hubspot.com/marketing/ecommerce-marketing (archived at https://perma.cc/6U9J-CFBH)

Instapage (2020) How your team can save money on advertising campaigns with Instapage during an economic slowdown, available at: https://instapage.com/blog/save-money-advertising (archived at https://perma.cc/NXD3-F32P)

LEK Consulting (2015) Better together: The new logic of retail partnerships, *Executive Insights*, **XVII**, 39, available at: https://www.lek.com/sites/default/files/insights/pdf-attachments/Retail-Partnerships_LEK-ExecutiveInsights-1739.pdf (archived at https://perma.cc/6PWN-THGF)

Marketing91 (2021) Top 25 ecommerce trends to watch for in 2021, available at: https://www.marketing91.com/tag/ecommerce/ (archived at https://perma.cc/K4JY-28RG)

Nomalys (2019) 28 surprising CRM statistics about adoption, features, benefits and mobility, available at: https://www.nomalys.com/en/28-surprising-crm-statistics-about-adoption-features-benefits-and-mobility/ (archived at https://perma.cc/ACQ2-UYM3)

Oberlo (2020) Pricing your products – pricing strategies for ecommerce businesses, available at: https://www.oberlo.co.uk/blog/pricing-strategy-for-ecommerce (archived at https://perma.cc/SM96-KHEK)

Oberlo (2021) The ultimate guide to starting your first ecommerce business, available at: https://www.oberlo.com/ebooks/starting-ecommerce (archived at https://perma.cc/2VSX-S5YY)

12

Providing customer service that delivers high review scores and builds loyalty

Introduction

In today's world, delivering outstanding customer service is the key to growing your business and building brand loyalty. Prioritizing customers' needs elevates their experience on the whole, which ultimately increases your revenue. Customer service can be the key to your success or downfall, especially if you've had a hard time retaining customers. Providing good customer service shows that you value your customers and that you're willing to act as a resource.

Customers want various channels available to communicate with your brand when seeking guidance or support. Make yourself available to solve their problems and give them a reason to talk about your brand with their friends and relatives. Positive customer experience increases the odds that they'll buy again and again, becoming loyal, returning customers.

To provide better customer service, you need to analyse the likes and dislikes of your core customer groups. Once you understand their problems, you can decide on the appropriate type of response.

The most effective and basic type of customer service is usually delivered by phone. This is probably the most popular choice. Speaking directly to a person can strengthen relationships with your customers and have a more meaningful impact than talking over text.

Other popular customer service avenues include email, live chat, on-site service or social media contacts. Some of these options may be more appealing to certain demographics. For example, young people who are often on Twitter might find it easier to send a DM than to call in to discuss an issue.

Now that you understand the fundamentals, let's get to the core issues and look at some strategies for improving your customer experience.

TOP TIP

Reviews

Customer reviews influence the decision-making process for others. Any business has to receive both good and bad responses to properly assess its strong and weak points.

Reviews are critical, but how exactly do they influence prospective buyers? Positive reviews give visitors more confidence in the product or service, reduce doubts as to the legitimacy of the company or quality of the product or service, and ultimately lead to more conversions.

Negative reviews are just as important as five-star ratings. If you don't have a single unsatisfied customer, others may think your positive reviews are fake.

In addition, reviews can be an excellent way to demonstrate that your customer service works well. Your immediate responses and actions to correct an issue will show potential clients that you truly care about their opinions.

Step one: Understanding customer expectations

Every company wants to meet and exceed customer expectations, so let's take a closer look at what customer expectations are. Customer expectations are the perceptions a customer has of a product, service or brand. For instance, customers that buy an iMac instead of a PC have a set of expectations about the sleek design of that product.

Consumer expectations are created in the minds of consumers based on their pre-existing experience and knowledge. These opinions and values may vary depending on your specific industry. Consider the roles of cost, reliability, function and convenience as they apply to your specific product or service.

Performance standards

Customer service performance standards establish how customers should be treated. Educating employees on these standards helps to improve your operations and gain loyal customers. Define the ideal experience you want customers to have and use that to create your standards.

Assess your service model in depth. Think about how well your employees can fulfil any tasks that customer experience depends on, and consider how these processes can improve. Also, ensure staff are friendly when dealing with customer concerns.

Ensure employees have adequate guidance on how to respond to customer queries. This could mean providing them with scripts, as well as giving them all the information they need about processes, technical matters or whatever it is that customers may inquire about.

Professionalism

Professionalism is the foundation for engaging with customers and the general public. A professional person stays calm, no matter what. They approach their interactions in a different manner from what their instinctive reaction may be. For example, if a customer snaps at you, you may be tempted to snap back, thinking to yourself, 'How could they talk to me like that?' As a professional, that is not the way to respond.

The aim is always to reassure the customer that the issue is being handled and will be resolved. The aim is to resolve the situation in the most effective way possible and prevent it from escalating. Maintaining a professional demeanour prevents raised voices, arguing and mirroring a customer's negative tone.

Even if your customer is angry, taking an immature approach or overreacting, there is still a valid reason they are unhappy. Thus, focus on solving the problem. Your calm persona automatically provides reassurance that they needn't worry, and that their issue is being dealt with. No matter how much they argue, do not argue back. With the most difficult customers, you may choose to let them get it all out of their system; after that, they tend to be more cooperative.

Some companies choose to collect customer experience data via surveys. This feedback gives you the ability to recognize if one of your employees is causing an issue due to a lack of interpersonal tact or professionalism. You can set this up as an automated survey or invite customers to respond with a web address.

Fairness

When we think about being fair, it is important to keep the following goal in mind: Always advance your respectful understanding of customers as human beings. Customers want to know that you will be reasonable when they have a concern.

By actively monitoring your own errors, you can reach out to customers in advance to make things right. When addressing customer issues, you need to make every effort to leave your customer with the feeling that they have been treated fairly. Remember – customer service can have a more significant impact on your customers' perceptions than any other facet of your business.

Here are some recommendations to ensure fairness:

- Be efficient and friendly.
- Treat all customers equally.
- Be proactive and give yourself the tools to anticipate future issues.
- Acknowledge your own mistakes.
- Issue recalls or refunds for known deficiencies.

Consistency leads to reliability

Provide customers with a consistent level of service. Reliability and consistency will hook customers to keep them returning for more. Retaining customers enhances a company's profitability, since many people will default to a brand they know, even if it costs more money. If you are in a saturated business field, offering your customers the reliable support they require is the easiest way to differentiate your business from competitors.

In a crowded marketplace, consumers want different things at different times. Customers love to be surprised. When we offer customers something above and beyond their minimum expectations, they will often remember when they need a product or service again. A small discount or reward could be enough to promote customer loyalty.

Remember too, that it doesn't matter if you are in a store, on the phone or online – no one likes to wait. The response times of your customer service channels should be reasonable.

TOP TIP

Take it offline

Customers have taken to highlighting their issues with a company on social media. It's beneficial to take the conversation away from social media immediately, and move it to direct message, email or phone. This avoids a public back-and-forth that only enhances the digital footprint of the complaint and gives it further reach. A simple message to say, 'We're sorry and we're contacting you to resolve' is sufficient. Then move the conversation away from public socials so that the team can hear the customer and come up with a solution.

CASE STUDY: CONTROLLING BUT ENCOURAGING REVIEWS – A HOSPITALITY COMPANY)

The challenge

A hospitality company in Europe was delivering a significant number of experiences for individuals around the world. Their service delivery was very good and as a result they received regular positive feedback, but, like most companies, they also received complaints from time to time. In the hospitality industry, reputation is a major factor for consumer decision making.

The solution

The company focused on managing its reviews closely. Using multiple review platforms, such as Trustpilot and Google, the company was able to quickly develop a large number of very positive reviews. Encouraging customers to submit reviews was the first step and this drove thousands of reviews in just a few months. It also drove negative reviews, however. The company dedicated one of their team to looking after these reviews and this meant that negative reviews were taken offline, dealt with quickly and often removed by the customer due to the great service received by the team.

The results

The company quickly grew to be the market leader on both volume and score of the reviews. Company growth increased by 21 per cent over the first 12 months.

Step two: Identify customer service challenges

Delivering quality products alongside outstanding customer service can be quite a feat. While specific questions and concerns will vary, a few challenges are definitely more common than others.

Effective customer feedback methods

To stay ahead of competitors, continually track and analyse customer feedback – positive and negative.

EMAILS AND CUSTOMER CONTACT FORMS

Email is the most straightforward way to gather honest customer feedback. It also allows you to gain more personal feedback. With surveys, for example, you're addressing a group; with emails, it's on an individual basis.

To increase the likelihood of customer response, think about adding a brief note at the end of your emails, advising how soon customers can expect a response from you.

CUSTOMER FEEDBACK SURVEYS

There are several forms of customer feedback surveys. They may be brief, in the format of polls or sliders; or they may be longer, more traditional surveys. If you want your customers to complete a survey, make sure you follow these tips:

- Ask a question that helps you meet your goals.
- Include open-ended questions.
- Avoid leading questions.
- Create consistent rating scales.
- Offer an incentive, such as a discount code or other form of reward – this also draws customers back to your business.

Analysing customer support data

There are many opportunities to gather data, such as social media, live chat or any other interaction customers have with your customer team. Consumer service teams use different key performance indicators (KPI) to evaluate the quality of their work:

- **Average first response time:** This KPI refers to the time taken for a customer to receive the first response to their initial request. Customers expect a reply to social media questions within 24 hours; live chat queries should get a near-instant answer. Customers prefer a quick response time, even if it doesn't solve the issue immediately. For a quick response, send an automated message regarding the contact. It is a handy trick to reassure customers that their request has reached the target, making their wait more bearable.
- **Average reply time:** This is the average time taken for your customer service team to respond to clients across all interactions. For complicated issues, this may take longer, as employees conduct research or work out how to approach a problem.
- **Average number of replies per request:** This measures the number of touchpoints required to solve a single customer request. A high number of touchpoints could be a sign that tickets are being directed inappropriately, causing your customer to have to work harder to get their problem solved. Ensure that customers do not have to repeat themselves to multiple representatives.
- **Average time of resolution:** This figure shows how long it takes to close an open case or resolve a concern. This KPI can be affected by the number of staff available and the number of tickets, among other factors.
- **Average rate of resolution:** Calculate the average rate of resolution by dividing the number of resolved cases by the total number of cases. Some cases may never be closed if employees aren't able to find an answer to an issue. This metric is a measure of productivity and efficiency.
- **Customer satisfaction score (CSAT):** This lets you ask your customers to rate their satisfaction with your product, service or business. The CSAT scale doesn't have to only consist of numbers; it can includes stars or smiley faces, for example. You can select various scale ranges, but keep in mind that simpler scales are particularly effective.

- **Net promoter score (NPS):** This parameter evaluates the power of your referrals. Ask customers, 'How likely are you to recommend us to a colleague or friend, on a scale from 1 to 10?' Their replies will fall into these categories: promoters (9–10), passives (7–8), detractors (0–6). Then, calculate the percentage of promotors and the percentage of detractors. Subtract the percentage of detractors from the percentage of promotors – the result is the NPS. There are some tools available with email questionnaires if you don't want to develop your own. You could try Trustful NPS for a free solution and Promoter.io for a paid option.
- **Customer retention rate (CRR):** This KPI refers to a business's ability to keep a paying customer over a set period of time. It shows the percentage of customers retained over a given period. Customer acquisition can be costly; 5 to 25 times more costly than customer retention. Thus, holding your customer for a longer period is important. CRR can be calculated on a weekly, monthly, or annual basis:

$$\text{Customer retention rate} = ((CE - CN) / CS) \times 100$$

Where: CE = Number of customers at the end of the period;

CN = Number of new customers acquired during the period;

CS = Number of customers at the start of the period.

QUALITATIVE CUSTOMER SUPPORT DATA

Analysing qualitative data, such as responses to open-ended survey questions, is also vital. It gives us insights about the reasons behind metrics and scores. Qualitative data offers you in-depth knowledge of customer's issues and can help solve customer problems.

CUSTOMER SUPPORT TICKETS DATA

Omni-channel customer service is increasing, allowing customers to reach out via several different methods. For support teams, this indicates that incoming tickets may arrive via mail, live chat, social media, mobile apps and phone calls.

There are various help desk software options available, such as Zendesk, Google Data Studio, Freshdesk and Front. Specialized software can help you organize your workload as it stores incoming support tickets centrally by displaying requests from different sources in one area.

AI in customer service analytics

Systems powered by artificial intelligence drive business innovation and allow companies to automate the process and get relevant insights about their data. Practical applications of AI in customer service include:

- tagging tickets and routing them to the appropriate personnel;
- detecting urgent issues;
- collecting valuable insights and qualitative data.

Machine learning models can extract and arrange large volumes of unstructured data in a matter of seconds. Different models can be created depending on the task, such as keyword extraction (identifying the most relevant words in a ticket) or sentiment analysis (an automated process that identifies and extracts opinions from messages). These methods help to uncover the most frequent technical issues, or monitor similar technical problems easily.

Identifying the most urgent requests is critical to proper prioritization of concerns. In addition, analysing urgent tickets can help you recognize patterns, such as a sudden spike of urgent queries around a specific time of year.

TOP TIP

Be quick

Satisfying customers with speedy service is another essential step for the success of your business.

According to a survey from Zendesk (2021), 69 per cent of customers judge the quality of a customer experience based on response time and quick resolution to their inquiries. Give people the option to get instant answers to basic questions.

- Use an automated process, such as online chat or automated voice response, to react to minor issues. Website FAQs can also handle common questions.
- For complex issues, consider having 24/7 customer service with trained representatives. Hire professionals who can provide real expertise in your industry.
- Measure customer-service-oriented key performance indicators for speed. This will help you achieve continuous improvement.

- Anticipate customer concerns before they occur. For example, companies like Evinent Analytics offer machine learning tools to optimize websites and analyse customer behaviour. If data shows that customers are immediately leaving your site without making a purchase or getting in touch, it may indicate that you're not providing the right value.
- Another way to achieve fast customer service is to integrate your communication channels into an omni-channel strategy. This needs to be done carefully to avoid eliminating the efficiencies associated with each method.

Step three: Identify and set up customer service channels

Which customer service channels do you provide? Many people think that having more channels will result in a better customer experience. Providing more channels helps you serve customers to the best of your ability, but a customer's priorities are speed and convenience. Thus, you should be able to guide customers to channels that meet their specific preferences.

Human interactions in customer service

Agents give the customer the sense that they're concern is being addressed immediately, as opposed to waiting to get past the gatekeeper – the chatbot. Many customers prefer chatting with agents because live chat or human responses are often perceived as personalized and friendly. The flexibility in responses and the ability to show empathy to customers is unique to human representatives.

A survey by Forbes (2016) shows that 50 per cent of customers say having humans available to answer questions is an essential feature when deciding on purchasing. Humans are emotional and solve problems with a personal touch that makes customers more satisfied. Apart from this, humans can make changes and deliver an improved customer experience based on inputs.

Over time, humans learn about various situations customers may encounter and can therefore deliver better service. Best of all, unlike chatbots, humans can handle irritated, angry or disappointed customers. Chatbots can't understand things like tone or word selection. Understanding anger, sarcasm and other emotions helps service providers respond appropriately.

PROS AND CONS OF HUMAN CUSTOMER SERVICE

Pros

- Understanding of human emotions.
- Ability to perceive tone.
- Best for complex technical issues.
- Experience-driven approach.
- Flexibility of response.
- Better overall customer relationship.

Cons

- Slow response time.
- Inability to handle multiple requests at a time.
- Potential for errors.

AI chatbots

AI chatbots are going head-to-head with customer service providers. The debate about whether AI chatbots are better than human representatives is ongoing.

In situations with simple tasks, an AI chatbot may be the better option. A bot is less likely to make mistakes with things like payments, maths or numbers. They reduce customer service costs and offer better responses and quick resolutions. They also eliminate the language barrier by offering multiple language choices for better processing. Chatbots can work limitlessly and handle multiple requests at a time and provide service around the clock.

However, AI chatbots lack the nuance to handle complicated questions. They might not be familiar with synonyms or other keywords that customers are using to describe their problems.

PROS AND CONS OF AI CUSTOMER SERVICE

Pros

- 24-hour service.
- Instant response.
- Quick resolution of simple queries.

- Efficient customer experience.
- Cost savings.

Cons

- Data security issues.
- Inability to understand human emotions and nuances.

Chatbots and human customer service are competing. Some customers are happy to deal with a bot, while others like to talk to a human. The crux of the matter is that both are crucial for providing optimal customer service.

Social media customer service

Social media customer service offers support through social channels such as Facebook. It lets you quickly answer questions; but providing support via numerous social media can be difficult for many companies, in both B2C and B2B contexts.

Your support team must be available on the platforms your customers use. You can use Facebook, Instagram, Twitter, Pinterest and LinkedIn. To find out which platforms your customers prefer, search for mentions of your brand on each one. Also check for tags and likes.

A social media strategy should follow this basic road map:

1. Set up brand monitoring on social media platforms. You can set up brand monitoring tools to recognize posts and comments that contain specific words. This will allow you to focus on the relevant content related to your company.
2. Determine which types of comments customers respond to. Collect feedback from multiple platforms.
3. Compile feedback into a central location. Review the data to see if there are any clear trends. If so, consider your company's known strengths and weaknesses in relation to the feedback from customers.
4. Determine whether you'd like to respond to comments. Ensure you respond to negative comments as well as positive ones.
5. Build a system to get questions answered instantly. Organize a system with dedicated social media customer care members. Set it up so that all customer issues are resolved in one place. Delegate and assign work based on each customer's specific request.

Try to understand which social media posts should be resolved privately. If a conversation is likely to get tense, you don't want to handle it publicly. In these cases, engage with the customer in private.

Live web chat

Live chat is a popular contact channel for young audiences as it provides in-depth, tailored responses to queries instantly, and facilitates the development of customer relationships. It serves as a venue for meaningful conversations to take place in a convenient way. It also offers insights into the customer's website use and gives them the option to escalate issues where necessary.

Businesses seeking to add live web chat should take the following steps:

- Prepare canned responses to enhance resolution and reduce confusion.
- Collect feedback after each conversation.
- Outline the key KPIs and metrics for services via chat.
- Deliver quick live chat support.
- Provide training to ensure adequate product knowledge.
- Design a live chat window that matches your branding.
- Make it easy to use on any device.

Keep track of results. Monitor live chat to understand how to improve customer experience to meet business objectives, such as increasing sales.

Home assistant: innovation in the world of customer service channels

Channels such as Facebook Messenger and interactive SMS are becoming go-to options for basic tasks like leaving customer feedback or changing account details. Consumers want the quickest way to interact with a business, and businesses are searching for cost-effective channels to resolve customer issues effectively.

With the recent popularity of virtual or voice-activated assistants like Siri (Apple), Cortana (Microsoft), Google Now (Google) and Alexa (Amazon), the way we search for services has changed again. People who prefer to hear a voice on the other end of the phone don't automatically have to talk to another human being. Instead, these virtual assistants make it easy to find solutions without placing a traditional call.

Amazon's Alexa is fast becoming a familiar household feature, with millions sold. Alexa-enabled devices, such as Amazon Echo, Echo Dot, Amazon Tap and Fire TV, are always listening for inputs.

Big retail brands are beginning to see the value of voice. Many companies have introduced voice ordering through Google Home. This type of convenience can be tough to beat for companies that haven't adapted to these modern trends. To remain competitive, ensure your websites and apps can accept voice-enabled searches. Where possible, optimize your sales funnel to accommodate different styles of ordering.

You can also integrate data from Amazon Alexa to provide relevant messages via email and send push notifications to customers. However, Alexa is restricted to the home, so far, so try to combine geolocation technology with spending-habit information to create a digital experience for on-the-go consumers.

Step four: Plan corrective actions

Transforming your customer service will take some time, commitment and planning. Meanwhile, the growth of e-commerce doesn't mean that retailers should give up on having physical stores. Customers may prefer to shop in person for things they need to try out first or items that would be costly to ship back. E-commerce has set high expectations for customer experience. Thus, it is crucial to enhance your customer service standards if you intend to remain a physical entity.

If applicable, assess your business for these niches and determine how you can leverage those strengths to compete with e-commerce companies.

Speed

Provide fast, convenient customer support. Ensure that agents taking calls answer promptly – within three to four rings. Ensure too that recorded menus are clear to understand, so that customers get through to the right people.

Use positive language during customer interactions. When attending to customer problems, using positive language with a good attitude takes the stress away. For instance, phrases like 'great question' can keep the customer from feeling like their question is not valuable.

Communicate with purpose

Reduce email response times as much as reasonably possible and set a goal for your ideal response time. You can send automatic mail to speed things up. For example, your response can include a simple confirmation: 'We've received your mail! We're on it!'

Project the right image to customers and others who call your business. Use greetings that sound professional. Build trust with customers by going the extra mile to make accommodations and being transparent. Provide your customers with all the required information, including clear pricing and limitations, and hire staff who are highly-trained and experienced.

Provide resources

Update your website frequently. Customers may be frustrated if information is out of date. For example, a shopper who realizes that a discount code on your website has expired after they've selected several items may not respond in the future to coupons.

If your business deals with complicated products or confusing topics, consider offering a blog to answer more in-depth questions. These resources can show customers how to address common problems without having to contact a representative.

Use of language

Encourage employees to start using the right language with customers and avoid giving the impression that they cannot solve the problem. In addition, practise active listening and refrain from interrupting the customer.

Talk to your staff if your customer service is suffering from low ratings. Depending on the size of your company, you could schedule a weekly update or periodic performance reviews. Customer service representatives may be providing poor support because of an internal issue, not from a lack of effort.

Hiring practices

Hire people who have a genuine interest in providing high-quality service. Look for employees who communicate, listen well and manage their time efficiently. Once again, active listening is crucial – this quality has the potential to change unpleasant situations into positive ones for the customer.

Customer service automation

Customers are purchasing online at a far greater rate than ever before. The increased workload that may result can make it difficult for customer service and fulfilment teams to keep on top of things. The resulting stress increases chances of mistakes that can reduce customer satisfaction. Also, employees may become overwhelmed and respond negatively during direct customer interactions.

E-commerce businesses can use help-desk automation to counter this challenge. Common e-commerce customer service automation options are:

- **White glove treatment:** If you are not careful, unhappy customers can leave after a single incident. Frustrated consumers tend to use similar phrases when they express their feelings. Use a repository of trigger words as a starting point. This will help you assign a higher priority to those cases so that irritated customers get a response more quickly.
- **Social sentiment analysis:** These tools help you determine how much people are talking about your brand. Conduct a social media analysis to collect data, then monitor that data for results. There are some powerful tools available, such as Hootsuite Insights, Mentionlytics and Digimind. You can use these resources to make the process of analysis faster, easier and more accurate.
- **Customer reviews:** Customer reviews are more powerful than ever. Consumers want to be acknowledged, and they want to hear other opinions about their experience with a business, and its products and services. Reviews allow you to better understand what your customers think of your brand. Unlike word-of-mouth opinions, online reviews can last indefinitely, making it especially important to address negative experiences.
- **Smart search:** Offering a variety of search options means that customers aren't wasting time searching your website. Options like voice search or auto-filling search bars add convenience for customers.
- **Topic classifiers for recurring issues:** Businesses deal with a huge volume of unstructured text every day. Support tickets, social media posts and online feedback are just a few examples. Manually analysing a large amount of text data is nearly impossible. Sorting by hand also leads to mistakes and inconsistencies. Instead, AI-guided topic analysis makes it easier to sort incoming queries and tickets to ensure that each reaches the most suitable representative.

WHAT TO WATCH

Tone

In customer service, your tone is the main factor in how customers will perceive your words. There are some golden rules that customer service providers should follow:

- Inject energy into your voice. Positivity will translate to your customers and show that you're interested in finding a solution. This will make them feel more comfortable.
- Speak to a customer in a natural, calm, and personable manner. If customers are upset, stay cool and collected.
- Maintain a level of professionalism. Try to find the balance between being formal and casual. This will help you turn boring conversations about the status of an inquiry into a memorable and pleasant exchange.
- When your customer is explaining their story, show empathy and sincerity. Reassure them that you are listening.

A lot of customers prefer to make a call when they need the support of customer service. They choose to use the phone because they're seeking out a human connection instead of turning to impersonal alternatives like email or a chatbot. Remember that as you're engaging with the customer.

Speaking too fast makes it seem you are in a rush, and speaking slowly makes it seem like you don't care. Speak at a consistent pace with a confident voice. In addition, check for understanding while you are speaking to show that comprehension is important to you. Avoid actions like sighing that can indicate disinterest in the conversation. Your background should be clear of extra noise or distractions as much as possible.

Show the customer that they are your top priority – your business depends on it.

References

Forbes (2016) It's alive: Why chat is so important for brands, available at: https://www.forbes.com/sites/steveolenski/2016/08/10/its-alive-why-live-chat-is-so-important-for-brands/?sh=2353ad4253d1 (archived at https://perma.cc/3PNB-DVFY)

Zendesk (2021) Providing great social media customer service, available at: https://www.zendesk.co.uk/blog/customer-service-through-social-media/ (archived at https://perma.cc/7KBT-GTWR)

INDEX

Note: page numbers in *italic* indicate figures or tables